Theory and Policy
in International Relations

Written under the auspices of

THE CENTER OF INTERNATIONAL STUDIES,
PRINCETON UNIVERSITY

A list of other Center publications appears
at the back of the book

Theory and Policy
in International Relations

*Edited by Raymond Tanter
and Richard H. Ullman*

PRINCETON UNIVERSITY PRESS

PRINCETON, NEW JERSEY

This book is being issued separately as a
supplement to *World Politics*, Vol. XXIV, 1972.

This book has been set in Linotype Granjon
Printed in the United States of America
by Princeton University Press

CONTENTS

THE CONTRIBUTORS

RAYMOND TANTER, Associate Professor of Political Science and Director of the International Data Archive project at the University of Michigan, served during 1967 as Deputy Director of Behavioral Sciences of the Advanced Research Projects Agency, Department of Defense, and is presently a consultant to the Rand Corporation. His special interest is the creation of computer-based systems for modelling and managing international conflicts.

RICHARD H. ULLMAN, Professor of Politics and International Affairs at Princeton University, is the author of a three-volume study of Anglo-Soviet relations in the aftermath of the First World War. He has served on the Staff of the National Security Council, and on the Policy Planning Staff in the Office of the Assistant Secretary of Defense for International Security Affairs.

GRAHAM T. ALLISON, Associate Professor of Politics in the John F. Kennedy School of Government at Harvard University, is the author of *Essence of Decision: Explaining the Cuban Missile Crisis.*

MORTON H. HALPERIN, a Senior Fellow of the Brookings Institution, was formerly a member of the Senior Staff of the National Security Council and a Deputy Assistant Secretary of Defense. He is currently at work on a book on bureaucratic politics and foreign policy in the United States.

NAZLI CHOUCRI, Assistant Professor of Political Science at the Massachusetts Institute of Technology, is the author and co-author of numerous articles on the analysis and forecasting of international conflict behavior.

ROBERT C. NORTH, Professor of Political Science and Director of Studies in International Conflict and Integration in the Institute of Political Studies, Stanford University, is the author of *Moscow and Chinese Communists* and other books and articles concerned with international relations, international conflict, crises, and the antecedents of war.

EDWARD L. MORSE, Assistant Professor of Politics and International Affairs at Princeton University, is the author of a forthcoming book, *France and the Politics of Interdependence, 1962-1969.*

NORMAN FROHLICH and JOE A. OPPENHEIMER are assistant professors of Government at the University of Texas. They are co-authors (with Oran R. Young) of *Political Leadership and Collective Goods,* and are currently working together to develop an axiomatic theory of coercive relationships.

ORAN R. YOUNG is Professor of Government at the University of Texas. His most recent book is *Political Leadership and Collective Goods* (with Norman Frohlich and Joe A. Oppenheimer). He is currently working on models of strategic interaction and bargaining.

DAVIS B. BOBROW is Professor of Political Science and Public Affairs and Director of the Center of International Studies, University of Minnesota. Prior to that, he was Special Assistant for the Behavioral and Social Sciences in the Office of the Director of Defense Research and Engineering, and Acting Director, Behavioral Sciences, Advanced Research Projects Agency. His major current interests are in indicator systems for anticipating and evaluating international policy and the design of public institutions.

THE CONTRIBUTORS

ALLEN S. WHITING, Professor of Political Science and Associate for Chinese Studies at the University of Michigan, is the author of *China Crosses the Yalu: The Decision to Enter the Korean War*, and of other studies on Chinese and international affairs. He served in the Department of State from 1962-66 as Director, Office of Research and Analysis for Far East, Bureau of Intelligence and Research. From 1966-68 he was Deputy Consul General in Hong Kong.

STEPHEN M. SHAFFER is a Ph.D. candidate in Political Science at the University of Michigan. His major interests are in international relations, with particular focus on formal modelling and multivariate analysis. He is currently doing research on coalitions and alliances in world politics.

Theory and Policy
in International Relations

INTRODUCTION:
Theory and Policy in International Relations

IT is a commonplace observation—certainly among practicing members of the foreign policy community, but also among academic students of world politics—that policy-makers have seldom given much heed to the writings of theorists on international relations. Particularly in recent years, when academic writing on international relations has grown increasingly technical in nature and more impenetrable to a reader without specialized training in one or more social science disciplines, the theorist *as theorist* has had little communication with the policy-maker. It is also true that many practitioners, and many from the academic side as well, would tend to agree that, by and large, the policy-makers have not missed much.

This supplementary issue of *World Politics* is intended as a very modest effort to bridge the gap between the community of policy-makers and the community of theorists. Its purpose is to present some new approaches to international relations theory. But its contributors have been explicitly concerned, as their academic colleagues often have not, with relating various theoretical approaches to the concerns of the policy-making community. This is not to claim that their contributions are not, on the whole, abstract, or even that they are particularly easy to read. But it is to say that, both in its sum and in its several parts, the present volume attempts to suggest some ways in which the practitioners of international relations might benefit from the work of their academic colleagues whose concerns are theoretical rather than operational.

The first five of these articles—by scholars for the most part younger and less published than is usually the case with symposia of this sort—represent different approaches to international relations theory. In each case we have asked the authors to identify the ways in which their theoretical approaches might be useful to the policy-making community. The remaining three articles serve a different purpose. All are concerned, from different viewpoints, with the general relationship between theory-building and policy-making. One (by Oran R. Young) sets forth criteria for theorizing. The other two, by scholars with extensive experience in government (Davis B. Bobrow and Allen S. Whiting), comment as well upon the theoretical approaches put forward in the first five contributions.

We have not attempted to include here representatives of every theoretical approach or method which we ourselves feel to be either useful or important. Missing, for instance, are contributions employing game theory, simulation, mathematical models, content analysis, psychological models, and explicitly ideological (such as Marxist or Maoist) paradigms. In some cases, the omission is due to our feeling that the approach in question has already had ample exposure, in others to our inability to secure a contribution from a particular theorist whose work we regard as especially important, and in still others to our judgment that the payoffs for the policy-maker from a given approach have been and continue to be slight. Just as we have not included every school, we have not attempted to impose on our contributors any given format. We asked them only to point out the relevance of their particular theoretical approach to the world of practice.

A thread which runs at least in some measure through all of these papers is a concern with *why* foreign policy actors behave as they do. All of the five substantive contributions ask "why" questions which require some theoretical model for explanation of the phenomena under investigation. Raymond Tanter, for example, asks why an alliance in conflict would respond more to its own prior behavior than to the behavior of its opponents. Similarly, why would an alliance respond more to its opponent than to its own prior behavior? He suggests an organizational processes model to explain the phenomenon of an alliance responding to its own behavior and an event interaction model to explain an alliance's response to its opponent's behavior. Tanter concludes with a suggestion for a computer-based system for conflict modelling and management. Such a system assumes that it is possible to compare prior conflict situations with present or simulated ones and to generalize historical precedents across cases to a current situation. Any such computer-based system, he says, should include a process model of organizational restraints on decision-making.

Graham T. Allison and Morton H. Halperin also focus on organizational processes. They ask why a given foreign policy action occurred, and why certain strategies are likely to be successful in inter-nation interactions. They propose a bureaucratic politics model for explaining foreign policy actions and interactions among nations. A central feature of their model is bargaining along regularized circuits among players located hierarchically within a government. Their essay concludes with a list of suggestions for policy-makers—reminiscent, perhaps, of Machiavelli's advice in *The Prince*. There is a stress on levers of influence which would allow a political leader to achieve his objectives, taking account of his own domestic situation *and* that of his opponent.

Although the essay by Nazli Choucri and Robert North does not emphasize domestic *political* constraints, their paper also describes domestic levers that political leaders may use to alter the characteristics of international conflict. They look at such variables as population size, relative availability of resources, and levels of technology. They ask why patterns of conflict often shift from one mode to another. That is, what causes the shift from national expansion to competition and finally to crisis? They suggest an "anticipated gap" model to explain these break-points in the characteristics of international conflict. Their model places great emphasis on gaps, or differentials, in population, resources, and technology in explaining shifts in international conflict over long periods of time.

Edward L. Morse's essay focuses upon one type of international conflict and cooperation—that stemming from the existence within the global economic system of separate national economies pursuing distinct and often competing national goals. He asks, for example, why crises have become characteristic features of the international economic relations among Western nations. He suggests a model of economic interdependence and rational political calculation to explain why economic diplomacy has been characterized by deliberate attempts to provoke and manipulate crises.

Where Morse to some extent relies implicitly on a rationality model in seeking explanations for international economic crises, Norman Frohlich and Joe A. Oppenheimer use rationality more explicitly in answering the following questions: (1) Why do nations sharing a common good such as a defense establishment decide to contribute less than their "fair" share? (2) Why do political leaders of one country transfer resources for development to other nations? (3) Why do political leaders of one nation undertake a military intervention in another to remove an unwanted opposition movement? To answer such questions they propose an entrepreneurial model which assumes political interactions to be akin to the relations between entrepreneurs, who supply goods for profit, and their public. They suggest that political leaders in fact seek to maximize their utility functions in a manner not dissimilar to the behavior of "economic man," long a creature of economic theory.

In contrast to the rational-choice model posited implicitly by Morse and explicitly by Frohlich and Oppenheimer, Tanter and Allison-

Halperin posit a model whereby an actor's ability to pursue rationality is constrained by his bargaining with other persons, by organizational processes, and by his inability to obtain complete information on goals, alternatives, and consequences of actions. Choucri and North, however, may offer a method of explanation drawing upon both the rationality of economic man and models which posit more limited rationality. It may well be that men may maximize their utility function according to the dictates of rationality during the "national expansion" stage. As nations develop internal organizational routines and compete for scarce resources, however, this bargaining and competition prevents them from acting rationally in pursuit of their objectives. Finally, as they become locked into an action-reaction crisis spiral, they may have the least opportunity to act rationally.

In summary, then, all of the first five essays in this volume ask "why" questions and suggest theoretical models for answering them. As the essay by Oran R. Young points out, however, the road to deductive theory remains long and largely untravelled. Furthermore, as Bobrow and Whiting suggest, the policy relevance of academic models in general is thus far quite minimal. Recognition of the primitive state of theory and its inadequate relation to the concerns of policy-makers is only a first step, however. If there is to be a dramatic improvement in the quality of policy-relevant theory in international relations, there must be much greater attention to the model-building enterprise, with a stress on formal deductive models with high applicability to empirical cases.

The costs of producing this supplementary issue of *World Politics*, and of placing it in the hands of the journal's regular subscribers, have been borne by the Ford Foundation, to which we, as editors, would like to express our gratitude. We come away from our editorial task with mixed feelings. On the one hand, our search of the existing literature of international relations theory has rather forcibly impressed upon us that academic theorists and working practitioners have had, and appear to continue to have, relatively little to say to one another. On the other hand, the papers we have assembled here give us at least some basis for hope. If theorists were to address their efforts to the concerns and needs of practitioners more frequently, both groups might find that the basis for a valuable exchange in fact exists.

RAYMOND TANTER
RICHARD H. ULLMAN

INTERNATIONAL SYSTEM AND FOREIGN POLICY APPROACHES:

Implications for Conflict Modelling and Management

By RAYMOND TANTER*

... The international system is an expanding version of the notion of two-actors-in-interaction. .... Interaction analysis focuses on the outputs of national systems. The national systems, themselves, are black-boxed.
—Charles A. McClelland[1]

If a nation performs an action of a certain type today, its organizational components must yesterday have been performing (or have had established routines for performing) an action only marginally different from that action.

—Graham T. Allison[2]

INTRODUCTION

THE quotations from Charles A. McClelland and Graham T. Allison represent two distinct approaches to the study of international relations: (1) international system analysis; and (2) foreign policy analysis. Essentially, international system analysts seek to explain interactions between nations by phenomena such as their prior interactions and the structure of the system. Foreign policy analysts, on the other hand, seek to explain foreign policy behavior as the output of subnational organizations following standard operating procedures or engaging in a problem-solving search. Given the international system and foreign policy approaches as contrasting points of departure, the goals of the present study are:

* Acknowledgments to ONR Contract Number N00014-67-A-0181-0026, ARPA #1411 for support; to Cheryl Kugler, Hazel Markus, Michael Mihalka, Stephen Shaffer, and Lewis Snider for research assistance; to Patricia Armstrong for typing; to Graham T. Allison, Robert R. Beattie, Morton H. Halperin, Nazli Choucri, Robert C. North and Robert A. Young, whose ideas helped guide this inquiry; to Lutz Erbring, Edward L. Morse, Richard H. Ullman and Oran R. Young for helpful critique; to Charles A. McClelland, whose ideas and World Event/Interaction Survey provided a basis for the modelling and coding procedures used in the study; and to Walter Corson for providing his data, scaling system, and helpful interpretations.
[1] Charles A. McClelland, *Theory and the International System* (New York 1966), 20, 104.
[2] Graham T. Allison, *Essence of Decision: Explaining the Cuban Missile Crisis* (Boston 1971), 87.

1. to evaluate models based on an international system approach, a foreign policy approach, and a combination of both approaches as they are used to study alliance behavior in conflict situations; and

2. to infer from the evaluation of these models some implications for conflict modelling and management.

International system approaches may imply interaction models, whereas foreign policy approaches may suggest decision-making models. For example, J. D. Singer posits that by focusing on the international system, we can study the patterns of interaction which the system reveals,[3] while game theoretic approaches to the study of conflicts of interest blend both interaction and decision-making concepts through their emphasis on strategic interaction and rational choice behavior.[4] Game theory deals with strategic situations in which the consequences of action are uncertain; several different outcomes may result from a given action.[5] Players in a game confront others who are assumed to be rational and whose choices also affect the outcome of the game. A game theoretic approach to conflict thus emphasizes strategic interaction and bargaining under conditions of risk.[6]

An alternative set of conflict models widely employed in world politics concerns arms race processes. The most familiar is the Richardson process model, named after Lewis Richardson.[7] Richardson's model stresses interaction processes between nations but ignores rational choice behavior. The outcome of Richardson's model ". . . is what would occur if instinct and tradition were allowed to act uncontrolled."[8] The model ignores choice processes internal to a state and stresses the automatic response of one nation to the arms expenditures of another. The model

[3] J. David Singer, "The Level-of-Analysis Problem in International Relations," in Klaus Knorr and Sidney Verba, eds., *The International System* (Princeton 1961), 80. It should be noted that the *interaction* approach is often distinguished from the *international system* approach. The latter orientation is based on the assumption that international politics is more than the sum of converging interactions and transactions; properties of the system as a *whole* are assumed to influence the behavior of individual nations.

[4] The term strategic interaction in game theory often refers to the outcome of competing strategies. Here, interaction means the *process* where each actor pays attention to and responds to the prior patterns of his opponent.

[5] See Herbert Simon, "Some Strategic Considerations in the Construction of Social Science Models," in Paul Lazarsfeld, ed., *Mathematical Thinking in the Social Sciences* (Glencoe 1954), 388-415. Also see Herbert Simon, *Models of Man: Social and Rational; Mathematical Essays on Rational Human Behavior in a Social Setting* (New York 1957), 241-60.

[6] See Anatol Rapoport, *Two-Person Game Theory* (Ann Arbor 1966).

[7] Lewis F. Richardson, *Arms and Insecurity: A Mathematical Study of the Causes and Origins of War* (Pittsburgh 1960).

[8] *Ibid.*, 12.

is deterministic and described in terms of "social physics."[9] There are a variety of arms race models which have attempted to improve on Richardson's formulation. Martin McGuire's model, for example, incorporates rational choice behavior.[10]

Less formal than the game theoretic and Richardson process models are the mediated stimulus response (S-R) and event/interaction models of Robert North and Charles McClelland respectively.[11] North's model focuses on perception as an explanatory concept intervening between a stimulus and a response. McClelland, on the other hand, emphasizes prior international event/interaction sequences and systemic configurations as explanations for present international interactions.[12]

The game theory model assumes rational choice behavior; the mediated stimulus response, the event/interaction, and Richardson process models allow for irrational (misperception) or non-rational (recurring event sequence) behavior.[13] Nevertheless, all four classes of models have in common the interaction theme. That is, each model explains present interaction on the basis of prior interaction with a minimum of focus on the internal attributes of the actor.[14] Of these four interaction models,

[9] Anatol Rapoport, *Fights, Games and Debates* (Ann Arbor 1960), 15-107; and "Lewis F. Richardson's Mathematical Theory of War," *Journal of Conflict Resolution*, I (September 1957), 249-99. See also Kenneth E. Boulding, *Conflict and Defense: A General Theory* (New York 1962); Paul Smoker, "Fear in the Arms Race: A Mathematical Study," in J. N. Rosenau, ed., *International Politics and Foreign Policy* (2nd ed., New York 1969), 573-82.

[10] Martin C. McGuire, *Secrecy and the Arms Race* (Cambridge, Mass. 1965).

[11] Robert C. North, "Research Pluralism and the International Elephant," in Klaus Knorr and James Rosenau, eds., *Contending Approaches to International Politics* (Princeton 1969), 218-42; Robert C. North, "The Behavior of Nation-States: Problems of Conflict and Integration," in Morton Kaplan, ed., *New Approaches to International Relations* (New York 1968), 203-356; Charles A. McClelland and Gary D. Hoggard, "Conflict Patterns in the Interactions Among Nations," in Rosenau (fn. 9), 711-24.

[12] Charles A. McClelland, "The Acute International Crisis," in Knorr and Verba (fn. 3), 182-204; "Access to Berlin: The Quantity and Variety of Events, 1948-1963," in J. David Singer, ed., *Quantitative International Politics* (New York 1968), 159-86. Event/interactions are international actions such as threats and promises (words) or uses of force and offers of proposals (deeds). Event/interactions are different from transactions such as trade and mail flows between nations. The present study deals only with conflictive event/interactions since there were too few cooperative interactions during the Berlin conflict of 1961 to perform statistical analysis.

[13] See below, however, for a discussion of how recurring event sequences may be subsumed under learning models and how such models explain limited rational search behavior.

[14] The mediated S-R model draws on internal attributes (perceptions) more than the other models. Similarly, game theory models applied to world politics focus on the rational intentions of decision-makers, which tap internal attributes of nations. A major criticism of game theory models, however, is their treatment of an actor as a black-box, ignoring psychological and behavioral attributes. See John C. Harsanyi, "Rational-Choice Models of Political Behavior vs. Functionalist and Conformist Theories," *World Politics*, XXI (July 1969), 513-38; Michael Shapiro, "Rational Political Man: A Synthesis of Economic and Social-Psychological Perspectives," *American Po-*

the present study draws most from the event/interaction model. A hypothesis derived from this model is that the current behavior of the Warsaw Treaty Organization (WTO) in an East-West conflict is a consequence of a prior pattern of North Atlantic Treaty Organization (NATO) actions, and vice versa.

Recall the earlier suggestion that international system approaches suggest interaction models while foreign policy approaches may imply decision-making models. An early decision-making scheme is the one pioneered by Richard Snyder and his associates.[15] Although their original decision-making scheme allows for international system determinants of foreign policy behavior, the scheme mostly relies on the organizational roles—communication, information, and personality variables, especially motivation—which constitute the internal setting of decisions.[16] As with game theory, the decision-making scheme assumes rationality, but rationality is a more limited concept than the comprehensive version assumed in game theory. In game theory goals are ranked, all alternatives are specified, consequences are calculated, and rational choice consists of selecting the value-maximizing alternative. In the decision-making scheme, however, men are bounded by: (1) the lack of an explicit preference ordering; (2) incomplete information on alternatives; and (3) inadequate computational skills to calculate the consequences of each option. All three limitations violate the requirements of comprehensive rationality.[17]

The Snyder scheme focuses on the attributes of individuals as well

litical Science Review, LXIII (December 1969), 1106-19. Simon modified game theory by incorporating attributes of the actor and then inferring a new decision-rule—"satisficing" (Simon, fn. 5, 241-60). Experimental gaming explicitly treats properties of the actors such as competitiveness, risk, and temptation, as well as rewards and punishment. Melvin Guyer, "A Review of the Literature on Zero-Sum and Non-Zero-Sum Games in the Social Sciences," Mental Health Research Institute, University of Michigan, Mimeo, n.d.

[15] Richard C. Snyder and others, eds., Foreign Policy Decision-Making (New York 1962); James A. Robinson and Richard C. Snyder, "Decision-Making in International Politics," in Herbert C. Kelman, ed., International Behavior (New York 1965), 433-63; Glenn Paige, The Korean Decision (New York 1968); Charles F. Hermann, Crises in Foreign Policy: A Simulation Analysis (Indianapolis 1969); J. A. Robinson and others, "Search Under Crisis in Political Gaming and Simulation," in D. G. Pruitt and R. C. Snyder, eds., Theory and Research on the Causes of War (Englewood Cliffs, N.J. 1969), 80-94.

[16] Richard C. Snyder and Glenn D. Paige, "The United States Decision to Resist Aggression in Korea: The Application of an Analytical Scheme," in J. N. Rosenau, ed., International Politics and Foreign Policy (New York 1961), 196.

[17] Simon (fn. 5); James G. March and Herbert A. Simon, Organizations (New York 1958); Richard M. Cyert and James G. March, A Behavioral Theory of the Firm (Englewood Cliffs, N.J. 1963).

as on their foreign policy organizations. The decision-making model explicated by Graham Allison primarily stresses organizational processes.[18] Allison's model explains government behavior as the output of large organizations functioning according to standard operating procedures and search processes. Like Snyder's scheme, Allison's model assumes limited rationality rather than the comprehensive rationality of game theory models. Allison's organizational processes explanation asserts the following principle: Stop searching with the first alternative that is good enough—the "satisficing" rule.[19] The present study draws more on the Allison work than on Snyder's efforts. Consider Allison's inference from an organizational processes model: "The best explanation of an organization's behavior at [time] t is $t - 1$; the best prediction of what will happen at $t + 1$ is t."[20] Following Allison's model, a hypothesis is that the current behavior of WTO in an East-West conflict is a consequence of its own prior pattern of actions, and similarly for NATO.

The international system and foreign policy approaches may both yield adequate explanations of international behavior. Similarly, event/interaction and organizational processes models may apply to the same situation. Thus, the study evaluates: (1) an event/interaction model; (2) an organizational processes model; and (3) a combined interaction/organizational model. Consider the following illustrations of these three models. The event/interaction model assumes that WTO behavior was a reaction to the prior pattern of NATO events. That is, WTO countries decided to construct the Berlin Wall as a result of prior NATO provocations, e.g., the encouragement of a mass refugee flow from East Germany to West Germany via Berlin. Similarly, NATO behavior was a reaction to prior WTO events. NATO countries increased their defense budgets and sought alliance agreement on economic sanctions in reaction to Soviet threats to sign a separate peace treaty with the East Germans and to turn over control of Berlin access routes.

An organizational processes model, on the other hand, might stress such variables as standard operating procedures and the problem-solving search processes of organizations as explanations for alliance actions. Consider this explanation of an official U. S. reply to the Soviet *aide*

[18] Allison (fn. 2).   [19] Simon (fn. 5).
[20] Allison (fn. 2), 87. Allison's "explanation" of present behavior as determined by prior behavior is not an explanation in the sense of specifying *why* the present behavior occurs. A learning model may be able to explain why organizations repeat or deviate from prior patterns.

memoire and subsequent U. S. actions during the Berlin conflict of 1961: For weeks President John F. Kennedy waited to reply to a Soviet threat to Western access routes to Berlin which was implied by a Soviet *aide memoire*. The Department of State drafted a reply; Kennedy rejected it as stale and uninspired. He asked Theodore Sorensen to draft a new reply. Then Kennedy discovered the new reply could not be released without going through complicated allied and interdepartmental clearances. He gave up the new attempt and issued the earlier State Department reply.[21] The organizational processes model anticipates standard operating procedures and helps explain some of the foreign policy output. Perhaps *partly* as a result of his dissatisfaction with the perfunctory U. S. reply, Kennedy searched for more direct ways of answering the Soviet *aide memoire*, e.g., by increasing the military budget.[22]

The interaction/organization model combines the reaction and organizational process explanations into a single model. Prior studies suggest that a combination may be more powerful as an explanatory device than either the international system or foreign policy approach taken separately. Consider the studies by Nazli Choucri and Robert North. Although Choucri and North seek to explain international conflict behavior over longer periods of time, their work is nevertheless relevant here. Between 1870 and 1914, they find that a nation's role in international conflict was less a consequence of changes in that nation's own capabilities (i.e., the foreign policy approach) than of the changing distances between itself and rival nations, particularly its closest rival (i.e., the international system approach). They conclude, however, that neither the foreign policy nor the international system approach alone is adequate to explain the international conflict process.[23] Thus, the present study combines the international system and foreign policy type approaches in creating an interaction/organization model. A specific hypothesis based on the interaction/organization model is that WTO behavior in an East-West conflict is a consequence of both its own prior actions and prior NATO actions, and similarly for NATO.

The following three working hypotheses, thus, are: (1) an alliance's behavior in conflict situations results from the prior pattern of actions of its opponent (event/interaction); (2) an alliance's behavior in conflict situations results from its own prior patterns of actions (organiza-

---

[21] Theodore C. Sorensen, *Kennedy* (New York 1965), 587.

[22] This interpretation of the organizational model seems to imply that Kennedy increased the U.S. military budget because of his dissatisfaction with the State Department. External factors such as the WTO threat clearly should be considered to explain the increase in the military budget in this case.

[23] See the essay by Nazli Choucri and R. C. North in this volume.

tional processes); (3) an alliance's behavior in conflict situations results from both the opponent's prior pattern of behavior and its own prior pattern of actions (interaction/organization).[23a]

An Event/Interaction Model

McClelland has laid the theoretical framework for the event/interaction model in a series of essays. In the 1961 special issue of *World Politics*, his essay on "The Acute International Crisis" explicates an event/interaction model.[24] He suggests that events in conflicts might form a chain of interaction sequences, and the discovery of these sequences would permit comparisons across cases. McClelland's model describes the state of the international system in terms of its pattern (process), structure, and performance. Needed data are of two types: relationships to tap structure, and interactions as indicators of system process.[25] In a later article, McClelland evaluated several propositions with interaction data concerning access to Berlin, 1948-1963.[26] For example, he evaluated one of the ideas put forward in the 1961 article: the greater the number of intense conflicts between two actors, the more likely each will develop routines for minimizing violence. These routines develop as bureaucrats learn standard operating procedures to process repetitive conflicts.[27] Although the 1968 design does not provide an explicit test of the learning idea, there is some evidence supporting it in the Berlin case. Finally, an assumption of McClelland's event/interaction model is that there are certain international processes, such as arms races, which occur regularly with specific international situations such as intense conflicts. The task of the analyst of the international system is to discover the processes which accompany various situations and to forecast future processes.[28]

[23a] The distinction between event/interaction and organizational processes is for the sake of convenience of presentation. In a sense, there is only one model that contains interaction and organization parameters. Interaction parameters may be relatively more important at times, while organizational factors may be more significant at other times. See Tanter, 1972, for a more complete synthesis of interaction and organizational parameters than given here.

[24] McClelland, in Knorr and Verba (fn. 3).

[25] McClelland (fn. 1), chapter 4.

[26] McClelland, in Singer (fn. 12) 159-86.

[27] McClelland, in Knorr and Verba (fn. 3), 200-201. Note that one can explain event/interaction processes with an organizational model, a partial synthesis of the approaches of McClelland and Allison. Also, McClelland actually uses the term *crisis* where the interpretation in the text above refers to conflicts. The word crisis refers to the most intense phase of a conflict in the present study.

[28] Robert A. Young, "Prediction and Forecasting in International Relations: An Exploratory Analysis," unpub. Ph.D. diss., University of Southern California (June 1970).

McClelland's event/interaction model is the least formal and the least explicitly theoretical of the interaction models discussed above. It makes the simple assumption that an interaction pattern will continue under the conditions of a specific international situation and structure. Recall Allison's inference from his organizational processes model: "The best explanation of an organization's behavior at [time] t is $t - 1$; the best prediction of what will happen at $t + 1$ is t." McClelland's model makes a similar statement but it explains continuity of patterns by referring to the international situation and structure. McClelland's model, however, does not explain the continuation of a pattern by referring to axiomatic assumptions regarding rationality or learning, assumptions which would provide closure for either a deductive or inductive explanation. For example, game theory draws upon rationality in a deductive argument to explain rational choice. The power of game theory lies in its elegant deductive explanation of a wide range of rational choice behavior. When applied to the complexities of world politics, however, game theory loses its elegance as well as its deductive power. In a model of world politics, one cannot have deductive power without sacrificing the empirical fit of the model. There are definite trade-offs between logical closure on the one hand and empirical fit on the other hand. One can gain some closure by assuming that event/interaction patterns will continue as a consequence of prior reinforcement—a learning model. The learning model explains inductively the continuity of specific event patterns.

Regarding inductive and deductive explanations, Abraham Kaplan asserts, ". . . we know the reason for something either when we can fit it into a known pattern, or else when we can deduce it from known truths."[29] Kaplan states that the inductive pattern type of explanation may be appropriate to a more mature science. Even in the early stages, however, the generalizations explaining a continuing pattern can function as general laws in a deductive argument. In addition, the patterned behavior can be written as a tendency statement and then operate in an inductive explanation.[30]

A learning model can explain why event/interaction patterns repeat. In behavioral psychology, an individual's patterns result from prior socialization. Kenneth Langton states that, ". . . the continuity of many

[29] Abraham Kaplan, *Conduct of Inquiry* (San Francisco 1964), 332.
[30] Carl G. Hempel, "Deductive-Nomological vs. Statistical Explanation," in H. Feigl and G. Maxwell, eds., *Minnesota Studies in the Philosophy of Science* (Minneapolis 1962), 98-169.

patterns over time and place suggests that the individual has been modified in the course of his development in such a way so that he often
exhibits persistent behavior apart from the momentary effect of his
immediate environment. This behavior results from the socialization
process: an individual's learning from others in his environment the
social patterns and values of his culture."[31] Hence, socialization models
seem appropriate to explain why an event/interaction pattern will hold
in the future. One can classify learning and game models as similar
explanations of rational behavior. Simon asserts that, "Implicit in any
theory of learning is a motivational assumption—i.e., that learning consists in the acquisition of a pattern of behavior appropriate to 'goal
achievement,' . . . In parallel fashion, game theory . . . (is) concerned
with discovering the course of action in a particular situation that will
'optimize' the attainment of some objective or 'payoff'."[32]

Since learning and game models both explain rational choice behavior, it may be possible to subsume event/interaction patterns under
a more general model based on rationality.[33] Thus, an event/interaction
sequence only appears to be non-rational. It may not be the least theoretical of the interaction models discussed above. An event/interaction
analyst, however, need not pay attention to the implicit assumptions
concerning learning and/or rationality. For example, McClelland and
his associates identified recurring patterns in the flows of events with
little reference to assumptions about learning or rationality which
might have explained such patterns.[34] Given their purpose of forecasting from these patterns, it may be adequate just to know the existence
of patterns rather than why the pattern existed.

If one does not know why the pattern exists, he may have difficulty
anticipating changes in patterns. Learning models may explain why
international event patterns exist or change. In world politics, just as
in behavioral psychology, one may need to know prior reinforcement
and present behavior to forecast future behavior. Behavioral psychologists initiate their investigations and/or therapy by establishing prior reinforcement schedules. Thereafter, they monitor and reward present
behavior in relation to the prior schedules. McClelland and his associ-

[31] Kenneth P. Langton, *Political Socialization* (New York 1969), 3.

[32] Simon (fn. 5), 274.

[33] Learning models, unlike game theory, use a more bounded concept of rationality.
Goals may not be ranked, and *search* for an alternative which satisfies a goal replaces
choice of an optimal alternative.

[34] McClelland, in Singer (fn. 12); McClelland and Hoggard, in Rosenau (fn. 9),
711-24.

ates would be on more solid theoretical ground if they first attempted
to discover the prior reinforcement schedules of nations and *then* discovered their performance records.[35]

The present study attempts to infer prior reinforcement from present
interaction patterns. For example, if WTO tends to respond to NATO
in the most intense phase of the Berlin conflict, this might reflect the
experience of prior situations when WTO leaders were rewarded for
responding to NATO actions during the intense phases of prior conflicts. Indeed, an assumption in this regard is that alliance leaders are
more likely to recall learned behavior from the most intense phase of
a prior conflict than from less intense phases. Moreover, as conflictive
intensity increases, the greater may be the perception of interdependence among the actors. Oran Young, furthermore, suggests that actual
interdependence increases during the most intense phase of conflict because each actor is able to exercise less and less control over the interaction. As a result, each actor increasingly considers both the actual and
potential actions of the other party.[36]

Nazli Choucri and Robert North also stress the interdependence of
interactions during periods of high conflict intensity. In their contribution to this volume, Choucri and North discuss three models of international conflict behavior that deal with national expansion, competition, and crisis. The national expansion model assumes that a nation
generates its own dynamic of conflict behavior irrespective of its rivals.
The competitive model assumes that a nation's level of conflict may be
a consequence of the difference in power capability between itself and
its nearest rival. The crisis model assumes that a nation's involvement
in conflict is a response to the behavior of the opponent. The crisis
model anticipates reaction processes, as does the Richardson model. In
arguing for a mixed model, Choucri and North assert that the earlier
stages of a conflict are dominated by dynamics internal to the nation,
as explained by the national expansion model. During later stages,
processes of competition become more evident than the internal self-

[35] Acknowledgments to Judith Tanter for assistance with the behavioral modification
analogy. Subsequently, McClelland and his associates have begun to use learning models
in their World Event/Interaction Survey. Thanks to Gary Hoggard and John Sigler
for bringing these learning models to the author's attention. See McClelland's "Verbal
and Physical Conflict in the Contemporary International System," Mimeo, August 1970,
especially 4-8.
[36] Oran R. Young, *The Politics of Force: Bargaining During International Crises*
(Princeton 1968), 19, 28; Thomas C. Schelling, *The Strategy of Conflict* (Cambridge,
Mass. 1960), 15-16. Note also that evidence suggests that perceptions become more
important the more intense the conflictive interactions. See Ole Holsti and others,
"Perception and Action in the 1914 Crisis," in Singer (fn. 12), 123-58.

generating forces. Even later come the interdependent interactions characteristic of crises. Some of their most important discoveries are the "breakpoints," where external dynamics begin to dominate internal dynamics as determinants of conflictive interactions.

Following Choucri and North, the present study hypothesizes that internal attributes are more important in pre- and post-crisis phases.[37] The present study divides the Berlin conflict into three phases (pre-crisis, crisis, and post-crisis) in order to consider whether interdependent behavior between WTO and NATO increases during the crisis phase in contrast to other phases. During the crisis phase, an event/interaction model should explain alliance behavior more adequately than an organizational processes model. In short, limited rational actors learn patterns of interdependence from prior conflicts. They generalize these patterns and, particularly at the most intense phase of an ongoing conflict, tend to repeat the learned behavior.

AN ORGANIZATIONAL PROCESSES MODEL

Recall Charles McClelland's description of the international system. He ignores the internal attributes of the actors and stresses prior interactions as an explanation for current behavior. Graham Allison's foreign policy approach, on the other hand, ignores prior interaction and emphasizes standard operating procedures and the search behavior of complex organizations within each actor.[38] An event/interaction model can employ the concept of learning to explain recurrent patterns *between* actors; the organizational processes model can use learning to explain organizational routines and search processes *within* actors.

One important set of organizational routines are standard operating procedures (SOP's). The existence of standard operating procedures implies that the actor is adaptively rational. Although the actors are business firms, Richard Cyert and James March suggest that standard operating procedures are the result of a long run adaptive process through which a business firm learns.[39] Standard operating procedures are internal characteristics of the actor. If the actor has a need to behave adaptively in the changing environment of a conflict, however, he has

---

[37] The temporal domain of the present study differs from the Choucri-North study. They base their study on observations covering the period 1870–1914, while the present study concerns the eight-month period immediately prior, during, and after the intense conflict over Berlin in 1961. While the important events in the Choucri-North study unfold over a period of *years* or even *decades*, the theoretically meaningful unit of time in the present study is a period of *days*.

[38] Allison (fn. 2), explicitly acknowledges other models of foreign policy decision-making, e.g., Allison's rational actor model explicitly includes interaction.

[39] Cyert and March (fn. 17), 101 and 113.

to take into account the dynamic nature of that environment. Standard operating procedures are not tailored to specific environments. Rather, they are generalized routines which have been applied previously to similar problems.[40]

When a conflict occurs, standard operating procedures may not be an adequate basis for decision-making. In routine situations, the explanation of the output of an actor may depend heavily on standard operating procedures. During a conflict, rational adaptation suggests that the actor search for more innovative solutions than those provided by standard operating procedures. As Julian Feldman and Herschel Kanter assert: "The major variable affecting the initiation of search is dissatisfaction—the organization will search for additional alternatives when the consequences of the present alternatives do not satisfy its goals."[41] The concept of search fits nicely with the idea of "satisficing"—an actor searches until he finds an alternative which is satisfactory.[42]

During a conflict, the organizational standard operating procedures tend to give way to search processes which are more likely to respond particularly to the external environment. Even these search processes, however, occur primarily in the neighborhood of prior or existing alternatives because of the prominence of these options and the ease of calculating their consequences. In this respect, search simply builds incrementally on standard operating procedures relying on prior cases to provide alternatives that may satisfy organizational goals.

Organizational processes models are to event/interaction models as decision-making models of the firm are to some economic explanations of firm behavior. That is, some economic explanations stress the environment external to the firm as the basis of rational choice. Regarding event/interaction models, the market-determined firm is equivalent to the international system-determined nation. The external environment in a market economy consists of all other competitive firms, e.g., all firms are striving to maximize net revenue, given certain prices and a technologically determined production function. Similarly, consider nations as firms, where nations seek to maximize their national interest. If the market determined each firm's behavior irrespective of internal organizational processes, domestic attributes would be irrelevant to an explanation of a nation's foreign policy decisions. Cyert and March provide an alternative to the market-based ideas just as Allison provides

[40] Allison (fn. 2), 85.
[41] Julian Feldman and Herschel Kanter, "Organizational Decision-Making," in James G. March, ed., *Handbook of Organizations* (Chicago 1965), 662.
[42] Donald W. Taylor, "Decision-Making and Problem Solving," in March, *ibid.*, 662.

an alternative to international system ideas. Cyert and March supplement market analysis with an explanation of the internal operation of the individual firm. Indeed, their analysis indicates that a firm's resource allocation decisions are very dependent upon prior patterns of allocation.[43] In a related inquiry, Aaron Wildavsky finds that the most important determinant of the size and content of a given year's budget is the previous year's budget—a type of organizational incrementalism.[44]

Organizational processes models are to event/interaction models as decision-making models of budgeting are to community power studies. For example, John P. Crecine's study of municipal budgeting employs a decision-making model that stresses organizational factors. His findings provide empirical support to the organizational processes model of Cyert and March. Crecine finds that the lack of adequate data on agency performance leaves the decisionmakers with little choice. They must use prior budgets as a reference for current budget decisions. Crecine also discusses external citizen demand in the budgeting process. This kind of external demand has a counterpart in the event/interaction model of the present inquiry. Crecine acknowledges that external citizen demand may determine the pattern of expenditure within certain accounts. But he finds that there is no direct connection between political pressure and departmental budget levels. Crecine does suggest, however, that external pressures may have a cumulative, long run effect on governmental problem-solving.[45] In contrast, community power studies assume a process of mutual interaction comparable to the event/interaction model presented here. Community power studies do not allow for organizational explanations of the process by which local governments allocate values. The community power studies assume that a business dominated elite, or multiple elites specializing in particular issues, determine governmental resource allocation.[46] In other words the elitist and pluralist community power models both assume that resource allocation in the polity is a consequence of external factors, an assumption comparable to the logic of the event/interaction model.[47]

[43] Cyert and March (fn. 17).

[44] Aaron B. Wildavsky, *The Politics of the Budgetary Process* (Boston 1964), 11 ff.; also cf. Charles E. Lindblom, "The Science of Muddling Through," *Public Administration Review*, XXXVI (Spring 1959), 79-88; David Braybrooke and Charles E. Lindblom, *A Strategy of Decision: Policy Evaluation as a Social Process* (New York 1963).

[45] John P. Crecine, *Governmental Problem-Solving: A Computer Simulation of Municipal Budgeting* (Chicago 1969), 219; "Defense Budgeting: Organizational Adaptation to External Constraints," RAND Corporation (March 1970).

[46] Floyd Hunter, *Community Power Structure: A Study of Decision Makers* (Chapel Hill 1953).

[47] Robert A. Dahl, *Who Governs? Democracy and Power in an American City* (New Haven 1961).

There are several implications from organizational studies which are relevant to the present inquiry.[48] One such inference is that most actions taken by alliances may consist of the repetition or continuance of what was done in the past. In the absence of some reason to change behavior, alliances may simply continue doing what they have been doing.[49] An organizational processes model assumes that most present behavior is a result of prior behavior and organizational routines. Explanation of an action begins at the base line of prior behavior and routines, noting incremental deviations.[50] The incremental deviations may result from the external environment. Thus, the organizational based studies also suggest a combined interaction/organization model.

Recall the specific hypothesis emerging from a foreign policy decision-making approach: an alliance's behavior during a conflict results from its own pattern of actions. Given the discussion of conflict phases above, consider the following expansion and modification of this hypothesis: an alliance's behavior in pre- and post-crisis results from its intra-organizational standard operating procedures and search processes. Specifically, WTO should respond more to its own prior behavior than to NATO during the pre- and post-crisis phases of the Berlin conflict, and similarly for NATO. Finally, the interaction/organization model simply combines the event/interaction and organizational processes models.

Design and Analysis Decisions

A fundamental assumption of the design is that indicators can tap unmeasured concepts. That is, the data are the intensities of conflictive interactions between the WTO and NATO alliances. No data are presented here on such theoretically interesting concepts as learning, rationality, standard operating procedures, or search processes. Nonetheless, the design assumes that event/interaction patterns can be used as indicators of these theoretically significant concepts.[51]

If an alliance's current actions are a response more to its own prior behavior, the inference is that organizational processes are more important than interaction patterns. Conversely, if an alliance's current

---

[48] SOP's in bureaucracies imply long-term stability of behavior, while the present analysis treats continuity of action over periods of several days. Nonetheless, the organizational literature may provide useful analogies for the study of short-term conflict.

[49] Morton H. Halperin, *Bureaucratic Politics and Foreign Policy*, The Brookings Institute (March 1970).

[50] *Ibid.*; Allison (fn. 2).

[51] Hubert M. Blalock, Jr., "The Measurement Problem: A Gap between the Language of Theory and Research," in Hubert M. Blalock, Jr. and Ann B. Blalock, eds., *Methodology in Social Research* (New York 1968), 5-27.

actions are a response more to the other alliance's prior behavior, then the inference is that interaction patterns are more important than organizational processes. In both cases, measured indicators (actions) tap unmeasured concepts (e.g., event/interactions and organizational processes). *By no stretch of the imagination, then, does this design test models or their implications. Rather, the design simply evaluates the models which seem to be implied by certain patterns in the data.* This design is inductive in orientation, but it does more than search for regularities in the data. The study uses patterns as a point of departure for making inferences about models. In short, the design seeks to develop an interface between strategies that stress logical closure via tight models and those which search for empirical regularities.[52]

Specifically, the design allows for the evaluation of the following hypotheses:

1. Prior WTO conflictive action intensities determine current WTO action intensities.[53]
2. Prior NATO conflictive action intensities determine current NATO action intensities.
3. Prior WTO conflictive action intensities determine current NATO action intensities.
4. Prior NATO conflictive action intensities determine current WTO action intensities.
5. Prior WTO and NATO conflictive action intensities determine current WTO action intensities.
6. Prior WTO and NATO conflictive action intensities determine current NATO action intensities.

The first four hypotheses correspond to the paths in Figure 1. Hypotheses five and six combine paths one and four as well as paths two and three respectively. Paths one and two are called vertical paths while three and four are the diagonal paths in this study. If the diagonals are greater than the verticals, this might indicate that an event/interaction model is more valid than an organizational processes model. If the verticals are greater than the diagonals, this might indicate that an organizational processes model is more valid than an event/interaction model. If both the diagonals and verticals are equally strong, this might indicate that the interaction/organization model is the valid one relative to its components. If neither the diagonals nor the verticals are

[52] See the article by Oran R. Young in this volume regarding strategies that stress logical closure and those that emphasize the search for empirical regularities.
[53] The term action intensity includes both word and deed intensities.

strong, this might indicate one or two things: (1) the models specified here are invalid; (2) a significant amount of measurement error is present in the data.

FIGURE 1

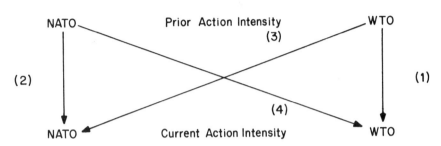

With the six hypotheses diagrammed in Figure 1, the author hopes to account for the systematic variance in the study. Other variance may be due to error or is systematic variance which is extraneous here. The design, therefore, seeks to minimize error variance and rule out extraneous variance, e.g., rival hypotheses which might explain the dependent variables. One plausible rival hypothesis, for example, is that the actions of the Chinese People's Republic might determine the interactions between WTO and NATO. There is some evidence of a close connection between the *long term* conflictive actions of the C.P.R., U.S.S.R., and the U.S.[54] An assumption of this study, however, is that the relationship between the WTO and NATO countries in a given conflict is not a result of their respective interactions with China.

A further design decision concerns the measurement of conflict intensity and the identification of the distinct phases of the Berlin conflict. Walter Corson made available his conflict intensity scale and coded data from the Berlin conflict of 1961.[55] Corson divides the Berlin con-

[54] Walter H. Corson, "Conflict and Cooperation in East-West Relations: Measurement and Explanation," paper delivered at the 66th Annual Meeting of the American Political Science Association, Los Angeles, September, 1970. Also, see Allen S. Whiting, "United States–Chinese Political Relations," The University of Michigan, Mimeo, 1970, 17.

[55] Corson constructed the scale in two phases. He administered questionnaires to 53 citizens of 13 non-Western and Western countries. In the first phase, there were 54 conflictive actions arranged in irregular order. With each action printed on a separate card, respondents arranged the actions in rank-order of increasing intensity. The responses from these questionnaires constituted information to compute a mean rank-order for each action, resulting in a 54-item rank-order conflict intensity scale. In the second phase, respondents had 14 conflictive actions selected from the original group of 54; these actions covered the full range of intensity. They were printed on separate cards and presented to respondents in irregular order. Respondents assigned a number to each action proportional to its intensity as they perceived it. Using the responses

flict into five phases on the basis of changes in the *types* and *intensities* of both conflictive and cooperative behavior. Corson's second criterion for disaggregating the total interaction process is events which act as obvious thresholds.

The present study draws partially on Corson's criteria to specify the phases of the Berlin Conflict. In contrast to the Corson analysis, the present study excludes cooperative interaction patterns.[56] Instead, total conflictive intensity scores are used for NATO and WTO by day from 1 May 1961 to 31 December 1961.

The data show that conflictive intensity remains low until 25 July when President Kennedy announced major U.S. military preparations. Conflictive intensity peaked for WTO on 13 August when the East Germans sealed the border, and for NATO on 17 August when France and Britain strengthened their armed forces and NATO demanded an end to the travel ban. The last high conflict peak occurred on 17 September when the U.S.S.R. protested West German air intrusion over Berlin. Beginning with the meetings between Soviet Premier Khrushchev and Belgian Foreign Minister Spaak on 18 September over the German treaty, events of moderate cooperative intensity occur with relative frequency. The time from 25 July to 17 September is thus delineated as the crisis phase for three reasons: (1) conflictive interaction is more intense during this 56 day period than during any other; (2) although this phase has several clear peaks, the intensity remained high for several days; and (3) the crisis phase begins on 25 July with an event of high conflictive intensity and ends with an event on 17 September of high conflictive intensity. Figure 2 presents all three phases of the 1961 Berlin conflict.[57]

The design evaluates the three models of conflict (event/interaction, organizational processes, and a combination of both) and their corresponding hypotheses by regressing each alliance's current conflictive action intensity (dependent variable) on both its own prior conflictive

---

from these questionnaires, the geometric mean for each event reflected its intensity across respondents. From these data, he developed a 14-item conflict intensity scale and assigned intensity values by interpolation to the remaining 40 conflictive actions. Details of the scaling project are given in Walter H. Corson, "Conflict and Cooperation in East-West Crises: Dynamics of Crisis Interaction," unpublished Ph.D. thesis, Harvard University, December, 1970.

[56] The conflict phases outlined in this paper are based on empirical data from a specific conflict and describe only that conflict. Work is under way by the author and his colleagues on the development of a process model of conflict which will draw on this analysis but not be limited to it.

[57] Corson originally identified five conflict phases: pre-crisis, intensification, peak, reduction, and post-crisis. For the present analysis, crisis includes intensification, peak, and reduction. Corson (fn. 55).

FIGURE 2

PHASES OF THE 1961 BERLIN CONFLICT

Phase	Period	No. of Days
All Phases	1 May 1961 – 31 December 1961	245
Pre-crisis	1 May – 24 July	84
Crisis	25 July – 17 September	56
Post-crisis	18 September – 31 December	105

action intensity and the other alliance's prior action intensity for each phase of the Berlin conflict. These operations yielded the path coefficients reported in this analysis.

A crucial substantive and design problem confronted in this paper is the meaning of *time*. As a variable and unit of analysis, time is usually measured in terms of increments of solar time—minutes, hours, days, weeks, months, years, and so on. Yet it is very likely that time holds a different meaning for decisionmakers caught up in a crisis. Time, thus, could be thought of as "diplomatic time" and measured in a variety of ways including aggregating solar time to periods of specific duration on the basis of explicit theoretical criteria, or abandoning solar time units altogether. A variety of studies of crisis[58] converge in their identification of two criteria integral to the nature of crises: (1) action intensity, and (2) elapsed time between actions.

Corson finds that the elapsed time between actions varies inversely with total conflictive intensity in his study of the 1961 Berlin conflict.[59] This implies that as events increase in conflictive intensity, they also become more frequent. However, a day is the unit of time in this study for three reasons: (1) the author knows of no theory relating the frequency of events with the intensity of conflict in a continuous fashion;

[58] Holsti and others, in Singer (fn. 12); Hermann (fn. 15); Corson (fn. 55). Thanks to Paul Smoker for his thoughts on the study of time.

[59] Corson (fn. 55), 186. Corson speculated that time period should be an aggregation of days rather than a single day. The criteria he employed are three: (1) if total conflictive intensity for NATO and WTO on a given day was less than 30 on the Corson scale, the intensity of conflictive actions on that day and the preceding six days predicted the intensity of conflictive actions for the next three days; (2) if total given intensity on a given day was between 30 and 150, action intensity on that day and the preceding four days predicted action intensity for the next three days; and (3) if total intensity on a given day was greater than 150, action intensity on that day and the preceding two days predicted deed intensity for the next two days. There are at least three difficulties with this method. First, it is difficult to implement this aggregation scheme without overlapping time periods. Second, the method is discontinuous when it should most properly be of the form

$$t = a/I$$

where t is the aggregation period, I, the conflictive intensity, and, a, the proportionality constant. As the intensity gets large the aggregation period gets small. Third, the method only represents more intuition than empirical finding.

(2) if time periods were aggregated, stronger relationships would be found according to the "ecological fallacy;" (3) the multi-lagged models tested did not contribute any additional information over and above the single-lagged models.[60] Thus, the study predicts current action intensity by prior action intensity across each day of the conflict.

A further decision was to aggregate data to the alliance level of analysis.[61] An initial decision was to study only Soviet-American behavior in the Berlin conflict. It became apparent, however, that East and West Germany would have to be included. Then what does one do with relevant actions by other countries during the conflict? These actions should also be taken into account. Hence, the alliance became the unit of aggregation. The alliance unit of aggregation may be more valid for a case such as Berlin than for a case such as the Cuban Missile Crisis of 1962. There, alliance participation was secondary to the Soviet-American confrontation.[62]

Regarding the data, there are 337 events for the Berlin conflict from 1 May 1961 through 31 December 1961—245 days. Primary data sources included the *New York Times* front page, *Deadline Data on World Affairs*, as well as *The World Almanac and Book of Facts*, 1961, 1962. The present study does not use events *per se* in analysis. Rather, the daily intensities aggregated across events for each alliance comprise the data for analysis. The coding and aggregation design decisions prepared the data for analysis. The method used is path analysis, which consists of regression analyses of theoretically specified relationships using standardized data.[63] Path analysis is appropriate for determining the relative contribution of competing paths in explaining a dependent variable. The assumptions of the method compare nicely with the measurement

[60] Multi-lagged models were run under two hypotheses: (1) the conflictive intensity on any given day would be some linear combination of the conflictive intensities of the previous six days; (2) conflictive intensity would have a decreasing effect as time from the present increased. Neither of these two hypotheses were supported by the models or the data. The only different model which arose out of this analysis is found in footnote 73.

[61] Aggregating to the alliance level as in the present study may result in a lack of fit between an organizational model and the alliance. The study assumes, however, that organizational models are equally valid irrespective of the level of analysis.

[62] In the Berlin conflict of 1961, 28% of WTO actions recorded involved other WTO members acting with or without the U.S.S.R.; 48% of all NATO actions recorded involved other NATO members acting with or without the United States. See *ibid*.

[63] Here is a summary of the methodology: The independent variables are prior WTO and/or prior NATO action intensities. Both word and deed intensity comprise the action category. The author standardized action intensity within the three conflict phases for each alliance, e.g., action intensity had a mean of zero and a standard deviation of unity, pre-conditions for path analysis. Standardized NATO and WTO action intensities were each regressed on standardized prior NATO and WTO action intensities, resulting in the path coefficients.

system and theoretical specification of this study. For example, path analysis assumes interval scale data and specification of some of the paths. The Corson scale probably meets the interval level assumption, and the present study specifies most of the paths explicitly.

ANALYSIS AND RESULTS

Here is a very brief historical overview of key events in the Berlin conflict from 1 May 1961 through 31 December 1961, followed by the path analysis whose purpose is to evaluate the three proposed models.[64] During May of 1961 (pre-crisis) WTO countries began to intensify their demands that the West terminate its presence in Berlin. There was concern with the problem of the flow of refugees fleeing East Germany—almost 200,000 in 1960. The refugee problem was a major motivating factor in precipitating the conflict. Recall the inference from the Choucri-North study that during the pre-crisis phase it is likely that the focus would be on internal attributes of the actor rather than on the opponent's actions. Intra-alliance factors such as the refugee problem and potential unrest in East Germany appear to be more important than NATO actions as determinants of WTO conflict intensification. There followed a slow but steady intensification of conflict which, although self-generated, was modified by Western actions occasionally. The WTO "ultimatum" of June, the threat to sign a separate peace treaty with East Germany and end the legal basis for the Western presence in Berlin, illustrates a key event in the intensification.

In the crisis phase there seemed to be a greater amount of competitive action and reaction than in the pre-crisis phase. For example, the WTO actions of 13 August 1961 to erect the Wall may have resulted from WTO dissatisfaction with Western response to the demand for a separate peace treaty with East Germany. The Western response consisted partly of a reiteration of three essentials: (1) continued allied presence in Berlin; (2) unrestricted access routes to and from Berlin; and (3)

---

[64] For a historical overview of the Berlin crisis, see: George Bailey, "The Gentle Erosion of Berlin," *The Reporter* (April 26, 1962); Arnold L. Horelick and Myron Rush, "The Political Offensive Against Berlin," *Strategic Power and Soviet Foreign Policy* (Chicago 1965), chap. 10; John W. Keller, *Germany, the Wall and Berlin: Internal Policies During an International Crisis* (New York 1964); Jean Edward Smith, "Berlin: The Erosion of a Principle," *The Reporter* (November 21, 1963); Jean Edward Smith, *The Defense of Berlin* (Baltimore 1963); Hans Speier, *Divided Berlin* (New York 1961); Jack M. Schick, "The Berlin Crisis of 1961 and U.S. Military Strategy," *Orbis*, VIII (Winter 1965); Oran R. Young, *The Politics of Force* (Princeton 1966); Charles McClelland, "Access to Berlin: The Quantity and Variety of Events, 1948–1963," in Singer (fn. 12), 159-86.

freedom for West Berliners to choose their own form of government. The Western response consisted of concrete acts which strengthened NATO military forces and reinforced NATO troops in Berlin. (One could select an event from the post-crisis phase to illustrate the de-emphasis on interaction and the consequent reassertion of domestic factors, but it is not necessary to illustrate the point.) One problem with selecting historical incidents as illustrations is that it is generally easy to find an event which demonstrates the idea! Systematic comparative inquiry seeks to avoid such biased sampling "to prove" one's ideas. A comparison of action intensities across time, based on a universe of events, is more valid than the selective sampling of events in a verbal descriptive account, although both are necessary.

Another way of analyzing the Berlin conflict is to look at the level of conflictive intensities over time. For example, from 1 May through 24 July, total conflictive intensity was low for both alliances.[65] Disag-gregating conflictive action into its components for a moment, consider the period between 25 July through 12 August. WTO threats were much higher in intensity than WTO disapproval, demands, or deeds. In contrast, NATO conflictive deeds were much higher in intensity than its words: disapproval, demands, or threats.[66]

From 13 August to 17 September, conflictive intensities were at their highest levels. Disaggregating the conflictive actions from 13 to 26 August shows that WTO conflictive actions were comprised of low demand, high threat, and low to moderately intense deeds. In contrast, NATO's conflictive actions in this period had moderately intense deeds (includ-ing troop movements), high demand, and low threat intensity (includ-ing frequent protests of the border closing but few threats of action which would counter the closing). Between 27 August and 17 Septem-ber the nature of WTO and NATO conflictive intensity levels are sim-ilar: threats and deeds were relatively high, disapproval and demands were relatively low.[67] In the post-crisis phase, 18 September through 31 December, events of cooperative intensity were more frequent than those of conflictive intensity.[68] In summary, total conflictive intensity for

[65] For the purposes of this study, 1 May 1961 is the beginning of the Berlin conflict. This establishes a base line period several weeks prior to the WTO ultimatum in early June.

[66] Corson (fn. 55).

[67] Corson, *ibid.*

[68] The meetings between Soviet Premier Khrushchev and Belgian Foreign Minister Spaak on 18–19 September mark the transition to the post-crisis phase. The analysis ends on 31 December 1961 because the frequency and intensity of actions began to approach the pre-crisis level of June.

WTO and NATO averaged lowest in the pre-crisis phase (daily average = 14 points on the Corson scale), moderate in the post-crisis phase (29 points on the Corson scale), and highest in the crisis phase (96 points on the Corson scale).

Given this brief historical overview and the description of intensities of conflictive behavior, Figure 3 contains the results of the quantitative analysis. Recall the general proposition that the organizational processes model should explain alliance behavior in the pre- and post-crisis phases

FIGURE 3

RESULTS FOR THE 1961 BERLIN CONFLICT[69]

$$(N = 245)$$

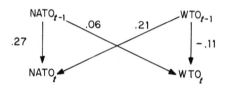

Pre-Crisis — Conflict Days 1-84 — N = 83

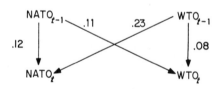

Crisis — Conflict Days 85-140 — N = 55

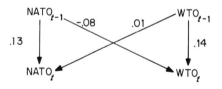

Post-Crisis — Conflict Days 141-245 — N = 104

[69] Note that when variables are lagged, you lose one degree of freedom. Thus, N is always smaller than the number of conflict days in each phase.

while the event/interaction model should explain such behavior during the crisis phase.[70]

The values in Figure 3 are path coefficients, which generally range from −1.0 to +1.0. They indicate the relative magnitude of each path in determining current alliance action intensity. High vertical path coefficients relative to the diagonals are consistent with an organizational processes model. Large diagonal coefficients relative to the verticals are compatible with an event/interaction model.[71]

How are the numbers to be interpreted in light of the hypotheses of the study? Paths may be thought of as flows of influence between variables, indicating both the direction of the "flow" and the strength of the dependence of one variable on another. Donald Stokes likens paths to a system of interlocking waterways with the flow of water through the paths directed by gates and the amount of water flowing through each gate determined by the magnitudes of the path coefficients.[72]

According to the organizational processes model for the pre-crisis phase, the vertical paths for both WTO and NATO should be stronger than the diagonals, and, indeed, this is generally the case. However, for WTO, the vertical path coefficient is only .06 while the diagonal is just −.11. These results suggest that the model is inadequate and/or there is large measurement error in the data. On the other hand, the vertical path coefficient for NATO is .27 while the diagonal is .21. Given the small difference between these two values, it would seem that both the organizational process model and the event/interaction model apply to NATO activity in this period, but one should not draw strong inferences because of the small magnitude of the coefficients.

The fit does not improve for the crisis phase, although, as one would expect, the event/interaction model has a slight edge in predictive power. For NATO, the diagonal path coefficient, .23, is twice as large as the vertical, .12, but given the small sample size the difference would

---

[70] Besides the organizational processes model, there are several other foreign policy type models that might explain incremental outputs during the pre- and post-crisis phases (cf. Allison and Halperin in this volume).

[71] The path coefficients for the entire period can be seen in the following diagram:

[72] See Donald E. Stokes, "Compound Paths in Political Analysis," The University of Michigan, Mimeo, n.d.

not be statistically significant.[73] The fit is even worse for WTO; the diagonal path coefficient, .11, is about the same as the vertical path coefficient, .08. Thus, one should be cautious in drawing any inferences.

In the post-crisis phase, the vertical coefficients are larger than the diagonals, but not of sufficient magnitude to suggest a reversion to standard operating procedures and the organizational processes model. For NATO the vertical coefficient is .13 while the diagonal coefficient is .01. For WTO the vertical coefficient is .14 while the diagonal coefficient is —.08.[74]

Given the inconclusive results of the data analysis, the author cannot select between the models. The organizational processes model may or may not be adequate for the pre-crisis and post-crisis phases; the organizational processes model might be as relevant or irrelevant to the crisis phase as the event/interaction model.[75]

There are at least three possible explanations for the inconclusive results. First, the models may be mis-specified; that is, not all of the predictive variables were included in the analysis. Recall that the refugee problem was a major motivating factor in precipitating the conflict. Thus, at least one major causal variable was left out of the model. Indeed, internal conflictive behavior was left out of the model. There is justification for expecting little relationship between domestic and foreign conflictive behavior, but now may be the time to re-examine the

---

[73] This study does *not* use statistical inference procedures in evaluating the models. Here is an alternate model for NATO in the crisis phase, the only instance where the author felt the multiple lags contributed new information:

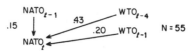

Here is an indication of the strength of the interaction relationships. NATO reacts strongest to WTO actions lagged by four days.

[74] Results of an earlier analysis using the aggregation periods defined in footnote 59 supported the hypotheses that organizational processes were more important in the pre- and post-crisis phases, and that organizational processes may have been important in the crisis phase as well. Because of the reasons stated in the text, most especially because of the ecological fallacy, these results are not presented here. Although the ecological fallacy demonstrates little effect on the functional relationship between variables, the regression coefficient, it has profound effects on the strength of that association, the beta weight. In path analysis only the beta weight is presented, which would be inflated because of the aggregation of days. Thus, it may be misleading to draw inferences, based as they might be on an artifact of aggregation. For a reference, see Hubert M. Blalock, Jr., *Causal Inferences in Nonexperimental Research* (Chapel Hill 1964), 97-114.

[75] Given the alternative model in footnote 73, it appears that the event/interaction model has more explanatory power for NATO during the crisis phase.

internal-external relationship, given the nature of the Berlin conflict.[76]

Second, the Corson scale as used here may be inappropriate. Summing conflictive intensities about interactions may not be sufficient to tap such theoretically interesting concepts as standard operating procedures. The Corson scale should be re-examined for its assumptions and its applicability to models of relevance to the current study.

Third, there is some question as to whether action intensity, which is the aggregate of both words and deeds, should be used as the indicator in the models. Action intensity was used initially as a means of tapping the total behavior of the actors, but this may be unsatisfactory for three reasons: (1) deeds have a longer preparation time than words; (2) international politics words can be disregarded with greater frequency than deeds—it is very difficult to ignore the Berlin Wall; (3) words are subject to greater misinterpretation than deeds. The author is at present addressing himself to the above problems in his forthcoming book on the 1948–49 and 1961 Berlin conflicts.[77]

Implications for Conflict Modelling and Management

The twin goals of this paper are to make a tentative evaluation of models based on an international system approach, a foreign policy approach, and a combination of these two approaches; and to infer from the evaluation of these models some implications for conflict modelling and management. The inconclusive nature of the above analysis only points up the problems facing the conflict manager, and in this section the author attempts to address the implications of the study of the Berlin conflict of 1961 for the more general problem of conflict management.

If one is to generalize about conflicts, it would make sense to have information on as many cases as possible. An analyst hopes to draw inferences from a limited number of cases which are representative of the larger universe of all conflicts. The Berlin conflict of 1961 may not be at all representative. As McClelland indicates, the Berlin conflicts of 1948, 1958, and 1961 may have been increasingly routinized as a consequence of a bureaucratic processing that became almost self-generating. That is, conflict over Berlin occurred so frequently that organizational processes assumed greater importance over time. Quite possibly, standard operating procedures grew up around the conflicts as a result of this

[76] Raymond Tanter, "Dimensions of Conflict Behavior Within and Between Nations, 1958–1960," *Journal of Conflict Resolution*, x (March 1966), 41-64.
[77] Raymond Tanter, *The Berlin Crises: Modelling and Managing International Conflicts* (forthcoming, 1972).

repetitive pattern.[78] Yet, in a case such as the Cuban Missile Crisis of 1962, the event/interaction model might be more valid within the crisis phase. Thus, it is important to create a universe of cases for the comparative inquiry of conflicts before drawing firm inferences from any one case. (The new conflict data should include information on the interactions and on organizational processes if possible.)

In addition to obtaining data on more cases, it is necessary to explicate further the present models and to develop additional models to explain conflictive interactions. The present models allow one to make little sense of patterns in the data. Certainly, this result of the data analysis indicates a need to develop further process models that would describe and explain the evolution of conflict situations.[79] In the interest of preventing the explosion of conflicts into crisis, it is extremely important to discern the connection, if any, between apparently dissimilar conflicts. This might be accomplished through the development of models and through the long and tedious process of making, rejecting, and accepting hypotheses based on these models.

The results of this study have other tentative implications for an effort at model-building. For instance, the evidence does not indicate that the author should ally himself with "disillusioned interaction analysts" and join the growing number of organizational analysts. Such a decision would be premature, especially since the times call for a synthesis of the two approaches. Perhaps the Thomas Schellings and Charles McClellands overemphasize the role of interaction processes; perhaps Graham Allison and Morton Halperin overemphasize organizational processes in relation to interaction notions. It is not for the author to say at this time; the jury is still out.

How would the organizational theorists view the Berlin conflict? Halperin, for example, might claim that "In periods viewed by senior players as crises . . . , organizations will calculate how alternative policies and patterns of action will affect future definitions of roles and missions. . . . [Organizations] will press for policies which they believe

---

[78] This study, however, does not compare intensities for the three Berlin conflicts; rather, it only has data on the Berlin conflict of 1961. Thus, there are no hard data presented here on the routinization of conflict decision-making.

[79] Process modelling is a research strategy designed to disaggregate a complex set of interrelated events and behaviors into stages representing discrete actions or distinct choice points. Process models serve several useful purposes. First, they direct our attention to processes such as learning, forgetting, or precedent search which underlie highly complex patterns of behavior. Thus, process models reduce complex situations to their basic elements, permitting an economy of description and explanation. Finally, process modelling could explain the breakpoints in a conflict—those points where the internal dynamics give way to external factors.

will maintain or extend their roles and missions, even if at some cost to the immediate objectives of the President. . . ."[80] Regarding the present study, Halperin's explanation *suggests* that alliances should respond more to intra-alliance than to inter-alliance considerations. Halperin's explanation also poses the question whether alliances are useful units of analysis to tap organizational processes. (See footnote 61.) If bureaucracies respond, as Halperin contends, to their roles as defined within a particular country, there is no reason to suppose that this response is consistent with other countries in the alliance. Indeed, one might suspect the contrary. The alliance problem may account for the relatively weak organizational process link found in the analysis of the Berlin conflict of 1961. To determine the effects of organizational processes, it might be better to examine individual countries and, especially, the various bureaucracies in those countries.

One of the more interesting aspects of this study comes from the examination of the plots of conflictive intensity. For the pre-crisis and post-crisis phases, activity is relatively minor; many of the days register no activity at all. This might conform to Halperin's statement that, ". . . most of the actions taken by bureaucrats . . . involve doing again or continuing to do what was done in the past. In the absence of some reason to change their behavior, organizations keep doing what they have been doing."[81] This notion of "bureaucratic incrementalism," explaining the performance of foreign service personnel around the world, is certainly intuitively appealing. Evidence from the budgeting studies, moreover, suggests that municipal politicians may have something in common with their statesmen counterparts in the foreign service.

There is a problem, however, with the incrementalist thesis. How can the incrementalist thesis account for an innovative sequence of interactions such as WTO's ultimatum to NATO, NATO's response increasing its conventional military capabilities, the Berlin Wall, and negotiations? Although these events are measured, the present quantitative analysis fails to account for such innovative sequences. Similarly, the budgeting studies which stress quantitative budget totals may overlook the quality of the programs. Thus, quantitative analysis needs to be supplemented by a study of the qualitative aspects. The latter may be more apt to yield event/interaction sequences.[82]

[80] Halperin (fn. 49), 50.

[81] *Ibid.*, 9.

[82] As stated previously, however, one must be careful to avoid selecting historical events in order "to prove" one's hypothesis. Thanks to Alexander George for the critique of the incrementalist thesis regarding the quality of programs.

In summary, this study implies that in modelling conflict an analyst should: (1) specify a universe of cases for comparative inquiry across conflicts; (2) further explicate the event/interaction and organizational processes models, emphasizing their formal axioms and data requirements; (3) develop process models that describe and explain the evolution of conflict in general—emphasizing breakpoints where internal dynamics give way to external factors; and (4) integrate qualitative evaluation of events with quantitative analysis, to ensure that one takes into account the nature of events.

A project underway by the author and his colleagues seeks to implement those modelling implications with the construction of a Computer-Aided Conflict Information System (CACIS). Coders are classifying major power conflicts since World War II in terms of environmental factors, policy options, national interests and involvement, goals, intentions, resources employed (military, economic diplomatic), and outcomes. CACIS will also include a capability for specifying event/ interaction and organizational models, among others, within the general framework of a process model of conflict. An important aspect of the process model will be its formal status. Rather than using the relatively loose verbal models of the present study, CACIS will emphasize tight, deductively oriented formal models.

One principal attribute of CACIS is that it is being built around four separate but interrelated modules:

1. The *memory* module which stores information about prior conflicts.
2. The *experience* module which stores evaluations of strategies used in prior conflicts, and the number of successes, failures, or indeterminate outcomes.
3. The *involvement* module which estimates the type and magnitude of interests (or values) of conflict participants.
4. The *operational* environment module which includes external events and domestic political factors. This module could serve as the basis for the evaluation of the relative potencies of internal processes vs. external events on the policy-making process, as well as provide parameters for an all-machine simulation of conflict decision-making.

A second major characteristic of CACIS is its reliance on the process of precedent search.[83] That is, a party to a conflict, in seeking a solution

[83] Hayward R. Alker, Jr. and Cheryl Christensen, "From Causal Modelling to Artificial Intelligence: The Evolution of a U.N. Peace-Making Simulation," Massachusetts Institute of Technology, Mimeo, n.d.

commensurate with its goals, will search for prior conflicts similar to the current conflict as policy guides. Precedent search behavior assumes the existence of rules or "precedent logics"[84]—i.e., criteria guiding precedent search—as well as the identification of dimensions of similarity and differences along which conflicts may be located.

CACIS supplements the Computer-Aided System for Handling Information on Local Conflicts (CASCON), developed by Lincoln Bloomfield and Robert Beattie.[85] CASCON focuses on local conflicts between small powers or between a small power and one major power, while CACIS will include mainly the CASCON cases and those conflicts involving more than one major power. Some overlap, however, is expected in the sample of cases selected. CACIS will offer more options to the analyst through the programming of multiple models rather than the single model of local conflict of Bloomfield and Amelia Leiss in CASCON.[86] Finally, unlike CASCON, CACIS is expected to have a machine simulation capability enabling the user to look at "what might have been" by recalling prior relevant cases, applying alternative policy options, and examining the simulated outcomes in relation to a current conflict.

Implications of the present study for conflict management are less certain. Glenn Paige faced a similar problem in deciding whether to draw implications for conflict management from a single case—Korea, 1950. He wondered ". . . whether it is not premature and irresponsible for the student of decision-making analysis to venture suggestions of an applied nature on the basis of a single case. . . ." Paige concluded that international crises are such important phenomena that it is well worth the risk to venture suggestions.[87] Following Paige's lead, the present study will also make inferences regarding conflict management, with similar caveats about over-generalizing.

The idea of conflict management assumes that conflicts are similar enough to plan for in advance. Some national security policy planners argue that the element of surprise places great constraints upon planning. For example, G. A. Morgan asserts: "The number of theoretically possible crises in the years ahead is virtually infinite. Even to try to plan systematically for all that are moderately likely would be a questionable

[84] *Ibid.*, 21.
[85] Lincoln Bloomfield and Robert Beattie, "Computers and Policy-Making: The CASCON Experiment," *Journal of Conflict Resolution*, XI (March 1971); Robert Beattie, and Lincoln Bloomfield, *CASCON: Computer-Aided System for Handling Information on Local Conflicts.* (Cambridge, Mass. 1969); also cf. Fisher Howe, *The Computer and Foreign Affairs* (Washington 1967).
[86] Lincoln Bloomfield and Amelia Leiss, *Controlling Small Wars: A Strategy for the 1970's* (New York 1969).
[87] Paige (fn. 15).

expenditure of resources."[88] Klaus Knorr and Oskar Morgenstern agree
with this, concluding that planning is difficult because intense conflicts
are ". . . essentially unpredictable. . . ."[89]

The notion that conflict planning is virtually impossible because of
unpredictability overlooks the fact that contingency planning takes
place in several areas where phenomena are not easily predicted. For
example, earthquakes are rarely predictable in advance. Nonetheless,
areas where they frequently occur have developed standard operating
procedures for processing the injured, alleviating congestion, and com-
municating in the absence of normal channels. Similarly, in international security planning, conflict need not be fully predictable for management plans to be written and used as general guides.

Social scientists should not feel uncomfortable at being unable to
make point predictions of specific events. Physicists often do not forecast individual events, but they are able to explain and forecast processes
and general classes of events. Social scientists also should seek to explain
and forecast processes and classes of events. Process models are promising ways of developing explanatory and predictive theory both for
processes and general event-classes. The development of conflict intensity scales is a way of constructing more general event-classes.[90] Computer based models and the acquisition of comparable data on a series
of historical cases promise to improve the generality of event concepts.

The creation of computer based models such as CACIS should
facilitate conflict management in several ways. For example, the results
of the coming inquiry might serve as a basis for specifying models in
CACIS. Suppose then, that these analyses found that an organizational
processes model explained WTO and NATO alliance behavior better
than an event/interaction model, especially in the pre- and post-crisis
phases. In such a case, a foreign policy decision-making approach may
yield more than an international system approach for the conflict. If a
new Berlin conflict were to erupt, an analyst might expect the predominance of intra- as opposed to inter-alliance factors. CACIS would allow
the analyst to compare recurring conflict over Berlin with what oc-

[88] G. A. Morgan, "Planning in Foreign Affairs: The State of the Art," *Foreign
Affairs*, xxxix (January 1961), 278. The thrust of Morgan's argument is for selective
planning. However, some authors advocate more planning—J. C. Ausland and J. F.
Richardson, "Crisis Management: Berlin, Cyprus, Laos," *Foreign Affairs*, xliv (January
1966), 291-303.

[89] Klaus Knorr and Oskar Morgenstern, *Political Conjecture in Military Planning*,
Princeton University, Center of International Studies, Policy Memorandum No. 35
(1968), 10-15.

[90] A conflict intensity scale produces more general classes than raw event data. That
is, the scales allow an analyst to aggregate across a variety of events to calculate a
general intensity score for the actor.

curred in 1948, 1958, and 1961, especially regarding the organizational processes of the actors. If such a comparison proved useful, the analyst might expect the bureaucratic patterns of the past to repeat themselves. As a result, the analyst can develop his plans anticipating standard operating procedures and search processes.

Another way that CACIS might facilitate conflict management is as an aid to memory in the form of an information retrieval system. The information would describe prior conflicts, the policy measures used, and their consequences. The institutionalization of prior crisis patterns, and the policy measures employed, is important for several reasons. First, the memory of complex organizations too often resides in now departed personnel who were instrumental in prior conflict problem-solving. CACIS would thus be an aid to memory in immediately accessible form. As an aid to memory, CACIS would facilitate the search for alternative options. Recall the search style of limited rational actors—they learn to search for alternatives until they find the one that satisfies goal achievement.[91]

It is also very important to institutionalize alternatives. During a conflict there is a higher probability that stress may cause the replacement of complex problem solving habits by more basic forms. That is, if stress is intense and persistent, there is a tendency for more recent and usually more complex behavior to disappear and for simpler and more basic forms of behavior to reappear.[92] Thus, there might be a tendency to revert to the standard operating procedures and other familiar organizational routines during periods of highest conflictive intensity. Rather than bringing about a greater sensitivity to the external environment, crisis induced stress may result in increased reliance upon standard operating procedures in the intense crisis phase.

Finally, institutionalization of alternatives would permit the examination of the consequences of conflict management attempts in prior cases. For example, Alexander George specifies seven principles of crisis management, some of which relate nicely to the present inquiry. He asserts that there should be: (1) high level political control of military options; (2) pauses in military operations; (3) clear and appropriate demonstrations to show resolution; (4) military action coordinated with political-diplomatic action; (5) confidence in the effectiveness and discriminating character of military options; (6) military options that

---

[91] James G. March, "Some Recent Substantive and Methodological Developments in the Theory of Organizational Decision-Making," in Austin Ranney, ed., *Essays on the Behavioral Study of Politics* (Urbana 1962), 191-208.

[92] Thomas W. Milburn, "The Management of Crisis," Mimeo, 1970.

avoid motivating the opponent to escalate; and (7) avoidance of the impression of a resort to large scale warfare.[93] CACIS may aid the control over military options by specifying alternatives (emphasizing political ones?) and estimating consequences. CACIS could be used to evaluate the effects of timely pauses in military operations in a current conflict by suggesting what the implications were for such pauses in prior conflicts. CACIS may help develop clear and appropriate demonstrations of resolution, as well as help discriminate among options based upon such intensity scaling as developed by Corson. In addition, an improved Corson scale might allow for a more subtle selection of politico-military options and decrease the probability of escalation.

Summary

The present study evaluates an international system and a foreign policy decision-making approach via their corresponding models: event/interaction, organizational processes, and interaction/organizational models. The design used actions between East and West in the Berlin conflict of 1961 to infer the unmeasured models. The Corson scale of conflict intensity provided a discriminator of politico-military options, even though there may be problems with the scale and the coding.[94] The Berlin conflict of 1961 provided a laboratory for the exploration of the three models. The resulting path coefficients did *not* support the original hypotheses. The magnitude of the coefficients is so low that the results are inconclusive.

The implications of this study for conflict modelling and management are tentative but potentially promising. Regarding modelling, the study concludes that analysts should: (1) specify a universe of cases for comparative inquiry across conflicts; (2) explicate the event/interaction and organizational processes models, emphasizing formal axioms and data requirements; (3) develop process models that describe and explain the evolution of conflict, emphasizing breakpoints where internal dynamics give way to external factors; and (4) integrate qualitative evaluation of events with their quantitative analysis to make sure that

[93] Alexander George and others, *The Limits of Coercive Diplomacy* (Boston 1971), 8-15.

[94] Cf. Edward Azar, "Analysis of International Events," *Peace Research Reviews*, iv (November 1970), 83. Azar asserts that, "We code events and measure their violence content with the 13 point interval scale. Although we realize that participants to a conflict situation do not use such an objective instrument, we maintain that they employ an implicit (or possibly explicit) scale which ranks signals by their violence content." Also see William A. Gamson and Andre Modigliani, *Untangling the Cold War: A Strategy for Testing Rival Theories* (Boston 1971), for an attempt to quantify and scale East-West interactions.

the quality of the policies is taken into account. Regarding conflict management, the study concludes that: (1) the results of the present inquiry could help specify models for a Computer-Aided Conflict Information System, which could be used to compare a current conflict with prior relevant cases; and (2) CACIS might institutionalize prior alternatives and estimate their consequences in similar cases. Such institutionalization should expand the political options short of military force available to decision-makers. Finally, CACIS should not be used to freeze options on the basis of historical precedents. Rather, CACIS should provide a fresh set of alternatives for the adaptively rational actor.[95]

[95] Also, see Sidney Verba, "Assumptions of Rationality and Non-Rationality in Models of the International System," in Knorr and Verba (fn. 3), 93-117. Acknowledgments to Dennis Doolin for calling attention to the danger of freezing options on the basis of historical precedents with a system such as CACIS. There is a great need for what Doolin calls ". . . creative politics—which is really the essence and true genius of politics—and there seems to be a danger in an approach that could view routinization as a rule of action." Letter from Dennis Doolin, 28 June 1971. CACIS attempts to address itself to Doolin's perceptive critique and to facilitate "creative politics."

BUREAUCRATIC POLITICS:

A Paradigm and Some Policy Implications

By GRAHAM T. ALLISON and MORTON H. HALPERIN*

DURING the Tet holiday of 1968, North Vietnamese troops launched massive attacks on a large number of South Vietnamese cities. *Why?*

In December, 1950, the Chinese Communists intervened in the Korean War. Today some Senators raise the specter of Chinese Communist intervention in the Vietnamese War. Will Communist China intervene in Vietnam? Specifically, if the U.S. were to renew the bombing of North Vietnam with a vengeance, destroying the dikes and closing Haiphong, and South Vietnamese troops were to invade North Vietnam—both unlikely contingencies—would large units of Communist Chinese troops enter the war?

In the mid-1960's, the U.S. put a lid on American strategic weapons: 1000 Minutemen, 54 Titans, and 640 Polaris, and a limited number of bombers. Administration officials announced these limits, recognizing that the Soviets would build up to a position of parity but hoping that Moscow would not go for superiority. If in the mid-1960's a Secretary of Defense had wanted to persuade the Soviet Union not to deploy an ICBM fleet that would seriously threaten U.S. forces, how might he have proceeded?

The first question asks for an explanation; the second for a prediction; the third for a plan. These are three central activities in which both analysts of international politics and makers of foreign policy engage. In response to the first question, most analysts begin by considering various objectives that the North Vietnamese might have had in mind: for example, to shock the American public and thereby affect the presidential election; to collapse the government of South Vietnam; to cause a massive uprising of military and civilians in South Vietnam, thus bringing total victory; or to take the cities and keep them. By ex-

---

* This presentation of a bureaucratic politics approach to foreign policy builds upon previous works of both authors. Specifically, it takes as a point of departure Allison's "Conceptual Models and the Cuban Missile Crisis," *American Political Science Review*, LXIII (September 1970) and *Essence of Decision: Explaining the Cuban Missile Crisis* (Boston 1971); and Halperin's *Bureaucratic Politics and Foreign Policy*, forthcoming. Here we focus on the further development of "Model III," recognizing that organizations can be included as players in the game of bureaucratic politics, treating the factors emphasized by an organizational process approach as constraints, developing the notion of shared attitudes, and introducing a distinction between "decision games" and "action games."

amining the problems that Hanoi faced and the character of the action they chose, analysts eliminate some of these aims as implausible. Explanation then consists in constructing a calculation that permits us to understand why, in the particular situation, with certain objections, one would have chosen to launch the Tet offensive. In attempting to predict whether the Communist Chinese will intervene in the Vietnamese War, and if so, in what fashion, most analysts would consider (1) Chinese national security interests in Vietnam, (2) the likelihood of the collapse of the North Vietnamese in the absence of Chinese Communist intervention, (3) the contribution of Chinese Communist troops to the North Vietnamese efforts, and (4) indications of Chinese Communist intentions, for example, warnings to the U.S., pledges to the North Vietnamese, statements about Chinese interests, etc. These considerations would then be combined in some intuitive fashion to yield a prediction. In recommending U.S. actions to persuade the Soviets to stop with rough parity, and not to push for "superiority," many analysts would have focused on Soviet national security interests. They would then consider American actions that would affect those interests in such a way that deploying larger strategic forces would be counterproductive.

Characteristic of each of these three answers is a basic approach: a fundamental set of assumptions and categories for thinking about foreign affairs.[1] This approach depends primarily on the assumption that events in international politics consist of the more or less purposive acts of unified national governments and that governmental behavior can be understood by analogy with the intelligent, coordinated acts of individual human beings. Following this approach, analysts focus on the interests and goals of a nation, the alternative courses of actions available, and the costs and benefits of each alternative. An event has been explained when the analyst has shown, for example, how the Tet offensive was a reasonable choice, given Hanoi's strategic objectives. Predictions are generated by calculating the rational thing to do in a certain situation, given specified objectives. Recommended plans concentrate on analyzing other nations' strategic interests and ways of affecting their calculations about the consequences of actions.

Let the reader consider, for example, how he would explain the Soviet invasion of Czechoslovakia in 1968, or North Vietnamese activity in Laos and Cambodia. One typically puts himself in the place of the nation or the national government confronted with a problem of foreign affairs and tries to figure out how he might have chosen the action in question. If I had been the Soviet Union faced with the threat of

[1] For an elaboration of the argument of this introductory section, see Allison, *op. cit.*

Czech liberalization, or the Czech threat to the economy of the Bloc, what would I have done? Moreover, this is not simply the way we react to current events. It is the way most analysts, most of the time, structure their most careful explanations and predictions of important occurrences in foreign affairs.

Few readers will find the simple assertion of this point persuasive. Obviously there are several variants of this basic approach. Obviously the approach does not capture the entire analysis of those who employ it. Obviously not all analysts rely on this approach all of the time. But as one of us has argued at much greater length elsewhere, this framework, which has been labelled Model I, has been the dominant approach to the study of foreign policy and international politics.[2] (Even analysts primarily concerned with discovering causal relations between variables—for example, between environmental or intra-national factors—and specific outcomes, when called upon to explain or predict, display a tendency to rely on the assumption of purposive unitary nations coping within the constraints established by these causal relations.)

This traditional approach to international politics has much to recommend it. As a "lens" it reduces the organizational and political complications of government to the simplification of a single actor. The array of details about a happening can be seen to cluster around the major features of an action. Through this lens, the confused and even contradictory factors that influence an occurrence become a single dynamic: the *choice* of the alternative that achieved a certain goal. This approach permits a quick, imaginative sorting out of the problem of explanation or prediction. It serves as a productive shorthand, requiring a minimum of information. It can yield an informative summary of tendencies, for example, by identifying the weight of strategic costs and benefits.

But this simplification—like all simplifications—obscures as well as reveals. In particular, it obscures the persistently neglected fact of bureaucracy: the "maker" of government policy is not one calculating decision-maker, but rather a conglomerate of large organizations and political actors who differ substantially about what their government should do on any particular issue and who compete in attempting to affect both governmental decisions and the actions of their government.

The purpose of this paper is to present an alternative approach that focuses on intra-national factors, in particular Bureaucratic Politics, in explaining national behavior in international relations. The argument is that these factors are very important, underemphasized in the current literature, yet critical when one is concerned with planning policy. Sec-

[2] For an elaboration of this point, see Allison, *op. cit.*

tion I of this paper presents the alternative approach: a Bureaucratic Politics Model.[3] Our hope is that the framework is sufficiently general to apply to the behavior of most modern governments in industrialized nations, though it will be obvious that our primary base is the U.S. government. Section II suggests how this approach can be applied to understand how one nation influences the behavior of another. Section III states a number of policy implications of this alternative approach.

Section I

A BUREAUCRATIC POLITICS MODEL

Our purpose here is to outline a rough-cut framework for focusing primarily on the individuals within a government, and the interaction among them, as determinants of the actions of a government in international politics. What a government does in any particular instance can be understood largely as a result of bargaining among players positioned hierarchically in the government. The bargaining follows regularized circuits. Both the bargaining and the results are importantly affected by a number of constraints, in particular, organizational processes and shared values.[4]

In contrast with Model I, this Bureaucratic Politics Model sees no unitary actor but rather many actors as players—players who focus not on a single strategic issue but on many diverse intra-national problems as well. Players choose in terms of no consistent set of strategic objectives, but rather according to various conceptions of national security, organizational, domestic, and personal interests. Players make governmental decisions not by a single rational choice, but by pulling and hauling. (This by no means implies that individual players are not acting rationally, given their interests.)[5]

The conception of national security policy as "political" result contradicts both public imagery and academic orthodoxy. Issues vital to national security are considered too important to be settled by political games. They must be "above" politics: to accuse someone of "playing

[3] In arguing that explanations proceed in terms of implicit conceptual models, this essay makes no claim that foreign policy analysts have developed any satisfactory empirically tested theory. In this essay, the use of the term "model" with qualifiers should be read "conceptual scheme or framework."

[4] For a review of earlier proponents of the bureaucratic politics approach, see Allison, op. cit.

[5] In order to highlight the distinctive characteristics of the Bureaucratic Politics Model (BPM), we contrast it with the traditional approach. Our argument is not, however, that the approaches are exclusive alternatives. The relationships between these approaches is discussed in Allison, op. cit.

politics with national security" is a most serious charge. Thus, memoirs typically handle the details of such bargaining with a velvet glove. For example, both Sorensen and Schlesinger present the efforts of the Executive Committee in the Cuban missile crisis essentially as rational deliberation among a unified group of equals.[6] What public expectation demands, the academic penchant for intellectual elegance reinforces. Internal politics is messy; moreover, according to prevailing doctrine, politicking lacks intellectual substance. It constitutes gossip for journalists, rather than a subject for serious investigation. Occasional memoirs, anecdotes in historical accounts, and several detailed case studies to the contrary, most of the foreign policy literature avoids bureaucratic politics.

The gap between academic literature and the experience of participants in government is nowhere wider than at this point. For those who participate in government, the terms of daily employment cannot be ignored: government leaders have competitive, not homogeneous interests; priorities and perceptions are shaped by positions; problems are much more varied than straightforward, strategic issues; the management of piecemeal streams of decisions is more important than steady state choices; making sure that the government does what is decided— and does not do what has not been directed—is more difficult than selecting the preferred solution.

This general orientation can be stated more sharply by formulation of the Bureaucratic Politics Model as an "analytic paradigm" in the technical sense developed by Robert K. Merton for sociological analysis.[7] Systematic statement of basic assumptions, concepts, and suggestive propositions will highlight the distinctive thrust of this style of analysis. In formulating the paradigm, wherever possible, we use words the way they are used in ordinary language. But the terms that constitute this paradigm are often given a more specific definition for purposes of clarity.

BUREAUCRATIC POLITICS PARADIGM

I. BASIC UNIT OF ANALYSIS

In thinking about problems of foreign affairs, what most participants and analysts are really interested in are *outcomes*—that is, selectively delimited states of the real world importantly affected by the actions of

---

[6] Arthur Schlesinger, Jr., *A Thousand Days* (Boston 1965); see Theodore C. Sorensen, *Kennedy* (New York 1965).
[7] Robert K. Merton, *Social Theory and Social Structures* (rev. and enl. ed., New York 1957).

governments. Thus, for example, the problem of proliferation for most participants or analysts is: how many nations will have what nuclear capabilities at some point in the future.* Similarly, an explanation of the Cuban missile crisis must allow one to understand why at some point, Soviet missiles were no longer in Cuba. The U.S. was publicly committed not to invade Cuba, and all this had been accomplished without nuclear war. The selection of variables is made by the analyst or participant with reference to his perception of some problem or issue. When explaining, predicting, or planning, an analyst, at least implicitly, specifies some characteristics of the real world—an outcome—that focus his attention.

The basic unit of analysis of the approach developed here is *actions* of a government which we define as the various acts of officials of a government in exercises of governmental authority that can be perceived outside the government. According to this definition, a presidential announcement of a decision to bomb North Vietnam, the subsequent movement of an aircraft carrier into a position near North Vietnam, and the actual dropping of bombs are actions of a government. Whereas a secret paper sent from the Secretary of Defense to the President recommending bombing of North Vietnam or a private presidential decision to bomb North Vietnam are not actions of a government. It is an assumption of the approach developed here that in order to explain, predict, or plan outcomes it is necessary to identify the actions of particular governments that affect the outcome, to treat these actions separately (including how one nation's actions affect another) and in this way to treat the event in its entirety.

In explaining, predicting, or planning actions of a government, one must identify the *action channels*—that is, regularized sets of procedures for producing particular classes of actions. For example, one action channel for producing U.S. military intervention in another country includes a recommendation by the ambassador to that country, an assessment by the regional military commander, a recommendation by the Joint Chiefs of Staff, an assessment by the intelligence community of the consequences of intervention, recommendations by the Secretaries of State and Defense, a presidential decision to intervene, the transmittal of an order from the President through the Secretary of Defense and

---

* More specifically, the outcome might be defined in terms of a set of variables: (a) the number of states that have formally renounced nuclear weapons, (b) the number of states that have announced intentions to acquire nuclear weapons, (c) the nuclear technology of various nations, (d) the number of states with a stand-by capability, (e) the number of states that have tested nuclear weapons, (f) the number of states that have nuclear stockpiles and the size of these stockpiles.

Joint Chiefs of Staff to the regional military commander, his determination of what troops to employ, the order from him to the commander of those troops, and the orders from that commander to the individuals who actually move into the country. The path from initiation to action frequently includes a number of *decisions*, that is authoritative designations, internal to a government, of specific actions to be taken by specific officials. Thus, a secret decision by the President to intervene, and the determination by the regional commander are both decisions, but a public announcement of either is an action of the government.

The action channel for major foreign policy decisions can be usefully divided into that portion which leads to decisions by senior players and that part which follows from those decisions. The latter is frequently referred to as "implementation" but we resist that terminology as too restrictive. Many elements of implementation stem from sources other than decisions by senior players. Thus, for example, the presence of U.S. troops in the Dominican Republic in 1965 stemmed from a decision by the President to send the Marines to that country, but the actions of the 18,000 Marines in the Dominican Republic (e.g., the precise positions that they occupied) followed from much lower-level decisions as well as from other factors. Moreover, many actions of governments occur in the absence of any high level decision. For example, in the earlier Dominican crisis that led to the overthrow of Juan Bosch, Ambassador John B. Martin's offer to Bosch to send in the U.S. Marines was not preceded by any high-level decision to make that offer.[8] Actions may also be affected by decisions on other issues and by *policy*, that is, authoritative aspirations, internal to a government, about outcomes. For example, Martin's behavior was influenced by the U.S. *policy* of supporting democratic governments in Latin America. The actions of the Marines, when they did intervene, were affected by prior budget decisions. For purposes of analysis we will identify the activity of players leading to decisions by senior players as *decision games*, activities leading to policy as *policy games*, and activities that follow from, or proceed in the absence of, decisions by senior players as *action games*.

Thus we have defined the following terms: outcomes, actions, action channels, decisions, policy, and decision games, policy games, and action games.

II. ORGANIZING CONCEPTS

The organizing concepts of this paradigm can be arranged as elements in the answers to three central questions: (1) Who plays? (2)

[8] John B. Martin, *Overtaken by Events* (New York 1966).

What determines each player's stand? (3) How are players' stands aggregated to yield governmental decisions and actions?

A. *Who plays? That is, whose interests and behavior have an important effect on the government's decisions and actions?*

In any government, there exists a circle of *senior players* in the national security policy game.[9] This circle includes the major political figures, the heads of the major national security organizations, including intelligence, the military and, for some purposes, the organization that manages budgetary allocations and the economy. Generally one of these players is the chief executive of the government. He may have a disproportionate share of influence on major decisions. The President of the U.S., for example, has a range of both interests and formal powers that set him apart from other players. Other individuals can enter this central circle, either on a more regular or a strictly *ad hoc* basis, because of their relation with the head of the government. Organizations and groups can for some purposes be treated as players, for example, when (1) the official papers that emerge from an organization can be summarized as coherent calculated moves of a unitary actor; (2) the actions of the head of an organization, whose goals are determined largely by that organization, can be treated as actions of the organization; and (3) the various behaviors of different individual members of an organization can be regarded as coherent strategies and tactics in a single plan.

Around the central circle of *senior players*, there are various circles of *junior players*. In the United States actors in the wider governmental game ("Congressional influentials," members of the press, spokesmen for important interest groups, especially the "bipartisan foreign policy establishment" in and out of Congress, and surrogates for each of these groups) can enter the game in a more or less regularized fashion. Other members of the Congress, the press, interest groups, and public form concentric circles around the central arena—circles that demarcate limits within which the game is played.

The mix of players will vary depending on the issue and the type of game. Action channels determine, in large part, which players enter what games, with what advantages and handicaps. Senior players will dominate in decision games. But in action games on the same issue quite junior players in the organization who are charged with carrying out the decision may play a major role.

---

[9] In the statement of this paradigm we focus primarily on issues of foreign policy that arise as matters of national security. Extension of the argument to other issue areas, e.g., foreign trade, is straightforward.

B. *What determines each player's stand? What determines his perceptions and interests which lead to a stand?*

Answers to the questions "What is the issue?" or "What must be done?" are colored by the position from which the question is considered.

A player is an individual in a *position*. His perceptions and preferences stem both from his individual characteristics (for example, attitudes shared with other members of the society and government and attitudes special to himself) and from his position.

The *interests* that affect players' desired results can be characterized under four headings: national security interests, organizational interests, domestic interests, and personal interests. Some elements of national security interests are widely accepted, such as the interest in the United States' avoiding foreign domination, and the belief that if the U.S. were to disarm unilaterally, other nations would use military force against it and its allies with very serious adverse consequences. But in most cases, reasonable men can disagree on how national security interests will be affected by a specific issue. Other interests can affect an individual's perception of the national security interest. Members of an organization, particularly career officials, come to believe that the health of their organization is vital to the national interest.[10] The health of the organization, in turn, is seen to depend on maintaining influence, fulfilling its mission, and securing the necessary capabilities. The latter two interests lead to concern for maintaining autonomy and organizational morale, protecting the organization's essence, maintaining or expanding roles and missions, and maintaining or increasing budgets. While many bureaucrats are unconcerned with domestic affairs and politics and do not ask themselves how a proposed change in policy or behavior would affect domestic political issues, some senior players will almost always be concerned about domestic implications. Finally, a player's stand depends on his personal interests and his conception of his role.

When an ostensible issue arises, e.g., when a new weapons system is proposed, players will come to see quite different *faces of the issue*. For example, a proposal to withdraw American troops from Europe is to the Army a threat to its budget and size; to the Budget Bureau a way to save money; to Treasury a balance of payments gain; to the State Department Bureau of European Affairs a threat to good relations with NATO; to the President's Congressional adviser an opportunity to remove a major irritant in the President's relations with the Hill. (Senior

---

[10] For an elaboration of the discussion of organizational interests see Halperin "Why Bureaucrats Play Games," *Foreign Policy* (Spring 1971).

players, especially, tend to see several faces of the issue simultaneously.) Given the face of the issue that he sees, each player must calculate how the resolution of this issue may affect his interests. This defines his *stakes* in the issue at hand. In the light of these stakes he then determines his *stand* on the issue.

Suggestive propositions

1. There are important differences between (a) governmental systems in which many players in the central game hold their positions because of political influence and aspire to the position of chief executive of the government and (b) governmental systems in which most central players have no thought of becoming the chief executive. In the former, most players' personal interest in remaining in the game and advancing toward the top frequently dominates their stand on most issues.

2. Beyond the circle of senior players, certain individuals (viz., non-career officials and those in organizations without organizationally-defined missions) are often motivated by the desire to participate *per se*. These individuals are likely to take stands that permit them to get into the game.

3. There are important differences between (a) governmental systems that are relatively closed to expressions of interest and pressures from outside the governmental game and (b) governmental systems that are relatively open as a result of elections. In the latter, such factors as dependency upon the approval or acquiescence of a wider circle of individuals, and vulnerability to pressures from this wider circle, force players to a larger conception of their interests.

4. Organizational interests weigh more heavily in the full set of interests of some senior players than in others. In the U.S. government there seems to be a rough spectrum of such weights from greater to lesser, for example, the Chief of Naval Operations, to the Secretary of Defense, to the Secretary of State, to the President's Special Assistant for National Security Affairs.

5. Organizational interests are often dominated by the desire to maintain the autonomy of the organization in pursuing what its members view as the essence of the organization's activity, e.g., flying for the Air Force.

6. Even, and perhaps particularly in crises, organizations compete for roles and missions.

7. Organizations rarely take stands that require elaborate coordination with other organizations.

8. Most players, especially senior players, have a very high discount rate: that is, a short time horizon on any issue. Players whose stands are heavily influenced by organizational interests, especially careerists, often have a much longer time horizon regarding the interests of the organization.

C. *How are the players' stands aggregated to yield decisions and actions of a government?*

We consider first how players' stands aggregate to produce policies and decisions by senior players; second, we consider how policies, decisions, and other factors produce governmental actions.

1. *Policy and decision games.* Sometimes an issue arises because a player sees something that he wants to change, and moves. Most often, however, the game is begun by the necessity that something be done, either in response to a *deadline* (e.g., the annual budget) or an event (external or domestic). When he becomes aware that a game has begun, each player must determine his stand and then decide whether to play (if he has a choice) and if so, how hard. These decisions require a calculation (often implicit) about both resources and reputation. Resources are finite and fungible, e.g., time and senior players' reputation with the President. Reputation depends on one's track record, thus players consider the probability of success as part of their stake.

Decision games do not proceed randomly, but rather according to fixed rules. Typically, issues are recognized and determined within an established channel for producing policies or decisions. Where a deadline or event initiates the game, that trigger influences the selection of the action channel. In most cases, however, there are several possible channels through which an issue could be resolved. Because action channels structure the game by pre-selecting the major players, determining the usual points of entrance into the game, and by distributing particular advantages for each game, players maneuver to get the issue into the channel that they believe is most likely to yield the desired result.

Each player's probability of success depends upon at least three elements: bargaining advantages, skill and will in using bargaining advantages, and other players' perceptions of the first two ingredients. Bargaining advantages stem from control of implementation, control over information that enables one to define the problem and identify the available options, persuasiveness with other players (including players outside the bureaucracy) and the ability to affect other players' objectives in other games, including domestic political games.

What emerges from the game is also importantly affected by constraints, in particular by the routines of organizations in supplying information and options, and by the shared values within the society and the bureaucracy.

The game consists of each player engaging in various maneuvers to achieve his desired results. Some players develop sophisticated plans, though most players seem to plan very little. All players can try to change other players' stands by arguments.

The resolution of an issue can be a policy, a decision, or the avoidance of a decision. Decisions may be very general or quite specific. In some cases, senior players will have no choice about who will carry out the action. But in other cases, the rules permit a choice of implementers. For example, negotiations with foreign governments are usually the domain of the foreign office; but they can be assigned to a special envoy of the head of government, or to the intelligence services. Bombing missions must be assigned to the military, but there may be a choice between Services or within a Service, e.g., between the Navy, SAC, or TAC. Monitoring functions may be assigned to an organization with an interest in the action, but with no capability to carry it out.

2. *Action games.* The actions of a government that affect an outcome typically include a large number of distinct elements. For example, recent U.S. government actions which affect the spread of nuclear weapons include: the State Department's efforts to gain adherence to the Non-Proliferation Treaty; Presidential offers of guarantees to non-nuclear nations against nuclear blackmail; Atomic Energy Commission tests of nuclear explosives for peaceful purposes (which provide a convenient shield for non-nuclear powers' development of nuclear devices); withdrawal of U.S. forces from the Far East (which may increase the concern of some Japanese or Indians about their national security); statements by the AEC about the great prospects for peaceful nuclear weapons (which are designed to influence AEC budgets); an AEC commissioner's argument, in the absence of any higher level decision, to a Brazilian scientist about the great virtues of peaceful nuclear explosives; and the U.S. government's refusal to confirm or deny the reported presence of nuclear weapons aboard ships calling in foreign ports. As this list suggests, actions that affect outcomes may be importantly affected by policies about that outcome, by decision games about that outcome, and by decision games about other outcomes. Actions that affect outcomes may also be actions in the absence of higher level decisions designed to affect an outcome, maneuvers in decision games, or routine behavior of organizations.

To treat the actions of a government that affect an outcome, the analyst needs to separate out these various strands of action and provide explanations for each. Obviously most actions are an amalgam of several strands.

If the action is in fact a result of routine behavior of organizations, one needs to explain the organizational standard operating procedures (SOP's) that produced that behavior.[11] If the action is a maneuver in a decision or policy game, one needs to identify the game and explain why the maneuver was used. If the action was taken without a high-level decision, one must identify the circumstances that permitted the player that leeway and explain what led the player to take that step. If the action resulted from a policy or a decision game unrelated to the outcome being analyzed, one must identify the relevant decision or policy game and provide an explanation for the decision and the action that followed. Finally, if the action flows from a relevant decision game, one needs an explanation of that action game.

Action games, which follow from decision games, do not proceed at random. The decision that triggers the game and the rules of the game assign the action to a player and pick the action channel. However, there are likely to be several sub-channels. Players will maneuver to get the issue into the channel they believe offers the best prospects for getting the desired result.

As in decision games, players' probabilities of success depend upon their power. In this case, bargaining advantages stem from: formal authority, control over the resources necessary to carry out the action, responsibility for carrying out the action, control over information that enables one to determine the feasibility of the action and its consequences, control over information that enables senior players to determine whether the decision is being implemented, and persuasiveness with other players, particularly those responsible for implementation. Action is also affected by the constraints imposed by the standard operating procedures of large organizations.

In some cases, players responsible for implementing decisions will feel obligated to implement the spirit as well as the letter of the decision. Even in such cases, the action may differ from the action that the senior players thought would result from their decision. This is in part because actions are carried out by large organizations according to existing routines, in part because decisions do not usually include an explanation of what the action is intended to accomplish, and in part

---

[11] For an elaboration of the discussion of organizational routines, programs and SOP's, see Allison, *op. cit.*

because when specifying details junior players may distort the action.

In most cases, players will feel that the decision leaves them considerable leeway in implementation. Players who supported the decision will maneuver to see it implemented. They may go beyond the spirit if not the letter of the decision. Those who opposed the decision, or who oppose the action, will maneuver to delay implementation, to limit implementation to the letter but not the spirit, or even to have the decision disobeyed.

The characterization of decision and action games captures the thrust of the bureaucratic politics approach. If problems of foreign policy arose as discrete issues, and decisions and actions were determined one game at a time, this account would suffice. But most "issues," e.g., Vietnam or the proliferation of nuclear weapons, emerge piecemeal over time, one lump in one contest, a second in another. Hundreds of issues compete for players' attention every day. Each player is forced to fix upon his issues for that day, deal with them on their own terms, and rush on to the next. Thus the character of the emerging issue, and the pace at which the game is played, converge to yield a collage of government decisions and actions. Choices by one player (e.g., to authorize action by his department, to make a speech, or to refrain from acquiring certain information), decisions and "foul-ups" (e.g., points that are not decided because they are not recognized, raised too late, or misunderstood) are pieces which, when stuck to the same canvas, constitute actions relevant to an outcome.

Suggestive Propositions

About Decisions

1. Decisions of a government seldom reflect a single coherent, consistent set of calculations about national security interests.

2. Decisions by definition assign specific actions to specific players, but they typically leave considerable leeway both about which subordinates should be involved and what specific actions should be taken.

3. Decisions typically reflect considerable compromise. Compromise results from a need to gain adherence, a need to avoid harming strongly felt interests (including organizational interests), and the need to hedge against the dire predictions of other participants.

4. Decisions are rarely tailored to facilitate monitoring. As a result, senior players have great difficulty in checking on the faithful implementation of a decision.

5. Decisions that direct substantial changes in action typically reflect a coincidence of (a) a deadline for a President or senior players that

focuses them on a problem and fuels the search for a solution and (b) the interests of junior players committed to a specific solution and in search of a problem.[12]

About Actions

1. Presidential decisions will be faithfully implemented when: a President's involvement is unambiguous, his words are unambiguous, his order is widely publicized, the men who receive it have control of everything needed to carry it out, and those men have no apparent doubt of his authority to issue the decision.[13]

2. Major new departures in foreign policy typically stem from some decision by central players. But the specific details of the action taken are determined in large part by standard operating procedure and programs existing in the organizations at the time.

3. Ambassadors and field commanders feel less obliged to faithfully implement decisions because they typically have not been involved in the decision game. They feel they know better what actions one should want from another government and how to get those actions.

4. The larger the number of players who can act independently on an issue, the less the government's action will reflect decisions of the government on that issue.

5. Where a decision leaves leeway for the organization that is implementing it, that organization will act so as to maximize its organizational interest within constraints.

III. CONSTRAINTS

The factors highlighted in this model assume a *ceteris paribus* clause. Other features, treated here as constraints, bias the outcome of the bureaucratic politics game. For some classes of governmental behavior (e.g., the detail characteristics of the behavior of large organizations), these other factors may be more important than those emphasized by the Bureaucratic Politics Model. Indeed, what is described here as an "organizational constraint" has been elaborated elsewhere by one of us as an alternative model.[14] The issue of typology, that is, what factors weigh most heavily for what classes of outcomes, is a central issue for further research.

[12] For this proposition we are indebted to Ernest R. May.
[13] This proposition is drawn from Richard E. Neustadt, *Presidential Power* (New York 1960).
[14] See Allison's "Model II," *op. cit.* The discussion of organizational constraints draws heavily on that account.

A. *Organizational Constraints*

The game among players (and organizations considered as players) proceeds within a context. A large part of that context is the existing configuration of large organizations, their established programs and standard operating procedures for performing various functions. These organizational routines are especially important in determining (1) the information available to the central players, (2) the options that the senior players consider, and (3) the actual details of whatever is done by the government.

How does *information* about most national problems become available to members of a government? For example, how did the U.S. government become aware of the Soviet construction of missiles in Cuba in 1962? For the most part, information is collected and processed by large organizations. In the Cuban missile crisis, the existence of the CIA and Air Force, with existing capabilities and processes, yielded a U-2 flight over Cuba according to a pattern that discovered the missiles in the second week of October.

The menu of *alternatives* defined by organizations in sufficient detail to be live options is severely limited in both number and character. The character of the alternatives available to a leader (i.e., the location of the set of alternatives in the universe of possible alternatives relevant to his objectives) differs significantly from the character of alternatives presented by a team of five disinterested experts. The difference is a function of the configuration of established organizations and their existing goals and procedures. Those alternatives that are built into existing organizational goals (e.g., incremental improvements in each military service's primary weapons system) will be adequate (i.e., compare favorably with the experts' list, though with less sensitivity to cost). However, alternatives that require coordination of several organizations (e.g., multi-service military operations or weapons systems) and alternatives in areas between organizations (e.g., weapons that are not represented by a major service component) are likely to be inadequate.

Action according to standard operating procedures and programs does not constitute far-sighted, flexible adaptation to "the issue" (as it is conceived by an analyst). Detail and nuance of actions by organizations are determined chiefly by organizational routines. Standard operating procedures constitute routines for dealing with standard situations. Routines allow large numbers of individuals on low organizational levels to deal with numerous situations day after day, without much thought. But this regularized capacity for adequate performance is purchased at the price of standardization. Specific instances, particularly critical instances that typically do not have "standard" characteristics, are often handled sluggishly or inappropriately. A program, that is, a complex cluster of standard operating procedures, is rarely tailored to the specific situation in which it is executed. Rather, the program is (at best) the most appropriate of programs in the existing repertoire. Since repertoires are developed by parochial organizations for standard scenarios that the organization has defined, the programs available for dealing with a particular situation are often ill-suited to it.

B. *Shared Attitudes*

Perceptions of issues or arguments about the national interest do not begin *ab initio*. Beneath the differences that fuel bureaucratic politics is a foundation of shared assumptions about basic values and facts. These underlying assumptions are reflected in various attitudes and images which are taken for granted by most players.

Shared attitudes and images provide common answers to such questions as: Who are the actual or potential enemies of the United States? What are their intentions and capabilities? Who are our friends? What are their capabilities and intentions? What influences the behavior of other nations? Among the attitudes and the images that have recently prevailed in the U.S. bureaucracy are:

- The United States should act to halt the spread of Communism.
- Only force will deter the Chinese from aggression.
- The loss of American gold to foreign central banks is a threat to U.S. prosperity and should be avoided.
- The capability for assured destruction is necessary to deter the Soviet Union.
- European unification is desirable.
- Good relations with Japan are important to U.S. security interests.

Most participants accept these images. Their idea of the national interest is shaped by these attitudes, and their arguments are based on them. Most participants tend to interpret the actions of other nations to make them consistent with held images, rather than reexamining basic views. Even those in the bureaucracy who do not share some or all of these values and images are inclined to act and to argue as if they believed them. They do this because to do otherwise would make them suspect by other members of the bureaucracy.

Section II

INTERACTION BETWEEN NATIONS

How does the behavior of one nation affect that of another?

Most analysts of international politics approach this question by applying a version of Model I to the behavior of each nation. This approach leads them to treat the interaction between nations as if it resulted from a competition between two purposive individuals. Each nation's actions are seen to be an attempt to influence the actions of the other by affecting its strategic calculus. The behavior of each nation is explained as a reaction to the behavior of the other.

Consider how analysts who take this approach explain arms races. Nation A builds military forces for the purpose of influencing nation B. If it fears that nation B is stronger and hence may be tempted to attack or to exploit its military superiority, nation A will increase the size of its own forces. Nation B, observing this buildup, and fearful of the increased strength of nation A, in turn increases its own forces.

The Bureaucratic Politics Model suggests an alternative answer to the question of how one nation's behavior affects the behavior of another. Explanation focuses primarily on processes internal to each nation. The actions of a nation result not from an agreed upon calculus of strategic interests, but rather from pulling and hauling among individuals with differing perceptions and stakes. These arise not only from differing conceptions of national security interest but also from differing domestic, organizational and personal interests. The influence of one nation's actions on another result from the actions' impact on the stands, or on the power of players in decision or action games in the other nation.

From this alternative perspective, the explanation of an "arms race" is to be found primarily within each nation—in particular in the process by which each one procures and deploys military forces. At any given time some players in nation A will take stands in favor of increasing defense expenditures and procuring particular weapons systems. The interests that lead them to these stands will be diverse. Career officers in the armed services, for example, will seek additional funds for forces controlled by their services. Other players' stands will be affected by their perceptions of how particular decisions will affect the influence of particular players. Actions by another nation will be interpreted by those seeking additional weapons to enhance their arguments and influence. These actions will affect decisions to increase defense spending if they affect senior players' perceptions of what is necessary for national security or of what is necessary to promote their other interests.

Model I analysis can be relied on to predict the fact that a large increase in nation A's defense budget will produce an increase in nation B's defense spending. But the size of that increase and, even more importantly, the specific characteristics of weapons purchased with the increase are better explained or predicted by the Bureaucratic Politics Model. In general, Model I is more useful for explaining actions where national security interests dominate, where shared values lead to a consensus on what the national security requires, and where actions flow rather directly from decisions. The bureaucratic politics model is more useful where there is data on the interests of players and the rules of the game, where organizational and domestic interests predominate, or where one wishes to treat the details of action.

The Bureaucratic Politics Model suggests a number of propositions about the way actions of one nation affect the actions of another. We shall attempt to formulate these propositions explicitly. But before presenting propositions, it should be useful to consider in a more general manner the process of national interaction as it looks through the lens of bureaucratic politics.

The Bureaucratic Politics Model's emphasis on intra-national processes stems not only from the fact that individuals within nations do the acting, but also from the observation that the satisfaction of players' interests are to be found overwhelmingly at home. Political leaders of a nation rise and fall depending on whether they satisfy domestic needs. Individuals advance in the bureaucracy when they meet the standards set by political leaders or by career ladders. Organizations prosper or decline depending on domestic support in that bureaucracy and beyond it—but within the nation. These struggles are what preoccupy players in foreign-policy bureaucracies. Threats to interests from rival organizations, or competing political groups, are far more real than threats from abroad.

This is not to say that players do not have national security interests. No leader wants to see his nation attacked, and few desire to send their soldiers off to fight in distant wars. Some leaders are committed to a conception of world order. Some players have a wide range of interests beyond the borders of the nation. Even when players are concerned about national security interests, however, they are likely to see the battles as being won or lost mainly at home. This has become a truism of the Vietnam war, but it is true for other policies as well. For President Harry S. Truman the problem of the Marshall Plan was how to get Congress to establish the program and vote the funds, not how to get European governments to take the money or use it wisely. For President Dwight D. Eisenhower the problem of arms control was how to get imaginative proposals from his associates. For planners in the Pentagon, the drive to get the forces necessary to defend the nation is stymied, not by foreign governments, but by rival services, the Secretary of Defense, and the President.

It is not that actions of other nations do not matter, but rather they matter if and when they influence domestic struggles. A player's efforts to accomplish his objectives—whether to advance domestic political interests, organizational interests, personal interests, or national security interests—are sometimes affected by what he and other players come to believe about the actions of other nations. A German chancellor whose domestic position depends upon his reputation for being able to get what the Federal Republic needs from the United States will be concerned about American actions that lead his colleagues and opponents to conclude Washington no longer listens to him. An American Secretary of Defense or President who wishes to cut defense spending will see that his position requires Soviet actions that permit him to argue that the nation's security can be protected with reduced forces. A State Department official who believes his government's security requires European unification will fear that his efforts to get the United States to promote this cause could be undercut by Common Market trade policies, since these offer an opportunity for others to point to the adverse economic consequences of European unification. Since actions by other nations can affect the stands players take, and thereby affect decisions and actions, we must consider how actions of other nations enter into the process of decision bargaining and how they affect actions.

Many nations are doing many things at any given time. Not all of these foreign activities become relevant to decision or action games within a nation. Those that do are the actions reported by the nation's foreign office or intelligence organizations, or by senior players directly. Intelligence organizations are not perfect and neutral transmission belts. They notice what their images of the world lead them to think will be important to senior players. They report events and opinions according to established procedures and in ways designed to protect their own organizational interests. Senior players notice what may help them or their opponents and relate mainly to the former. If a new interpretation of another nation's actions comes to be accepted among senior players, some players will see new opportunities to seek decisions or actions. Others will see threats to ongoing actions or desired new ones; still others will be unconcerned.

Reports of the actions of other nations will never be more than one of many influences on decisions and actions. However, when players are evenly divided, or new action suggests to many a substantial change in anticipated future actions, these reports of another nation's actions can be decisive. The Japanese attack on Pearl Harbor, to take an extreme example, affected the perceptions of many Americans about whether the national security required American forces to engage in war against Japan. The Soviet ABM deployment may well have tipped the balance in the hard-fought American controversy over whether to deploy an ABM. President Lyndon Johnson's estimate of the effect of not deploying an American ABM system on his reelection prospects may have been substantially changed by the possibility that he could be charged with permitting an "ABM gap."[15]

When the actions of one nation are effective in changing the behavior of a second, the new action is rarely what was intended by any player in the first nation. Changes in stands will lead to desired changes in action, which in turn will produce desired changes in the action of another nation only: when a clear signal is sent, when someone in the other nation already wants to take the desired action and the action increases that player's influence. More often, the effects are marginal or unintended.

Propositions About National Interaction

1. The actions of nation *A* that appear to an outside observer to be designed to influence the actions of nation *B* will in fact be a combination of: (a) routine patterns of behavior; (b) maneuvers in decision games that are incidentally visible to other nations or deliberately visible, since to be effective they must appear to be a "signal"; (c) actions by players in the absence of decisions; (d) actions following a decision game not related to influence nation *B*; as well as (e) actions following a decision game related to influencing nation *B*.

2. Reports and interpretations of these actions provided to senior players by participants in nation *B* (in the Foreign Office and Intelligence) charged with observing, reporting, explaining and predicting actions of other nations, will be affected by (a) the perceptual tendencies of all individuals; (b) the use of Model I analysis or (c) even if not, the lack of required data and understanding; and (d) the

---

[15] On the ABM discussion see Morton Halperin, "The Decision to Deploy the ABM," *World Politics,* xxv (October 1972).

standard operating procedures and interests of these organizations.

A. These players share the perceptual tendencies of all individuals. This means, for example, that

(1) New information will be fitted into their existing attitudes and images;

(2) Reports that should lead to a change in plans will be distorted so as to "save their theory";

(3) Clues that signal a significant change in the probabilities of events will be lost in the surrounding noise.[16]

Examples: Evidence of a Japanese attack on Pearl Harbor was explained away.[17] One senior military officer urged that the United States proceed to invade Cuba even after the Soviets agreed to remove their missiles.[18]

B. Because these players use Model I they tend to assume that the actions were: (1) designed and executed, in effect, by a single individual; (2) designed carefully to influence their nation; (3) designed with a world view like their own; and (4) designed without regard to the domestic and bureaucratic politics of nation *A*.

Examples: Khrushchev warned Kennedy of the difficulty he had during the Cuban missile crisis of convincing his associates that an American U-2 which crossed into Soviet territory was not an indication that the United States was about to attack.[19] The American intelligence community persists in predicting Soviet force structure on the basis of Model I analysis.[20]

C. Even if they employ a bureaucratic politics model they will lack data and understanding of nuances of what determines the actions of nation *B*.

Examples: Both in the Suez crisis of 1956 and the Skybolt crisis of 1961, senior players in the British and American governments frequently misread the meaning of actions because they lacked an understanding of the nuances of how the other system worked.[21]

D. Standard operating procedures and interests will affect what is reported.

(1) Standard operating procedures will lead to delays and to selections different from what senior players would choose.

For example: the procedures of the intelligence community led to

[16] See Roberta Wohlstetter, *Pearl Harbor* (Stanford 1962).
[17] *Ibid.*
[18] Robert Kennedy, *Thirteen Days* (New York 1969), 119.
[19] For examples from the Cuban missile crisis, see Allison, *op. cit.*
[20] This point has often been made by A. W. Marshall.
[21] On Suez and Skybolt see Richard E. Neustadt, *Alliance Politics* (New York 1970).

a considerable delay between the time evidence of Soviet missiles in Cuba entered the system and the time this evidence reached senior players.

(2) Standard operating procedures and interests may lead to disguising internal bureaucratic disagreements and the withholding of bad news.

(3) Information will be presented so as to imply an action recommendation.

For example: President Eisenhower was told during the Chinese attack on the offshore island of Quemoy in 1958 that the fall of Quemoy would have consequences more "far-reaching and catastrophic than those which followed" the fall of China. This report clearly signaled the action favored.[22]

(4) Information-gathering and reporting procedures will be designed to protect the interests of intelligence agencies, such as to protect the roles and missions of the CIA in relation to other organizations.

(5) Procedures will also be designed to protect the organizational interests of a parent operating organization.

For example: according to a former Defense Intelligence Agency (DIA) analyst, DIA estimates concerning Vietnam were written so as not to undercut the action recommendations of the U.S. Military Commander in Vietnam and the Joint Chiefs of Staff.[23]

3. The ability of senior players in nation B to pursue their interests will be affected by the actions of nation A only to the extent that the actions of nation A, as reported by the Foreign Office, Intelligence and other senior players, affect (a) who is in power in nation B, (b) the power *of participants* in nation A, or (c) these latter participants' perception of their national security interests.

Examples: President Lyndon Johnson may have believed that Soviet deployment of an ABM would hurt his chances of reelection in 1968. Kennedy's failure to get Soviet missiles removed from Cuba would have reduced his influence on the American government. President Johnson is reported to have believed that getting his Great Society legislation through Congress required that he not permit South Vietnam to fall to communism. The North Korean invasion of South Korea changed President Harry S. Truman's view of whether it was important to American security to keep South Korea non-communist.

4. If actions by nation A do affect a player in B's ability to pursue his interests he will at a minimum report on the action and interpret

[22] Dwight D. Eisenhower, *Waging Peace* (New York 1965), 692.
[23] Patrick J. McGarvey, "DIA: Intelligence to Please," *Washington Monthly*, II (July 1970).

it so as to advance stands previously taken. If the interpretation of the action accepted by most senior players affects the calculation of what stand would advance his interests, the player will change his stand and seek to advance his interest without affecting the actions of nation A (if this can be done) or by affecting nation A's actions if necessary.

Examples: When the North Koreans invaded South Korea in 1950 State and Defense were split on the desirability of an early peace settlement with Japan. Defense favored a delay because bases in Japan were required. Defense argued that the Korean War demonstrated the need for bases and hence strengthened the case for delaying signing the peace treaty. State argued that because of the attack, Japanese concern would make it possible to negotiate base rights after a Peace Treaty. Hence the United States should move quickly to sign a Peace Treaty.[24]

President Johnson did change his stand and decide to deploy an ABM in response to the Soviet ABM deployment in order to cancel the possible effect of the Soviet ABM on the 1968 election. By preventing an "ABM gap" issue this change accomplished its purpose without need to cause a particular Soviet reaction. On the other hand, Secretary of Defense Robert McNamara's proposal for SALT talks to prevent the American ABM deployment depended on a Soviet willingness to participate in negotiations.

5. Changes in the stands of one or more participants in nation A may affect the actions of nation B. But the change in behavior of B is unlikely to be well designed to secure the action by nation A which is desired by any single participant. This is because: (a) the generator of a proposal will not put forward an optimum signal; (b) the decision will deviate from the proposal of any single player; and (c) the actions will deviate from the decisions.

5.1 The generator of a proposal for action designed to affect the behavior of nation A will not put forward an optimum signal.

5.1.1 Even if a player's only interest is to design a signal to affect the actions of nation A he is likely to do a poor job because (a) he uses Model I or (b) he uses a Bureaucratic Politics Model but lacks the required data and understanding.

A. He is likely to employ a particular Model I framework which assumes that nation A:

(1) Will be heavily influenced by the behavior of his nation;

(2) Is listening closely and with sophistication and will understand the meaning of complex signals;

---

[24] On Korea, see Glenn Paige, *The Korean Decision* (New York 1968), and Joseph de Rivera, *Psychological Dimensions in Foreign Policy* (Columbus 1968).

(3) Is unaffected by domestic political constraints (embassy officials will generally not hold to this point, nor will senior players for nations whose leaders they know well);

(4) Shares the images of the world which his nation accepts.

For example: a dying Secretary of State John F. Dulles, giving his last advice to then Vice President Richard Nixon on how to communicate with Soviet leaders, assured him that "Khrushchev does not need to be convinced of our good intentions. He knows we are not aggressors and do not threaten the security of the Soviet Union. He understands us."[25]

B. Even if a participant uses a Bureaucratic Politics Model he is likely to lack data and an understanding of nuances about how processes work in nation A.

For example: British and American leaders during the Suez and Skybolt crises failed to design optimum signals because they did not understand the nuances of each other's system. A rare counter-example is presented in a memorandum prepared by Richard Neustadt on how to sell the MLF to a new Labour British government.[26]

5.1.2 Even if a participant is focused only on national security interests, he will be concerned about other audiences at home and abroad.

For example: during the 1958 Quemoy crisis Dulles wanted to make absolutely clear to the Chinese that we would defend Quemoy. But he was inhibited from sending a clear signal by his fear that others would also hear the warning. Domestic critics of U.S. policy might use it to effectively challenge his policy. And the Chinese Nationalists might use the warning as a handle to provoke a clash between the U.S. and the Chinese Communists.[27]

5.1.3 A participant who desires to send a signal will have other interests which will influence his proposal. He will know that other audiences will hear his signal. Their reaction will always be taken into account and may, depending on his interests, be of greater concern.

For example: Secretary of State John F. Dulles, in a private conversation where he sought to convey to British Prime Minister Anthony Eden what the American position on Suez was, recognized that the British leader, out of concern or appreciation, might telephone his old friend President Eisenhower to report the conversation. This report, Dulles feared, could set back his efforts to establish a relationship of

[25] Richard Nixon, *Six Crises* (New York 1962), 241.
[26] Richard Neustadt, "Memorandum on the British Labour Party and the MLF," *New Left Review*, LI (September 1968).
[27] On the 1958 Quemoy crisis, see Morton Halperin and Tang Tsou, "United States Policy Toward the Offshore Islands," *Public Policy*, XV (Cambridge 1966).

trust with the President. Thus he was not very explicit about American policy.

5.2 The decision of a government in a game designed to influence the behavior of nation A will deviate from the proposal of any single participant. Some of the disagreements among participants that affect decisions will relate to influencing the behavior of nation A. (a) Participants may defer on what actions by nation A are desirable; and (b) participants may differ on how to induce the desired behavior.

For example: at one point in the Suez crisis Dulles apparently proposed that the United States assure the British government that the U.S. would assume the financial cost of bypassing the Suez Canal if this became necessary. Neustadt suggests that Dulles had concluded (correctly, Neustadt argues) that this promise would reduce substantially the chance of the British resorting to force without any real probability that the United States would have to make good on its commitment. He was unable to convince Secretary of the Treasury George Humphrey. This was not because Humphrey did not want to stop the British, but because (Neustadt implies) Humphrey did not quite accept Dulles' complicated explanation of how the British cabinet functioned, and he did not want to yield his control of the funds involved.

5.3 Actions which follow from a decision related to affecting the actions of nation A will deviate from the decision. In part the deviation will be directly related to disagreements about influencing the actions of nation A, in that (a) participants may differ on what actions by nation A are desirable, and (b) participants may differ on how to induce the desired behavior.

Examples: When General Douglas MacArthur learned that Truman, hoping to end the war on compromise terms, was about to announce publicly the American desire for an armistice in Korea, MacArthur, who opposed a compromise, broadcast a surrender demand to the enemy. Former U.S. Ambassador to India Kenneth Galbraith reports in his *Journal* many occasions when his actions deviated from his instructions because he believed his actions were more likely to bring about the desired Indian action.[28]

6. Changes in actions of one nation will succeed in changing the actions of a second nation in a desired direction only to the extent that (a) the actions of the first nation send a clear, consistent, simple signal and (b) some participants in the other nation want, in pursuit of their own interests, to change behavior in the desired way, and (c) this signal serves to increase the influence of these participants.

[28] John K. Galbraith, *Ambassador's Journal* (Boston 1969).

For example: the American effort to get the Japanese government to surrender without invasion of Japan succeeded only because (1) the United States sent Japan some of the clearest signals in history, including dropping two atomic bombs, destroying Tokyo with fire bombing, destroying the Japanese fleet, and assembling an invasion force; (2) there was a strong group within the Japanese government, including the Emperor, his principal adviser, and the Foreign Minister who had opposed the war from the start and wanted to surrender; and (3) the American signals increased this group's sense of determination and willingness to run risks while discrediting and demoralizing their opponents. No major figure in Japanese ruling circles changed his mind about the desirability of war with the United States from the beginning of the war to the end. Those who wanted to begin the war remained opposed to surrender.[29]

7. More often changes in actions by one nation will have unintended and unanticipated effects on actions.

Pearl Harbor and Skybolt

In the months leading up to Pearl Harbor, competing groups in Japan and the United States needed different actions from each other's government in order to accomplish their objectives.[30] In Tokyo those who opposed war with the United States needed to be able to show that the United States would not interfere with Japanese expansion by cuting off sources of scrap iron, oil, and other materials. They also needed the United States to avoid actions which would have enabled their opponents to argue that war with the United States was inevitable. Those who favored war had quite different needs.

In the American government, proponents of war with Japan looked for Japanese actions which would demonstrate that Japan's objectives were unlimited and threatened American and British possessions. Roosevelt, who sought to avoid war with Japan, had quite different needs. He had to resist pressures within the government from those who wanted to go to war with Japan. At the same time he did not want to so demoralize them that they would resign or reduce their efforts to prepare for the war with Germany which he believed was necessary.

[29] See Robert Butow, *Japan's Decision to Surrender* (Stanford 1954), and Herbert Feis, *Japan Subdued* (Princeton 1961).

[30] On Pearl Harbor, see Dean Acheson, *Present at the Creation* (New York 1969); Robert Butow, *Tojo and the Coming of the War* (Princeton 1961); Herbert Feis, *The Road to Pearl Harbor* (New York 1962); Joseph Grew, *My Years in Japan* (New York 1944); William L. Langer and S. Everett Gleason, *The Undeclared War* (New York 1953); and Wohlstetter (fn. 16). On Skybolt, see Neustadt (fn. 21).

Thus Roosevelt's purposes required that Japan avoid: (1) flagrant violations of international law, (2) linking up with Germany in ways that made it impossible to resist arguments that war with Japan was a part of the war against the Fascist alliance, and (3) threats to the British or Dutch colonies which could be seen as a threat to the Allies in Europe.

Actions of both governments were designed with a variety of purposes. Japanese military moves followed decisions to expand the area under direct Japanese control without any direct interest in signals to the United States. On the other hand, the negotiating positions proposed (and in some cases implemented) by the State Department were designed, in part, to demonstrate to the President that a negotiated solution was impossible. The stand of the Japanese military on negotiations probably had a similar purpose. Roosevelt and Japanese Foreign Minister Togo proposed positions designed to keep open the possibility of negotiations with the hope of reaching a settlement.

In this context Japan moved to occupy all of French Indochina. This Japanese move was not intended to signal anything to the United States or to influence American actions. Nevertheless, it was incompatible with what Roosevelt needed from the Japanese government. He no longer felt able to resist the pressures to take some sort of action against Japan. Resisting pleas for a total embargo, he compromised by requiring licensing of all exports to Japan. Those who favored war, including then Assistant Secretary of State for Economic Affairs Dean Acheson, were able to control implementation of this decision. They did so by imposing a total embargo on oil shipments to Japan.

At this point the Japanese leaders opposed to war did not have what they needed from the United States to pursue their objective. A period of high-level and intensive negotiations began. Those opposed to war on both sides sought to persuade the other side to rescind the behavior that made it impossible to resist pressures to go to war. Roosevelt, recognizing that the State Department's interests differed from his, used his Postmaster General as a negotiating agent. He also intervened directly by dealing personally with the Japanese envoy. The peace party in Tokyo, with considerable difficulty, got through the Japanese government two watered-down offers. Plan "A" promised an ultimate Japanese withdrawal from China. Plan "B" offered an immediate Japanese withdrawal from southern Indochina in return for lifting the trade embargo. However, those in both capitals who saw war as necessary or inevitable were able to resist the proposed compromises. And the two governments found themselves at war.

Richard E. Neustadt's account of the Skybolt crisis tells a quite different tale of relations between allies with a relatively successful resolution. Nevertheless, the basic points are the same.

What British Prime Minister Harold Macmillan needed from the United States were indications that American leaders held him in high regard. He was particularly good at getting from the United States what was in Britain's interest. He also needed the Skybolt missile, since he had made that a symbol of his independent nuclear deterrent. He needed the deterrent to pursue his domestic interests. If he failed to get these things from the United States, Macmillan was threatened both by potential alternative leaders in the Conservative Party and by the next election.

Kennedy's needs from Macmillan were more modest. He needed to avoid a demonstration of beastliness to the British, or non-support for the needs of a Conservative government. Kennedy's needs stemmed from his desire to maintain the active and enthusiastic support of the eastern foreign policy establishment which was sympathetic to Britain in general and to particular Conservative Party leaders, especially Macmillan. He also needed to avoid evidence of extreme discrimination in favor of Britain in order to pursue his objective of improving relations with France. He also needed to maintain a semblance of consistency with his non-proliferation policy.

Kennedy's acceptance of the recommendation of Secretary of Defense Robert S. McNamara to cancel Skybolt was in no way intended as a signal to the United Kingdom. It was not intended to suggest a lack of friendship or respect for the British government, or its leaders, or any desire to remove Britain from its role as an independent nuclear power. Nevertheless, the cancellation of Skybolt was incompatible with Macmillan's pursuit of his interests. Thus, Macmillan's first hope was that the decision could be rescinded. If this failed, he would need some substitute for Skybolt to continue with what he could describe at home as an independent nuclear capability. He also needed a demonstration of American support of him and a demonstration of the willingness of the American government to respond to his needs. However, Macmillan could not, before the Nassau Conference, request Polaris. The British Navy was opposed, as was the Air Force. The British Navy was opposed because it feared a diversion of funds from the navy's basic program (aircraft carriers), and the Air Force wished to keep the strategic deterrent role for itself. Both services had important supporters on the back benches. More important, Macmillan was reluctant to go to his cabinet where opponents of the independent deterrent might join with those concerned about the added cost of Polaris and defeat him.

The needs of American officials were different. The Secretary of State, Dean Rusk, who might have favored continuing Skybolt, was unwilling to meddle in the affairs of his colleague, the Secretary of Defense. Robert McNamara was determined to cancel Skybolt; but he was prepared to give the British Polaris as a substitute. He was unwilling, however, to do battle with the Europeanists in the State Department—which he would have had to have done to offer the British Polaris before they demanded it.

As a crisis ensued Kennedy became directly involved. He saw that if the U.S. government persisted in its current course of action, what he, Kennedy, needed from Macmillan would be threatened. Macmillan was prepared to have a break over the issue. He demonstrated to Kennedy that Kennedy had to choose between getting what he needed from the U.K. and other costs to his interests at home. The compromise which ensued gave Macmillan virtually everything that he needed, while only marginally affecting Kennedy's domestic position. Britain got Polaris, which could be used independently in moments of supreme national concern. Kennedy could point to the British agreement to use Polaris as part of an integrated NATO force. The needs of both leaders were met. Other players were unhappy. The crisis receded.

The two cases, in their similarities and differences, illustrate the utility of the propositions for analyzing how the behavior of one nation affects the behavior of another.

In both cases the key event that triggered the serious crisis was not meant as a signal to the other. The Japanese occupation of Indochina and the cancellation of Skybolt both resulted from decision games designed to affect other outcomes. Analysts in Washington, Tokyo, and London did a poor job of explaining the meaning of these and other actions and of predicting future actions. Senior players attempted to interpret actions to support stands they had previously taken. For example, those in the United States who believed war with Japan was inevitable pointed with alarm to Japanese actions.

In the Skybolt case the stakes for leaders on both sides were largely domestic. Macmillan and Kennedy saw dangers to their power in the possible changes in actions of the other nation. For other players, particularly the armed forces, the face of the issue was roles and missions. Others saw national security interests related to proliferation and European unification. In the case of Pearl Harbor the stakes were national security interests of the highest order—preventing war. Actions of the other nation threatened the ability of leaders to veto actions of other players, which they feared would lead to war.

Changes in the behavior of each nation in each crisis, at least at first, led to unintended changes in the behavior of the other. This increased the threat to interests of senior players on both sides. The Japanese move made it impossible for Roosevelt to prevent an embargo. The embargo, in turn, so weakened the peace group in Japan that war could not be prevented. In the Skybolt case the first move—cancellation of Skybolt—threatened Macmillan's interests and almost led him to attack Kennedy publicly. This would have required further American action. The two leaders, meeting in Bermuda, were able to find a solution. They were then able to force their reluctant colleagues to accept that solution. In this case the price of failure would have been a more intense crisis and troubles for both leaders at home. In the Pearl Harbor case, the stakes were much greater. One wonders whether a direct meeting between FDR and the Japanese Prime Minister might not have produced a mutually compatible solution which each could have imposed at home.

Section III

POLICY IMPLICATIONS

We present here some illustrative policy implications of the Bureaucratic Politics Model in the form of policy advice to players in the U.S. government, in particular to senior players. The presentation takes the form of precepts without evidence or elaboration. In some cases we present examples to illustrate a point, or to show that some people believe the contrary. These precepts are divided into two parts: (1) advice about the behavior of other governments and the effect of U.S. behavior on other government actions, and (2) advice about the behavior of the U.S. government.

BEHAVIOR OF OTHER GOVERNMENTS

EXPLANATION OF THE BEHAVIOR OF OTHER GOVERNMENTS

1. Be suspicious of explanations that depend on the assumption that one can reason back from detailed characteristics of specific behavior to central government intentions or doctrine. For example, on the Soviet SS-9 deployment Secretary Laird has testified, that "they are going for a first-strike capability and there's no doubt about it."[31]

2. Recognize that in most cases the full range of behavior exhibited by a government was not intended by any single participant. In most

[31] *New York Times*, March 22, 1969, p. 16.

cases, the policy and action decisions were compromises. Actual behavior reflects programs, standard operating procedures, and interests of implementors, as well as the relevant decisions. For example, a Soviet analyst who neglected these factors would have come to erroneous conclusions about why the United States was deploying an ABM system. Secretary of Defense Robert S. McNamara's speech in October 1967 laid out the arguments against a large Soviet-oriented ABM system while announcing a limited deployment of ABM's.

3. Press those charged with providing explanations for detailed explanations based on a Bureaucratic Politics Model.

4. Recognize that leaders of other governments may have quite different images of the world, information, etc., that lead them to see events in a dramatically different light. For example, Chinese bombardment of the offshore islands in 1954 may have reflected fear on the part of some Chinese leaders of American encirclement due to the security treaties the United States was currently signing. This explanation was not even considered by U.S. leaders because they knew that the treaties were defensive.[32]

PREDICTION

1. Be suspicious of predictions based primarily on calculations about the national security interests and doctrines of another nation. Calculations of this sort may provide an appropriate surrogate in the case of some problems, for example, deterrence of nuclear war by a stable balance of terror. In most cases such predictions will not be satisfactory. For example, estimates of Soviet force postures have frequently gone astray for this reason.

2. Ask for a bureaucratic-political map of the factors that can affect an outcome, including in particular a list of the participants and their interests.

Andrew W. Marshall has provided a set of specific propositions related to predicting Soviet force posture: (1) Force posture for a nation is especially influenced by the organizational interests and behavior of sub-parts of the military establishment. (2) Internal Soviet security controls over the flow of information and the general privacy of the decision-making process leads to an even more bureaucratically influenced force posture than is usual in Western countries. (3) Parts of the Soviet military bureaucracy strive to keep their budgetary shares and are fairly successful in doing so. (4) The mechanics of the operation

---

[32] See Halperin and Tsou (fn. 27), and Leon Sigal, "The Rational Policy Model and the Formosa Straits Crisis," *International Studies Quarterly*, XIV (June 1970).

of the budgetary process have a substantial impact on the formation of force posture.[33]

PLANNING

1. Ask who in another government wants to do what you want for his own reasons. If you locate him, strengthen him. If you do not, despair.

2. Limit claims on other governments to outcomes reachable by them within a wide range of internal politics, under a variety of personalities and circumstances.

3. Recognize the low probability of success.

PLANNING WITHIN THE U.S. GOVERNMENT

GENERAL PLANNING PRECEPTS

1. Focus on changing governmental action.

2. Decide whether a change in governmental actions requires that some policy or decision be changed.

3. Be aware that if it does appear necessary (desirable) to change policy in order to change action, the change in policy in the great majority of cases is only a way-station to the desired outcome and not the outcome itself—often the policy change is only an early way-station.

4. Realize that others, who may desire different outcomes, may also be planning, and take their planning into account.

5. Be prepared to modify your choice of outcome, or your declared prediction of the consequences of that outcome, in order to induce others to cooperate. Take into account, however, that these modifications may (or may not) affect the nature of your game with third parties.

6. Be aware that such modifications (compromises) may give rise to outcomes which are less desirable than the existing state of affairs. If the probability of such outcomes is sufficiently high, the game should not be started, or, once started, ended. With this consideration in mind, review the state of play frequently.

7. In choosing the desired outcome, consider how many changes in individual or organizational behavior are required for its achievement.

8. Assess whether desired changes in behavior will be easily observed or monitored. Design outcomes so as to produce natural monitors (but don't count on them).

9. Try to design outcomes so as not to affect major organizational interests, particularly the autonomy of an organization or its ability to

[33] Andrew Marshall, unpublished paper.

pursue what it sees to be the essence of its function, promotions, roles and missions, and budgets.

10. Design proposals so that people can agree for different reasons. (Use arguments that appeal to one side and offend others only in private.)

11. Plan systematically. Either internalize or consult an explicit planning guide. See Appendix.

INTERESTS

1. Recognize multiple interest and faces ("where they stand depends on where they sit").

2. Recognize that stands on issues are determined by calculations of multiple interests of which national security interests are only one. Therefore, only in cases where national security arguments are clearly dominant are they likely to change a player's stance on a particular issue.

3. Recognize that where a participant is strongly motivated by organizational interests, he will resist actions that seem to threaten the autonomy of his organization to pursue what is conceived to be the essence of its activity. For example, foreign service officers have consistently opposed proposals giving the State Department operational control of foreign operations beyond representation, negotiation, and reporting, e.g., of foreign aid, military assistance programs, and foreign information service.

4. Recognize that players with strong organizational interests will also be importantly affected by the impact of an action of promotion patterns, roles and missions, and budgets.

5. These interests, particularly the interest in roles and missions, will affect these players' behavior in situations that are regarded by the senior players as major national crises in which all are obviously pulling together.

For example: the competition between the Air Force and Navy in reporting on the effectiveness of the bombing in North Vietnam.

INFORMATION

1. Assume that others will give you information that they think will lead you to do what they want, rather than information that you would prefer to have.

For example: prior to the Bay of Pigs, President Kennedy indicated that he might cancel the planned invasion from fear that it might be a total failure. He was assured by leaders of the intelligence community that this was impossible. If the effort to establish a beachhead failed, the landing forces, which had received guerrilla training, would move to the nearby mountains. Kennedy was not told that there was a swamp between the landing site and the mountains, that less than one-third of the force had any guerrilla training; and no one in the invasion party was told that they should move to the mountains if the effort was failing.[34]

Another example is provided by a former DIA analyst:

From 1964–65, when U.S. involvement in Vietnam began to be considerable, until late 1966 or early 1967, the generals in Saigon worked to build up U.S. troop strength. Therefore, they wanted every bit of evidence brought to the fore that could show that infiltration was increasing. DIA obliged and also emphasized in all reports the enemy's capability to recruit forces from the South Vietnamese population. In 1967 a second period began. The high priests of Saigon decided that we were "winning." Then the paramount interest became to show the enemy's reduced capability to recruit and a slowdown in infiltration due to our bombing. The tune and emphasis of reports from the field changed radically, and so did those put out by DIA.

It should not be concluded that anyone suppressed evidence. No one did. The military in Saigon sent all the facts back to Washington eventually. During the buildup period, infiltration data and recruitment data came in via General Westmoreland's daily cablegram. Data from field contact with enemy units came amid the more mundane cables or by courier up to five weeks later. Cables from Westmoreland, of course, were given higher priority in Washington. When we started "winning," detailed reports highlighting "body counts" and statistics on how many villages were pacified were cabled with Westmoreland's signature; recruitment studies were pouched or cabled with the reports on the fluctuating price of rice. It was all a matter of emphasis.[35]

2. Do not assume that there are not critical differences in these evaluations of information simply because a piece of paper reports unanimous conclusions of the group. For example, DIA differences with

[34] See Haynes Johnson, *Bay of Pigs* (New York 1964); Schlesinger (fn. 6), and Sorensen (fn. 6).
[35] Patrick J. McGarvey (fn. 23), 71-72.

General Westmoreland's evaluation of the Tet offensive as total defeat for the enemy were not reported.[36]

3. Recognize that technical evaluations and conclusions are frequently based on simple rules of thumb, rather than on complex technical calculations. The rules of thumb are often wrong. For example, the optimum characteristics for the first generation of American missiles, specified by the von Neumann committee as destructive power of one megaton, range of 5500 miles, and accuracy measured as a CEP of 5 miles, were based respectively on a round number, a quarter of the earth's circumference, and compromise between those who were optimistic and those who were pessimistic about accuracy.[37]

4. Don't assume that information that you pass on to other players is passed on by them to their subordinates or superiors.

OPTIONS

1. Recognize that the options presented will be based on the programs and standard operating procedures of the organizations that generate the options.

2. Recognize that options which require cooperation between two independent organizations are unlikely to be advanced by either of these organizations.

3. Recognize that organizations tend to assert that an option is feasible only if it permits the organization considerable freedom of action. Options designed by organizations will be designed to maximize their freedom of action. For example, in 1962 the Joint Chiefs of Staff were prepared to recommend the introduction of American troops into Laos only if the President issued them an assurance that nuclear weapons would be used if necessary.[38]

4. Recognize that options tend to be biased by simplistic and unstated hunches about domestic politics and bureaucratic politics.

5. Recognize that options will be designed on the basis of the assumption that other governments act as single individuals motivated primarily by national security interests. In some cases this assumption will be complicated by some feel for Foreign Office or domestic politics.

6. Don't assume that participants are in fact motivated by the arguments they put forward in favor of their stand.

[36] Ibid.
[37] Herbert York, *Race to Oblivion* (New York 1970), 89.
[38] See Roger Hilsman, *To Move a Nation* (New York 1967), Schlesinger, *op. cit.* and Sorensen, *op. cit.*

7. Recognize that the intensity of a participant's argument for a position may not reflect the intensity of his commitment to that stand.

IMPLEMENTATION

1. Recognize that people do not feel obliged to implement faithfully a chosen action.

2. Note that they have available a number of alternatives, including: implementing the letter and not the spirit, delay, outright disobedience, as well as overzealous implementation.

3. Examine with great care the instructions given by an organization to its members for the implementation of some decision.

4. Locate yourself, prospective helpers, and presumed opponents in relation to all action channels readily or possibly available for implementing the results you want, and block those you fear.

5. Recognize that in the short run, the behavior implemented will reflect existing organizational programs and standard operating procedures.

6. Recognize that if an organization is forced to change its behavior it will tend to change to another program or standard operating procedure in its repertoire, rather than devise a new and perhaps more appropriate operating procedure.

7. Note that changing personnel is more likely to lead to changing behavior than changing orders to existing personnel: one new ambassador (of the right persuasion) is worth a thousand cables.

8. Recognize that members of foreign missions will employ various devices to increase their independence of home authority:

(a) They will often attempt to present their governments with a *fait accompli*.

(b) They will exploit visits by high officials of their governments by getting these officials on record as supporting mission positions. They will then use the record as evidence of a national commitment.

(c) They will reinterpret or evade unwelcome directives from home, hoping that the issuing authority will be forgetful or inattentive. Ordinarily, these hopes will be fulfilled.

(d) If authorities at home insist on compliance with unwelcome directives, the mission will warn of "dire consequences," etc.[39]

[39] Ernest May, unpublished paper.

APPENDIX

Planning Guide

I. *What precisely do I want to accomplish?*

    A. First attempt to predict what will occur.

    B. Plan and implement only if
        1. Disaster appears likely (possible);
        2. Substantial improvement is likely.

    C. Identify precisely the outcome I seek.

    D. Why do I seek it?
        1. Good in itself given my values. (If so, do I wish to reconsider my values?)
        2. I believe it will lead to a further outcome which I value. (If so, can I state the causal chain so I can retest?)
        3. I believe it will lead to behavior by other governments. (If so, consider that the other government is not a unitary actor and that its bureaucracy will do only what is in their interest in their own terms. Influence is most likely to take the form of altering incentives and power. Consider also how reliable my information is about the other government.)

    E. How likely am I to get the outcome as I desire it?
        1. Withhold judgment until working out paths to action and strategy.
        2. Consider relevant programs and standard operating procedures.
        3. Consider internal and external biases.

    F. How important is this outcome to me as compared to others?

II. *Alternative paths to action*

    A. Map out alternative routes to the desired outcome.

    B. Recognize that a change in policy may be neither necessary nor sufficient.

    C. Seek to change policy only if
        1. Necessary to remove an absolute barrier to changing action;
        2. Useful as a hunting license;
        3. Necessary given my access to those who must perform the action;
        4. Likely to lead easily to a change in action.

    D. Consider how high I need to go. (Do not involve the President unless necessary or he is likely to be sympathetic, i.e., unless he has a problem this may solve.)

    E. If seeking a change in policy, plot the action path from there to changes in actions.

    F. Consider for each path who will have the action. (Is there any path in which I will have the action?)

    G. Specify the formal actions which are necessary.

    H. What resources do I have to move action along each path with success? (Re-judge after considering tactics.) Relative advantages of each path.

    I. How will resources expended to get to one way-station outcome affect ability to get to further stations?

    J. What additional information will help? Can I get it? At what cost?

III. *Framing tactics—maneuvers and arguments—to move along a path*

    A. Identification of the participants and their interests, including those beyond the executive branch.
1. Who will inevitably be involved according to the rules of the game?
2. Who might seek to play but could be excluded?
3. Who might not seek to play but could be brought in?
4. What are the likely interests of the various participants, what face of the issue will they see, how will they define the stakes? Consider organization, personal, political, and national interests.
5. Who are natural allies, unappeasable opponents, neutrals who might be converted to support, or opponents who might be converted to neutrality?

    B. How can I lead a participant to see that the outcomes I desire are in his interest as he sees it?

    C. How can I change the situation to have an outcome conflicting less (or not at all) with participants' interests as they see them?

    D. Do I have the resources for this purpose? If not, can I get others to use theirs?

    E. What specific maneuvers should I use at what stages?

    F. What arguments should I use:
1. In general?
2. On a discriminatory basis?

    G. If I must get a large organization to change its behavior, I must consider the interests, standard operating procedures, and programs of that organization.

    H. Should I try to bring in players outside the executive branch? If so, how?

    I. How can I tell how well I am doing?

IV. *Gauging costs and benefits*

    A. Reconsider all phases from time to time. Specifically:
1. How high up should one seek a decision?
2. How should the decision sought relate to the change desired, i.e., should it be a decision to change policy, to change patterns of action, or to take a single particular new step (or to stop an on-going action)?
3. By what means will the initial decision which is sought be converted into the desired action?

B. Plan of action.
1. How to move the action to the way-station and final outcome desired.
2. What maneuvers and arguments to use on or with the other participants.
3. A time sequence.
C. To what extent is this process consciously duplicated by participants seeking a change? Are some participants more likely to plan than others? To plan effectively?
D. How is the choice of way-station outcomes and route action made?

DYNAMICS OF INTERNATIONAL CONFLICT:

Some Policy Implications of Population, Resources, and Technology

By NAZLI CHOUCRI and ROBERT C. NORTH*

INTERNATIONAL conflict has been accounted for in many different ways—in terms of aggressive "instincts," territoriality, population growth, the search for basic resources or seaports, the protection of trade routes, psychopathological deviations, plunder and profit, a drive for imperialist control, and so forth. Some theorists have considered grievances, competition, anxieties, tension, threat, and provocation to be of special importance. Others have laid heavy emphasis upon national power or capability, military preparedness, strategic considerations, and the competition for dominance.[1] No doubt most if not all of these variables are relevant, but this recognition does not help much in the development of a theory of war, its dynamics, and contributing causal networks. In the long run all factors need to be pulled together in some systematic way. A serious difficulty emerges from the fact that the various "causes" that contribute to war tend to be highly interactive, that is, they affect each other in various ways and often in many different directions. The problem is to find out, if possible, which variables are contributing most to international violence and in what proportion. The purpose of this paper is to take an early step in this direction by

* We would like to thank the editors for their extensive comments and suggestions. We are also indebted to James Foster, Daniel Lerner, Edward Morse, Ithiel de Sola Pool, Thomas Robinson, and Oran Young for their incisive criticisms, and to Hayward Alker and Richard Lagerstrom for their assistance on theoretical and methodological problems.

[1] See Raymond Aron, *Peace and War* (New York 1967); A.F.K. Organski, *World Politics* (New York 1968); Hans J. Morgenthau, *Politics Among Nations: The Struggle for Power and Peace* (New York 1964); Richard N. Rosecrance, *Action and Reaction in World Politics: International Systems in Perspective* (Boston 1963); R. J. Rummel, "Dimensions of Dyadic War, 1820–1952," *Journal of Conflict Resolution*, x (March 1966), 65-73; Raymond Tanter, "Dimensions of Conflict Behavior Within and Between Nations, 1958–1960," *Journal of Conflict Resolution*, x (March 1966), 41-64; J. David Singer, "Capability Distribution and the Preservation of Peace in The Major Power Sub-System, 1816–1965" (Paper prepared for delivery at the 66th Annual Meeting of the American Political Science Association, Los Angeles, September 1970); and Quincy Wright, *A Study of War* (Chicago 1942). We are particularly indebted to Professor Organski for a treatment of the concepts that provided the basis for our investigations.

reporting on some empirical research currently under way and by presenting some tentative findings which suggest partial explanations and some implications and difficulties for national policies.

In general there seem to be at least three major types of dynamic processes tending toward conflict and warfare among nations: *the dynamics of the expansion of national or imperial interests; the dynamics of antagonistic competition and the arms race; and the dynamics of crisis.* In this paper we shall examine the processes of national expansion and some of their implications. We shall also somewhat sketchily examine the processes of military competition. A primary emphasis will be upon some of the basic dilemmas associated with important variables and upon the recurring paths to large-scale violence. Some of these are readily manipulable by national policy-makers and some are not. The dynamics of crisis will be touched upon briefly, not for purposes of analysis but only as they relate to expansion and competition.

An important question, of course, remains as to the role of rationality and the rational calculus in national interactions. Many of the dynamics we shall be considering are beyond the range of such a calculus. Some are not. Isolating the variables that are readily manipulable by the policy-maker (or manipulable at relatively low costs) provides some insight into the issue of control over decision outcome.

I

Early investigations by the Stanford Studies in International Conflict and Integration into the dynamics of conflict and warfare have centered on crises and the eruption of large-scale violence. A crisis, however, is only the small tip of an obscured iceberg of competitions, antagonisms, relatively non-violent conflicts, arms races, and previous crises. Is it possible, then, to look into the antecedents of a crisis of war, to identify in some systematic way the longer-range causal networks, and to isolate the points where alternative paths may have made a difference in the long run? Could some key variables have been manipulated in ways that would have yielded different outcomes?

We do not suggest that crisis studies ought to be abandoned. On the contrary, it is of the utmost importance that as much as possible be understood about the dynamics of both arms races and crises. Nevertheless, an adequate comprehension of crises is not likely until theoretical and empirical linkages are established between crises and the longer-run dynamics of international competition and conflict—between the tip and the part of the iceberg farthest below the surface of the water. This linking up remains to be done; and it is not an easy undertaking.

A sounder and more empirically verifiable framework needs to be developed as a proper context for investigations of crisis phenomena.

In large part, longer-range sequences can be accounted for in terms of submerged phenomena such as population differences, technological growth, differential access to (and competition for) resources, trade, markets, and influence, the expansion of national interests, and so forth. These considerations may yield useful and even invaluable insights into the dynamics of conflict and warfare.

This essay is a report on research in progress. This research, if pursued in greater depth and on a broader front, may be of potential importance to long-range policy-making. This work proceeds from the assumption that there is an operational milieu in which national leaders and their advisors and deputies conceive and effect policy. It is also assumed that the elements of this milieu ought to be examined to see which are relatively constant and which are relatively manipulable— given the costs of manipulation.[2] The concept of such an operational milieu is interdisciplinary in its broad implications, drawing on the theories, data, and analytical techniques of the demographer, ecologist, economist, human geographer, and even the physicist, as well as the political scientist and other specialists in foreign policy.

For some years now we have been compiling extensive sets of annual data, some going back to 1870, for major powers and for some lesser and small powers. This collection includes data on national areas, populations, indicators of technology and production, military budgets, men under arms, colonial territories and expansions, trade, casualties, and so forth. For some countries over certain time periods we have gathered, coded, and analyzed data on conflict and cooperation. Gradually, and in an experimental fashion, we have developed a theoretical framework. We have been analyzing parts of these data using various types of multivariate analysis; and we have done a limited amount of computer simulation. In this paper we report our findings to date.

The specific problem we address ourselves to is this. From the policy-maker's viewpoint it may be theoretically interesting to know, for example, that in any particular situation population growth (the sheer numbers of people and their rates of increase) is more (or less) important than technological growth (the levels, distribution, and rates of advance of knowledge and skills among the people) in producing high conflict outcomes. However, the head of state or foreign minister (or an advisor or deputy) is not likely to consider this relevant to

[2] Harold Sprout and Margaret Sprout, *Foundations of International Politics* (Princeton 1962).

policy—although perhaps he should. Research such as ours will be of much more interest to a policy-maker if it identifies independent variables that are manipulable—defense budgets, for example, or alliance links—and if it informs him of the costs of manipulating these variables. He will also be interested in ways of using such variables for the achievement of his (or the nation's) purposes. In this paper we attempt (1) to specify the theoretical framework which provides the basis for our investigations, (2) to distinguish between those variables that are readily manipulable and those that are less manipulable or manipulable only at relatively higher costs, (3) to spell out some alternative long-range consequences of basic variables such as population growth, technological developments, and resource constraints, (4) to discuss our recent efforts to operationalize the conceptual framework and submit specific propositions to the empirical test, and (5) to specify some alternative implications for the policy-making community. It should be explicitly recognized, however, that our analysis is in a formative stage. Many of our findings are tentative at best. We expect revisions and modifications of both theoretical framework and empirical analysis in the course of further investigations.

II

We proceed on the following assumptions: that no one single cause ever determines international violence; that the over-all constellation of critical variables—psychological, sociological, demographic, economic and political—are not randomly distributed; and that it is possible to discern over-all patterns contributing to the outbreak of external conflict and war. We further assume that the outbreak of violence is the result of several developments which have their origins in the most basic attributes and capabilities of nations. We recognize also, however, that the leaders' perceptions of their nations' capabilities (accurate or inaccurate as the case may be) are equally, or perhaps even more, critical than this demonstrable reality. The leaders' perceptions are likely to be especially pertinent to an analysis of the *shaping* of a policy or decision. *Outcome* may well be more determined by the reality of things than by the perceptions of various leaders. The two, however, tend to be highly interconnected but the relationship is neither clear nor direct.

The basic proposition underlying our investigations of the dynamics of national expansion is that differential rates of population growth in combination with differential rates of technological growth contribute to international competition and sometimes to conflict, insofar

as competing nations have differential—grossly unequal—access to resources and capabilities. These relationships are not direct or simplistic.
Complex and intricate interdependencies dominate every stage in the
development of conflict situations. And we do not underestimate the
importance of human perceptions, values, preferences, goals expectations, decisions, and the like.[3] But a viable theoretical framework should
be able to accommodate both longer-range and shorter-range considerations. It should also offer possibilities for an eventual linking of objective and cognitive phenomena in the expansion, competition, and crisis
phases of international conflict.

After examining long sweeps of history we have developed a set of
further propositions about the dynamics of expansion which serve as a
tentative conceptual framework. This framework is based in part on
inferences drawn from history, in part on the writings of general systems theorists,[4] cyberneticists,[5] anthropologists,[6] and others,[7] and in
part on our own preliminary analyses of data from selected great and
smaller powers during the years between 1870 and 1970. Both the
framework propositions and our specific working hypotheses involve
some independent variables that are relatively non-manipulable by the
head of state or other responsible policy-maker or are manipulable only
at high costs (such as population and technology). Other variables
(such as military budgets and troop deployments) are from the policy-
maker's viewpoint more readily manipulated. Many of these variables
—particularly population, area, resources, technology, military budgets,
trade levels, and so forth—have in the past been regarded as important
by historians, sociologists, and political scientists. *The propositions we
are putting forward are not new, but they point to relationships among
these same variables recently perceived by ourselves and others as im-*

---

[3] In the shorter-run, during a crisis of a few days' or weeks' duration, for example,
the numbers of people or the broad levels of their knowledge will not vary appreciably.
In such instances, perceptions, values, preferences, goals, expectations and decisions
may be the crucial variables, with dimensions of population, level of technology, and
so forth, serving as constraining parameters. But in the longer-run, over years and
decades, the numbers of people, their rate of increase, their level of technology, their
rate of technological development, and the availability of natural resources in the environment, all seem to be powerful shaping and constraining influences.

[4] Ludwig von Bertalanffy, *General Systems Theory* (New York 1968); James G.
Miller, "Living Systems: Basic Concepts," *Behavioral Science*, x (October 1965), 337-79;
and James G. Miller, "Living Systems: Cross Level Hypotheses," *Behavioral Science*, x
(October 1965), 380-411.

[5] Norbert Wiener, *Cybernetics* (New York 1948), and *The Human Use of Human
Beings* (New York 1956).

[6] Elman R. Service, *Primitive Social Organization* (New York 1962); and Peter
Farb, *Man's Rise to Civilization as Shown by the Indians of North America* (New
York 1968).

[7] See especially Organski (fn. 1), and Sprout and Sprout (fn. 2).

portant for the analysis of national behavior. These propositions should be considered as a temporary framework subject to alterations as our operationalized hypotheses (the systems of equations presented later on) are tested in a variety of situations. By specifying the sequence of developments and the linkages between dynamics internal to the nation-state and those of a more external, international nature, we shall try to make explicit both long-range effects of critical variables and the short, more immediate considerations.

We assume that in formulating and carrying out policies national leaders are motivated in many ways. *To simplify the problem we may view them as operating to minimize, or close, one or a combination of three fundamental types of gap:* (1) *a gap between resources that are "needed" or demanded and those that are actually available;*[8] (2) *a gap between an expectation and the reality that materializes, as, for example, when climbing productivity tapers off;*[9] and (3) *a gap between the resources or growth rate of one's own country and that of a competitor or rival.* There are, of course, many other possible gaps that could be identified. The main point to be made here is that, in seeking to close any gap or combination of gaps, a national leader must either apply the specialized capabilities that are available to him, strengthen certain capabilities (perhaps at the expense of others), or develop new capabilities. The leader's ability to act, and his opportunity to employ one specialized capability rather than another (i.e., expanded trade rather than expanded agriculture, or heavy industry rather than light industry, or air power rather than sea power) will depend not only on available knowledge, skills, and resources, but also on how these capabilities have been organized and mobilized prior to the moment of his decision. In this way the leader is likely to be limited and constrained from action in some areas and influenced or even impelled toward other directions of activity. As we use the term in this paper, a constraint may not be absolute. We assume that, at the very least, (a) some additional amount of effort or other cost will be involved in overcoming it, or (b) some considerable amount of time, or (c) both.

The crucial, most basic "master" variables in our partial theory are population, resources, and technology, where technology refers to the level and rate of development of human knowledge and skills in a

---

[8] Alan Howard and Robert A. Scott, "A Proposed Framework for the Analysis of Stress in the Human Organism," *Behavioral Science*, x (April 1965).

[9] Raymond Tanter and Manus Midlarsky, "A Theory of Revolution," *Journal of Conflict Resolution*, xi (September 1967); James C. Davies, "Toward a Theory of Revolution," *American Sociological Review*, xxvii (February 1962).

society. A combination of growing population and developing technology places rapidly increasing *demands* upon resources, often resulting in internally generated *pressures*. The greater this pressure, the higher will be the likelihood of extending national activities outside territorial boundaries. To the extent that two or more countries with high capability and high pressure tendencies extend their interests and psycho-political borders outward, there is a strong probability that eventually the two opposing spheres of interest will intersect. The more intense the *intersections*, the greater will be the likelihood that competition will assume *military* dimensions. When this happens, we may expect competition to become transformed into conflict, and perhaps an *arms race* or cold war. At a more general level of abstraction, *provocation* will be the final act that can be considered as the stimulus for a large-scale conflict or *violence*. But an act will be considered a provocation only in a situation which has already been characterized by high lateral pressure, intersections among spheres of influence, armament tensions and competitions, and an increasing level of prevailing violence. Major wars, we shall argue, often emerge through a two-step process: in terms of internally generated pressure, and in terms of the reciprocal comparison, rivalry, and conflict, on a number of salient capability and behavior dimensions. Each process tends to be closely related to the other, and each, to a surprising degree, can be accounted for by relatively non-manipulable variables (or variables that are controllable only at high costs).

Because much of our empirical work rests on these hypothesized relationships it seems worthwhile to specify more fully the "causal" network and linkages between internal and external dynamics. We proceed from an assumption that man is much more a creature of his physical environment than is sometimes conceded. Recently biologists have been making explicit the extent to which each human being literally owes his life to the earth and ultimately to the sun.[10]

In any bounded environment, an island, a continent, or the world, *the larger the number of people, the greater will be the need and demand for some irreducible minimum of food and other indispensable resources.* There is no escaping this. For survival without serious damage to the human organism, each person requires approximately 2000

[10] Paul R. Ehrlich and Anne H. Ehrlich, *Population, Resources, Environment* (San Francisco 1970), 54-55, 82; see also Howard T. Odum, "Energetics of World Food Production," *The World Food Problem*, A Report to the President's Science Advisory Committee, III, Report of the Panel on the World Food Supply (Washington 1967); *Resources and Man*, Committee on Resources and Man, National Academy of Sciences, National Research Council (San Francisco 1969).

calories a day. A million people require at least a million times as much. Each human being also requires at least some minimal amount of water, air, and living space—and, again, a million people require a million times these irreducible amounts in order to survive without serious physical penalty.[11] The number of people in society (relative to resources and capabilities) is a critical variable, although the policy-maker is likely to accept the population of his country as a given. From his viewpoint this is a non-manipulable variable, or one that can be manipulated only at high costs. History presents numerous examples of large-scale population movements (forced or otherwise), and the creation of new polities based on massive immigration or emigration. But this has generally been a costly solution to political problems. And only infrequently can it be considered in short-range, low-cost terms.

Human beings rely on technology (knowledge and skills) in their efforts to meet physical, psychological, and emotional needs. A unique characteristic of man is his spectacular capacity for applying knowledge and skills to harness energy in the physical environment. At various levels of cultural development, man has derived energy from the burning of woods and charcoal, the generation of steam power, the tapping of coal and oil, and recently from the application of nuclear energy. Scientific and technological advances are among "the master variables, to which almost all other changes and transformations are directly or indirectly related."[12]

It appears self-evident that every practical application of technology (knowledge and skills) requires resources from the environment—although the amounts required tend to vary with the complexity of the tool, machine, or weapon. Thus, *the more advanced the level of technology—from the stone axe to the nuclear reactor—the greater the variety and quantity of resources needed by that society.* Applications of technology consume (or, more properly, "degrade") certain amounts of energy even when energy is being used for "positive" purposes, such as irrigating a desert.[13] As a rule, *the more advanced the level of tech-*

---

[11] Some societies obviously possess and "demand" considerably more than the irreducible minimum. Often, within a single society, some sectors of the population are affluent and others exist on the borderline of subsistence. In general, the societies with more affluence tend to be those which through one means or another, have access to relatively more resources and possess higher specialized capabilities. Useful suggestions for the analysis of complex relations are provided in W. Ross Ashby, "Constraint Analysis of Many-Dimensional Relations," in *General Systems,* Yearbook of the Society for General Systems Research, IX (Michigan 1964).

[12] Sprout and Sprout (fn. 2), 8.

[13] The consumption of resources (according to the First Law of Thermodynamics) does not mean the destruction of energy, but (according to the Second Law of Thermodynamics) usable energy is *degraded* with each transfer from more usable forms to a

*nology in a given society, the greater the range and quantity of things
people perceive themselves as "needing." Such societies with advanced
technology will also be more capable of securing much more than their
worldwide per capita share of resources.* We would expect these considerations to give rise to competition and conflict in many different situations.[14] This dependency, however, is certainly neither clear nor likely to be direct. One important problem lies in determining the nature of the intervening processes, and the extent to which differences in intervening processes give rise to different outcomes.[15] From the viewpoint of the policy-maker, the prevailing level of technology in his country, like the level of population, is likely to be accepted as a given, a less manipulable variable. Specific technologies, such as armaments, can be acquired in a relatively short period of time, and thus are readily manipulable. The general level of technology in a society—the distribution of knowledge and skills—is less easily manipulable. A major change may take decades or a generation.[16]

The point is that both population and technology use resources. Even technologies which acquire new resources require resources. Demands may refer not only to unsatisfied basic needs (food, water, space, and

---

less usable form. New applications of technology (the breeder reactor, for example, or nuclear fusion) may provide more efficient uses of primary energy. But such advances are likely to involve large amounts and a considerable range of other resources (such as minerals, fibers and so forth) in the construction of plants, machinery and auxiliary equipment and by way of raw materials for the production of artifacts. A more advanced technology is likely to be more efficient than a less advanced technology, that is, it is likely to produce more useable power per unit of input. However, the more advanced and efficient a given technology turns out to be, the greater is likely to be the variety and instances of the uses to which it is put, and consequently, the amount (as well as the range) of resources is likely to increase over-all.

[14] "Effects of Population Growth on Natural Resources and the Environment," *Hearings, Subcommittee of Committee on Government Operations*, House of Representatives, 91st Congress, 1st Session, September 15-16, 1969.

[15] We need not assume a fixed resource base to appreciate the full implications of these relationships. The interdependence of technology and resources is high. For example, resources may be discovered, or "created," where they were not known to exist. Or they may be acquired through trade, conquest, or other means. As long as the flow of resources is not severely impeded, or not perceived to be impeded, then the technology-resource-population relationship poses fewer problems for a society than otherwise. For elaboration of these points see especially *Resources and Man* by the Committee on Resources of Man and the Division of Earth Sciences, National Academy of Sciences, National Research Council, 1968.

[16] Over the course of human pre-history and history the broad advancement of knowledge and skills has tended to be exponential (extremely slow for many centuries, increasingly rapid in more recent times). However, at any given period, certain societies have tended to advance more rapidly than others. Often, a comparatively backward country, such as Japan around 1870, has displayed very rapid growth partly as a result of diffusion from more technologically advanced countries.

what is needed to supply tools, machines, and industrial processes) but also to such things as people *think* they need or yearn for (better food, housing, clothing, luxuries, and so forth). Objectively, resources may be available, but their usefulness may not be perceived. Or, resources may be present but not immediately available. Or, they may be available but as yet untapped. Making use of resources is, to a large extent, dependent upon the level of technology. To complicate matters further, "demands" are in considerable part a psychological variable. And only their empirical correlates are possibly subject to investigation.

In their efforts to meet what is needed or demanded, societies tend to allocate certain proportions of available capital, resources, and human energy in order to develop specialized capabilities.[17] Some of these allocations and investments are made by the government itself. Others are undertaken by the private sector. Both public and private decisions at an earlier point in time help to determine what the society can (and cannot) do, and also what it is likely to do at some subsequent period. Levels and changes in specialized capabilities are thus manipulable in part by national policy-makers (through budgetary allocations, governmental research and development programs, contract research, loans to private enterprises, and the like). But, on short notice, these specialized capabilities are non-manipulable, or manipulable only at very high costs. On the other hand, given an optimum foundation of basic capabilities, policy-makers can often manipulate appropriations and expenditures in the relatively short run of a few months or a year or so. This tends to be true of military capabilities (given either a sufficient industrial base, or the possibility of acquisitions from other nations), especially if the society as a whole has been alerted to some (real or fabricated) outside threat.

Countries have often increased their specialized capabilities rather quickly by forming an alliance with another country. This type of possibility amounts to a relatively manipulable variable, depending largely upon the discretion of the decision-makers (and on requirements of constituent support that differ considerably from one country to another). Alliances can impose serious constraints, however; or a country may be drawn into a conflict which its leaders or citizenry might prefer to avoid.[18]

[17] Howard and Scott (fn. 8).
[18] Such an interdependency of alliance commitments and obligations had a great deal to do with expanding what was a local conflict during the summer of 1914 into a major war. And the Cuban Missile Crisis of 1962 defined in a number of ways the limits beyond which neither Castro nor the USSR could move without risk of great cost to one or the other, or both.

The demands and specialized capabilities of a society combine multiplicatively to produce what might be called lateral pressure.[19] *This amounts to a tendency to undertake activities farther and farther from the original boundaries of the society, to acquire some degree of influence or control over a wider extent of space or among a larger number of people.* Such specialized capabilities as mechanized agriculture, commerce, finance, light industry, heavy industry, and military capability facilitate the meeting of demands. Without specialized capabilities of one type or another (or in some combination), a society will be hard put to acquire or achieve what is required and wanted. A society with few demands, and few specialized capabilities, will not generate much lateral pressure. Similarly, a society with a relatively large population, for example, may generate high demands. And if specialized capabilities are poorly developed, it will have difficulty satisfying such demands. It will not be able to expand major efforts very far beyond its borders.

Lateral pressure is thus a neutral term conveying the effort to extend in one or more directions (by exploration of territory, acquisition of new land, search for fishing grounds, expansion of trade, military conquest, and so forth), farther and farther beyond the original boundaries of the society. Alternatively, it is conceivable a society might invest its efforts and energies in tapping internal resources and capabilities, or move in both directions at once. However high their demands, a people cannot expand their efforts very far unless the appropriate capabilities have been developed.

The characteristics of the prevailing technology, and the specialized capabilities that a society has developed, will strongly influence its domestic, social, economic, and political institutions. It will also effect the mode in which lateral pressure is expressed—by settlement beyond its immediate frontier, by trade, by expansion of its frontiers, by conquest, by exploration of untapped internal resources, or by other means at its disposal.[20] For example, a strong commercial society may manifest lateral pressure through trade. It may also build an army (or navy)

---

[19] Again, what the correlates of lateral pressure are is subject to investigation. In contrast to "demands," explicit indicators of lateral pressure are readily available. See the *Research Note* below.

[20] Barrington Moore, Jr., *Social Origins of Dictatorship and Democracy: Lord and Peasant in the Making of the Modern World* (Boston 1967), 40. Moore emphasizes the importance to English institutions of relationships between the landed gentry and emerging commercial elements. Commerce and manufacturing lagged in France, as compared with England, and in consequence "All the main structural variables and historical trends in French society of the *ancien régime* differed sharply from those in England from the sixteenth through the eighteenth centuries."

and undertake conquest, acquire overseas colonies and establish settlements, or pursue a combination of these modes.[21] By extension, different societies may adopt different modes of lateral pressure. Alternatively, a society may choose to make use of one or more available modes.[22]

In these terms, then, we would expect a society with a rapidly growing population and rapidly advancing technology to generate high demands, develop strong specialized capabilities, and create considerable lateral pressure which would be manifested in a variety of modes.[23] A society with a rapidly growing population, but a seriously lagging technology, might be expected to generate high demands and suffer severe limitations in terms of specialized capabilities. The predicted outcome in the latter case would be low lateral pressure (Imperial China around 1900) in a society vulnerable to penetration by countries with greater capabilities.[24] Thus, during the late nineteenth and early twentieth centuries, traders, missionaries, engineers, gunboats, and marines proceeded *from industrialized western countries into China*— not the other way around.

Conceivably, a country of higher capability could turn inward. It might not require any great amount of resources from the outside.

[21] Thus Britain, as she became more and more a commercial nation, developed merchant shipping capabilities and a powerful navy. These specialized capabilities were critical factors in her achievement of an overseas empire. Russia tended, on the other hand, to expand her interests overland—eastward across Siberia—although she built fleets for Baltic, Black Sea, and Pacific service. See also Arnold J. Toynbee, *A Study of History*, III (London 1935).

[22] In these terms the concept of lateral pressure provides a link between theories of imperialism and colonialism on the one hand, and integration theories, functionalism, and federalism on the other. Much of the Marxist argument rests on the notions of surplus value and investment of energy outside territorial boundaries. In this context Hobson's interpretation seems as likely a hypothesis as the Leninist. Societies do not necessarily have to expand externally by adopting various modes of domination and conquest. It is conceivable, and possible, for societies to turn inward. By the same token, the mode in which lateral pressure is expressed does not necessarily have to be imperialistic, but could conceivably develop along lines of integration and building of political community. The history of the United States provides (as we note later on) a useful example of the interrelation between expansion, imperialism, and integration. Each of these processes reflects, in the terms described above, different dimensions or manifestations of lateral pressure. For a related discussion see Robert C. North and Nazli Choucri, "Population, Technology, and Resources in the Future International System," *Journal of International Affairs*, XXV, No. 2 (1971), 224-38.

[23] Such relationships would characterize Rome in the late republican and early imperial phases; Britain after the decline of Spain and again in the nineteenth century, as a consequence of her early initiatives in the industrial revolution; Germany in the late nineteenth and early twentieth centuries; Japan after the Meiji Restoration; the United States beginning a decade or so after the Civil War; and Russia in the late nineteenth century (despite her outmoded political and economic system) and increasingly after the Bolshevik Revolution.

[24] Moore (fn. 20).

New technologies could be used to uncover hitherto unavailable resources or to make new use of old resources. Sufficient fields for capital investment could be located at home, and hence foreign investment may not appear attractive. One has difficulty, however, identifying countries of high capability that are not manifesting lateral pressure (outwardly extending their activities and interests) in one mode or another. In general, the inward-turning countries seem to be those of low capability (China and Japan in the early nineteenth century, or modern Afghanistan or Bolivia).[25] If, on the other hand, a country is isolationist and has high capabilities (the United States during several phases of her history), we are likely to find it "spilling over" into relatively empty adjacent territory, filling out a continent, perhaps—and thus manifesting lateral pressure.[26] Or, countries turn inward with respect to many activities, but manifest lateral pressure in foreign trade or other essentially nonviolent, nonexploitative modes. It does not *necessarily* follow that lateral pressure always results in territorial expansion. Sweden presents a noteworthy pattern in this respect. There a growing, highly specialized technology, a relatively low and stable population, considerable forest and mineral resources, and limited amounts of arable land appear to be associated with highly developed commercial capabilities and a tendency to exert lateral pressure through somewhat distinct modes (by participation in United Nations peacekeeping forces, for example, rather than conquest or domination).[27]

In principle, a society can express lateral pressure in any mode provided the appropriate knowledge, skills, and resources are available and it is willing to incur the accompanying costs. Leadership seems to have free choice constrained only by whatever influences the rank and file of its constituents can bring to bear on policy-making. It is tempting to view lateral pressure as a variable which policy-makers—especially a powerful emperor or dictator—can manipulate almost at will. And this is, in fact, often the case, especially when a country is in a position to float a large foreign loan or move troops into foreign terri-

[25] It must be noted, however, that Afghanistan exerts some amount of lateral pressure toward Pakistan, although Pakistan probably exerts more toward Afghanistan. Something similar could probably be said about Bolivia.

[26] The full impact of United States' lateral pressure from around 1785 through the latter decades of the nineteenth century is sometimes obscured by the fact that the victims were largely Indian tribes. Hence, it was easy to think of the West as "empty." The same kind of observation is relevant to Russia's expansion eastward to the Pacific.

[27] Different parameter values associated with key variables are expected to yield different characteristic patterns of attributes and behavior. In other words, variation in the strength and relationship of key variables—population, technology resources—explain different modes of external behavior and differences between Sweden in comparison with Great Britain, France, or the United States.

tory. Yet important limitations, impulsions, and drifts are likely to emerge at almost every stage of the capability-building and interest-extending process. Because of lags and other reasons a head of state or policy-maker may not be able to influence either the level or rate of change of technology on a day-to-day basis. Specialized capabilities are more accessible to manipulation, but again, there are lag times involved. Many pertinent decisions are likely to be made in the private sector beyond direct governmental control.[28] Over longer periods of time, the major distributions of human energies, capital, and other resources tend to become institutionalized (both in terms of government budgets and private investments and distributions). They thus become parameters for the day-to-day decisions of state. They may be manipulable in a narrow sense—cut the military budget 10 per cent this year, raise education 2 per cent, and so forth—but to alter their distribution grossly is likely to be exceedingly difficult. Such distribution ratios may become virtually institutionalized and thus strongly incline a society toward the expression of lateral pressure in one mode (the expansion of military influence, for example) rather than another (nonexploitative trade, for instance). A major break, such as a revolution, may be required in order to alter such institutionalized priorities. Budgetary distribution thus provides a fairly accurate measure of a nation's operational, as opposed to its professed, values. At least it measures the operational values of the ruling group.

Nation-states and empires with high lateral pressure (whether generated by ruling elites, wide sectors of the populace, or by a combination of both) tend to extend their influence in search of raw materials, markets, or other needed resources.[29] *Also, high levels of energy and surplus capital often seek outside investment opportunity even when resources are relatively plentiful.* The nature of resources sought tends to change with the level and character of the technology of the country exerting lateral pressure. This includes the character of financial and commercial institutions, as well as the machines of production. In line with an earlier suggestion, something like the Law of the Instrument

[28] Policy-makers in socialist states are likely to have more control over specialized capabilities. But even Soviet and Chinese Communist leaders have been seriously constrained by the vast difficulties associated with the planning and management of developments in a bewildering array of specialized enterprises.

[29] The types of individuals, groups, classes, or levels of government instrumental in extending national influence may vary enormously from society to society, and even within the same society through time. Thus, the United States and the Soviet Union both extend their influence in search of raw materials and markets, but the modes and mechanisms are quite different. This is not to suggest that Soviet-American rivalry can be explained only in terms of competition for raw materials.

seems to operate: societies with high specialized capabilities, and high levels of human and mechanical energy, frequently have their capabilities put to expansive use—even if it means exploring the moon. In high-capability societies we would expect this predisposition for the deployment of available facilities, capacities, and power to operate on lower and middle-range bureaucratic levels, as well as at the top.

The higher the lateral pressure generated by a given state or empire, the greater the tendency to extend its interests into (and often domination over) territories and countries with lower levels of capability. This is illustrated by Rome's expansion in Europe, North Africa, and the Middle East; by the imposition of Spanish control in South America, Mexico, California, the Philippines, and elsewhere; and by the spread of British and French dominions. So, too, the United States, during its westward movement, pushed aside or destroyed Indian tribes and absorbed Texas, New Mexico, Arizona, California, and other territories belonging to Mexico. Along her northern border, the United States encountered a stiff British-Canadian lateral pressure and was somewhat constrained.[30]

The desire to achieve and maintain law and order (as defined by national leadership) and to protect national interests (or large private interests) in far-off places may lead to wars against low-capability societies (indigenous tribes, colonies, semi-colonies, so-called underdeveloped societies, regional warlords, and clients of rival states). It may also lead to efforts to attract, equip and partially finance client chiefs, princes, warlords, military leaders, other rulers, ruling groups, or classes benefitting from the presence of one's own national or imperial interests. The pattern is ubiquitous throughout history with extraordinarily close parallels in British, French, Dutch, German, Japanese, Russian, and United States practice. Prevailing modes are somewhat different today. But both the United States and the Soviet Union have sought to maintain "law and order" (as each defined the term) in their respective spheres of interest. Both have supported their own clients, and both have tried to deny the establishment of a client of the rival power.

If a high-capability, high lateral-pressure country extends its interests and defenses too far, however, its leaders may find costs proliferating on two fronts. As decisions, control, and defense *apparati* are extended farther from home territory, transportation, communication, and administration costs tend to rise, even though operations in some

---

[30] Conceptually one might consider one country's resistance to external penetration as the response to another country's lateral pressure.

parts of the world may be less expensive than in others. The resistance of hostile elements in a widening sphere of interest is also likely to become more difficult to control. If, at the same time, dissatisfied sectors of the home populace tend to raise overt objections, costs will tend to rise at both ends. Under such conditions a head of state is likely to find his decision latitude considerably constrained. Previously manipulable variables become less and less responsive to efforts at control.

To the extent that two (or more) countries with high capabilities and high lateral-pressure tendencies extend their interests and psychopolitical borders outward, there is a strong probability that sooner or later the opposing perimeters of interest will intersect at one or more points. There is often a feeling on the part of an aspiring, but still somewhat weaker or less prestigious, power that it is being "encircled" by rivals. When this happens, we may expect the competition to intensify. The intersection of Roman and Carthaginian interests in Sicily and Spain gave rise to the Punic Wars. Spanish and English interests intersected in the Caribbean and elsewhere, although the defeat of the Spanish Armada marked a sharp alteration in the "balance of power." English and French perimeters of interest intersected in North America, India, Africa, and so forth, English and Dutch in places as far apart as Manhattan and the East Indies. United States, Soviet Russian, and Chinese interests intersect today in Southeast Asia and elsewhere.

Competitions and conflicts between two or more high lateral pressure countries frequently lead (directly through colonial or client wars, or through some combination of local and more diffused conflicts) into arms races and crises. Again, Rome and Carthage, Spain and England, England and Holland in the late sixteenth and early seventeenth centuries, France and England, and England and Germany offer examples. To one degree or another, client forces were involved in nearly all these conflicts. Since World War II (with the decline of territorial imperialism and colonialism, and with the division of much of the world through cold-war conflicts) the tendency of major powers to rely upon client relationships has become critical and especially widespread.[31]

Countries may be in competition without developing hostile relations with each other. To the extent that their perimeters of interest

---

[31] The Korean and Vietnamese Wars; the Middle East Conflict; the Quemoy and Matsu crises; the division of Germany, Korea, and Vietnam into separate states; and the emergence of Communist and anti-Communist satellite systems are only a few of the more obvious examples of contemporary linkages between "colonial" or "client" conflict and arms races, crises, and wars involving two or more major powers.

intersect, however, competition—especially for resources that are perceived as scarce (including prestige, influence or power)—may give rise to "antagonizing," the process by which "each side forms an increasingly unfavorable picture of the other as evil, hostile, and dangerous."[32] Thus competition *may* lead to non-violent conflict, which *may* lead to an arms race, which is *likely to* lead to crisis, which is *likely to* increase the probabilities of war.[33]

Such a reaction process opens the possibility that a state's defense operations systems—undertaken for "deterrence" or for security, and not for aggressive purposes—may incite another state to responses which will, in the long run, bring about the warfare which the initial system was designed to inhibit. Such, in essence, were the circumstances in which Great Britain, Germany, France, and other European powers were operating throughout the decade or so prior to World War I.[34]

Among nation-states we find the reaction process functioning in commercial competition, competition for power, arms races, and in exchanges of threat and counter-threat at times of acute international crisis. United States Secretary of Defense Robert McNamara described nuclear proliferation in similar terms. "If Nation *A* acquires nuclear weapons, very likely her potential adversary, Nation *B*, must acquire them, and then Nation *C* is concerned because Nation *B* might possibly have aggressive intentions with respect to Nation *C*, and therefore Nation *C* acquires them. The result is there can be a very rapid and dramatic expansion in the number of nuclear powers."[35] Reaction in this situation does not depend upon the objective reality, but upon the leadership's perception of the nation and the relative position of its rivals.[36]

As competition between rival countries becomes more antagonistic, the intersection of perimeters of interest, or other confrontation, may initiate a crisis situation. The question of who is responsible, of who is at fault, of who is "right" and who is "wrong," is not of any great importance. Crucial are the dynamics of the crisis itself.[37] Involved in

[32] Arthur Gladstone, "Relationship Orientation and Process Leading Toward War," *Background*, VI (Fall 1962), 13-25.
[33] The objective of our research in the long run is to replace the qualifying terms by numerical probabilities.
[34] Kenneth E. Boulding, *Conflict and Defense* (New York 1962), 25.
[35] U.S. Department of State *Bulletin* (August 29, 1966), 305.
[36] Boulding (fn. 34), 35.
[37] Charles F. Hermann, *Crises in Foreign Policy* (Indianapolis and New York 1969); and Ole R. Holsti, "The 1914 Case," *American Political Science Review*, LIX (June 1965), 369-77.

such dynamics are the increasing anxieties, the apprehensions, fears, threats and counter-threats among those involved. Many escalations de-escalate. "There are down-escalators as well as up-escalators, and there are landings between escalators where one can decide to get off or to get on, to go up or down, or to stay there; or to take the stairs."[38] Nevertheless, once a nation is caught in the dynamics of a crisis, its leaders often face great difficulty in finding an easy way out.[39]

The occurrence of break-points—shifts from one set of dynamics to another, for example from the dynamics of expansion to the dynamics of antagonistic competition to the dynamics of crisis—accounts for the progression of a conflict situation in the direction of large-scale violence. Earlier stages of competition are dominated by dynamics *internal* to the nation-state. At a later stage processes of competition, reciprocal comparisons, and perceptions of immediate threat and counter-threat become salient. It is important to keep in mind that shifts in the underlying dynamics take place more than once. In practical terms it is often possible to distinguish among different stages in a conflict situation. The farther along the progression of conflict, the narrower the available alternatives are likely to appear. Later we shall present some empirical evidence for break-points during the forty years prior to war in 1914.

The general framework and accompanying propositions should be interpreted in probabilistic terms, and not deterministically.[40] If any determinism is operating it is not "ironclad," but the outcome of human ignorance, confusion, and habit. We are profoundly impressed by the power of resistance to significant change on the part of individual and social habit structures, institutions, and points of view. We believe that many perseverant behavior patterns—for example, many patterns of cooperation, organization, conflict, and resort to violence— make certain outcomes *highly probable*.

Some variables are less amenable to control than others. This recognition should be taken into account explicitly by the policy-maker. It then becomes the task of the national leader to control the effects of less readily manipulable variables while maximizing the effects of those

---

[38] Albert Wohlstetter and Roberta Wohlstetter, "Controlling the Risks in Cuba," *Adelphi Papers*, XVII (London 1965), 19.

[39] Lewis F. Richardson, *Arms and Insecurity* (Chicago 1960).

[40] It is entirely possible for two (or even three) of these dynamic processes to take place concurrently, but one may be more salient at a given time. These relationships and the broader partial theory upon which they rest need additional clarification and further tightening. This is only a first step toward the development of an empirically verifiable theory of international behavior.

variables that are more easily controllable. This is perhaps another way of saying that a policy-maker should act in such a way as to maximize his decision latitude with the understanding that under some conditions his actions will amount to little more than reaction to the actions of others. At such times every conscious effort should be made to "opt out" of the reaction process and reestablish decision latitude. These observations, however self-evident they may seem, become more compelling when one notes that even the configuration of less manipulable variables is subject to some decision, by some individual, at some point in time. In fact, with respect to most data, *each statistic is an indicator of—and a consequence of—a discrete decision by an individual human being governed by a value preference.*[41] Population growth, for example, may be viewed as the outcome of a large number of discrete private decisions over which the policy-maker is not likely to have much control. The determinism involved is thus a kind of social determinism. That is, a whole society is impelled, or simply drifts, in a predictable direction—sometimes almost in spite of the head of state or foreign minister—because thousands or millions of private citizens and lesser public servants are behaving in (often) legitimate, customary, routine ways.

Indicators of technology and technological growth, like population, can be viewed as the outcome of large numbers of widely dispersed decisions in the private sector—decisions (and inspirations) of individual scientists, inventors, designers, developers, and manufacturers. This is less true in socialist states. But even there a certain amount of invention, research, and development is likely to take place beyond the immediate and direct control of national leaders—although they may set or approve the budget. In the United States, on the other hand, invention, research, and development are much more a matter of public policy than they used to be. Large amounts are undertaken or contracted out by the Department of Defense, NASA, and other governmental agencies. The development of technology is thus somewhat less influenced by private individuals now and somewhat more influenced by organizations and bureaucratic decisions.

A considerable amount of routine, but often extremely influential decision-making, takes place in governmental bureaucracies. Departments and department heads, division and division chiefs, to say noth-

---

[41] Statistics involve descriptions of, and generalizations about, aggregates. It is extremely difficult, if not impossible, to trace the relationship of the individual to the aggregate.

ing of higher officers, often pursue immediate goals which have very little to do with national goals and policies.[42] Some of these may emerge from the subsystem (departmental or divisional) values, some from personal ambition, and so forth. There seems to be a general tendency for even lower-level bureaucracies to put to some use whatever power they can accumulate. The incremental accumulation of such decisions can exert constraints or contribute to "drifts." Much of the literature of organizational theory suggests that organizations determine outcomes. Or, rather, outcome is determined by groups of discrete individuals playing organizational roles. Outcomes are often not the result of conscious value-maximizing choices, but of inertia, habit patterns, or a mixture of personal and organizational purposes. In any case, social habit patterns at the general level can be considered as the outcome of some earlier, discrete (conscious or unconscious) individual choices made by members of the population at large, or by individuals in government, and so forth. In the intermediate term, the accumulation of such decisions produces parameters for national decision-making. Over the longer term, the accumulated decisions may appear as external constraints wholly beyond the direct or immediate control of national leaders.

Our earlier analyses have focused on individual leaders' perceptions and cognitions. At this point we are not at all sure that such a focus represents the best possible choice. Our strategy now is to explore the capabilities of longer-range models to their fullest. The residual would therefore be subject to investigation with other models, supporting different kinds of assumptions, offering alternative kinds of implications. Complications arise when the longer-range theoretical structure is itself subject to different models, an issue which we shall return to momentarily.

More basic than the above considerations is the problem of "linking up," in operational and theoretical terms, long-range dynamics with medium- and short-range decision-making, especially in crisis situations. It then becomes an important question whether or not policymakers *in fact* perceive the long-range variables (differentials in population, resources, technology, specialized capability, and so forth) as constraints. Does the policy-maker *in fact* compare his own capabilities

---

[42] See, for example, Graham T. Allison, "Conceptual Models and the Cuban Missile Crisis," *American Political Science Review*, LXIII (September 1969), 689-718. See also Herbert York, *Race to Oblivion: A Participant's View of the Arms Race* (New York 1970).

with those of rivaling states? Are there conscious efforts to manipulate less manipulable variables? Does the policy-maker resort to any kind of cost-benefit calculus?

In operational terms the linkages could perhaps be found in the policy-maker's rule book, if it were readily available. It would then become a relatively easy matter to test hypotheses concerning the nature of the linkages. Considerable work along these lines has already been undertaken using historical documents, namely the Parliamentary Debates in Great Britain between 1870 and 1914. In open documents such as these, policy-makers do *in fact* argue for appropriation of funds in terms of comparisons between their nation's capabilities and those of other states. The calculus is often very explicit and even expressed in numerical terms. Specific calculations of both long-range and short-range variables are undertaken, as well as projections of future alternatives and outcomes. This, of course, is nothing new. But from our particular perspective such information becomes a ready source of data relevant to linkages between long-range and short-range dynamics, data relevant to linkages with crisis situations.

Our theoretical structure is presented at a high level of abstraction. The cost of generality in this case is loss of relevance to short-range decision-making. We would be at a loss to advise the policy-maker in a crisis, or even with respect to much day-to-day decision-making. On the other hand, we can point out the long-term costs of some short-term manipulations, or the short-term obstacles to the control of less readily manipulable variables, such as population or level of technology. Yet the possibility remains that the policy-maker, if he can absorb the feel and impact of our partial theory and data, may stretch his decision latitude and achieve more of a reconciliation between short-term and longer-term outcomes.

In this context, the charge might be made that the prominence given in our propositions to population growth, demands for food, and demands for other basic resources amounts to biological reductionism. We take issue with this on the grounds that the other prominent variable, *technology* (or more precisely, the level of knowledge and skills), encompasses a wide range of other considerations. Technology contributes demands that are often more psychological and cultural than biological in their genesis and implications. Perhaps one most serious vulnerability is the exclusion of perceptual and other cognitive data. Any theory that tends to bypass or minimize cognitions, values, and decision processes is incomplete. In the last analysis, there is no doubt but that cognitive variables need to be taken explicitly into account. It is a matter of research strategy as to the particular timing of such additions to the present structure of the partial theory. Our preference is to build a reasonably sound and empirically verifiable substructure before including cognitive and perceptual data.

III

The transition from a general theoretical statement to a model capable of sustaining the empirical test is seldom easy. A first step is to identify those variables or conditions that are to be explained. These are eventually to serve as the outputs of the model. A second step is to specify as clearly as possible those effects that contribute to outcome variables by developing an equation designed to explain the behavior of the dependent variable. A third step is to develop similar specifications and related equations for each of the outcomes to be explained. At the present stage of our investigations we have attempted to formulate systematic "explanations" of the dynamics of *lateral pressure*, of *intersections* among spheres of influence, of *military competition*, and of prevailing levels of *violence*. Each of these considerations serves as an outcome variable. Each is dependent upon a series of explanatory variables and specific relationships.

Those explanatory variables that contribute to our understanding of the outcomes in question may be other dependent variables (lagged or unlagged); or they may be variables that are exogenous and not explained by the model. It is important to select variables (and, by extension, accompanying parameters) that are either manipulable by the policy-maker, a "given" in the situation, or influenced by "givens" or manipulables.[43] For obvious reasons, it would not be useful to select variables that are all "givens," or variables that are all manipulable only at very high costs. The particular mix of "given" manipulables and controllables is an important consideration in designing the model. The extent that a model is (or is not) useful in explaining variance in behavior of a given country in a particular situation is in large part an empirical question. It can be answered through analysis, provided the appropriate data are available.

Formulation of an identifiable model is a slow and arduous task. We have found it advisable to proceed with a considerable degree of

[43] Albert Ando and others, *Essays on the Structure of Social Sciences* (Cambridge 1963), 1.

caution. The operational question was first reduced to identifying a small set of variables and specifying inter-relationships and patterns of dependencies.[44] Only after a good deal of experimentation were more intricate formulations developed. It has been very useful, for operational and heuristic purposes, to "map out" the problem by moving explicitly from theoretical structure, to components of a model, to key variables, to operational definition of key variables, to the development of structural equations.[45] These steps are presented in Table 1. As a first approximation we have treated each component of the theoretical structure as generating one individual equation. In the longer run, these should be developed more appropriately into a set of block recursive structures. For example, lateral pressure then would be represented not by one equation but, conceivably, by a set of equations. Alternatively, it is quite possible for each equation to "fit" historical data. However, when coefficients are estimated simultaneously, errors may accumulate and bad fits will be obtained. For this and other reasons we would not expect individual equations adequately to represent dynamics as intricate as those described by the partial theory. Only by constructing the system bit by bit can a viable model be developed.

The development of an empirically verifiable model of the theoretical structure is only a beginning. Such a model may then be used to provide quantitative answers to particular questions, answers such as the effects of specific policy actions. The application of different exogenous variables, different decision rules and different initial conditions to the model would allow for experimentation with "what if" kinds of questions. This may help the policy-maker develop a feel for some of the middle- and longer-range components of actions which seem immediately desirable. Simulation techniques are important in this context because equations that cannot be solved by mathematical

[44] See Choucri and North, "The Determinants of International Violence," *Peace Research Society, Papers, Volume XII* (Cambridge 1968), 33-63; Choucri and North, "Aspects of International Conflict: Military Preparedness, Alliance Commitments, and External Violence," prepared for delivery at the Western Political Science Association Meetings, Hawaii, April 3-5, 1969; and Choucri and North, "Pressure, Competition, Tension, and Threat: Toward a Theory of International Conflict," prepared for delivery at the 65th Annual Meeting of the American Political Science Association, New York, September 2-6, 1969.

[45] Note the distinction between structural equations and model equations. This is especially important when evaluating the last column of Table 1: "A *structure* is a set of autonomous relationships sufficient to determine the numerical values of the endogenous variables, given the value of the exogenous variables." But a structure is meaningful only within the context of the model which makes explicit the nature of the equations and the kinds of variable included. See Carl F. Christ, *Econometric Models and Methods* (New York 1965) 21-22.

TABLE 1

Steps in the Development of Operational Theory

Theoretical Structure	Components of a Model	Key Variables	Operational Definition of Key Variables	Structural Equation* (as the base for model equation for analysis of the 1870–1914 period)**
DEMANDS	The constraints imposed by resources on the interactive effects of population and technology, giving rise to variable demands.	Population, technology, resources (growth and level).	Level and rate of national population, level and rate of industrial production (or more specialized variable), level and rate of resource variable (or area as approximation).	colonial population $= \Delta$ [home population/home area] $+$ [Δ steel per capita] $+ \Delta$ [home population/home area] . [Δ steel per capita $-$ Δ total trade per capita] $+$ [defense budget per capita] $+ u$
LATERAL PRESSURE	The combined effects of increasing demands and the availability of specialized capabilities giving rise to lateral pressure.	Differentials between variables that increase likelihood of lateral pressure and those that minimize or dilute (or which influence one mode of lateral pressure rather than another).	Combined effects of differential between population and resource (area), favorable trade, and specialized capabilities (merchant fleet and defense budget).	
INTER-sections	Variable expansionist tendencies in conjunction with specialized capabilities.	Variables indicating expansionist activities (either functional or literal).	Rates of increases in controlled territory of self and adversaries, or rate of penetration in areas, or economic control, or investments, and specialized capabilities (military).	Δ intersections $=$ [Δ expansion of self] $+$ [Δ expansion of others] $+$ [Δ defense budget of self] $+$ [Δ violence toward others] $+$ [Δ violence of others] $+ u$
MILITARY COMPETITION	Comparative calculations of capabilities and increases in armament provisions in combination with intersecting spheres.	Defense capabilities (budgets, men under arms, inventories) of nation and rivals (both rates and levels), expansion variables, gaps.	Rate of increase in defense expend., or men, or inventory, or advanced def. technology for self and rival, in combination with expansion variables.	Δ defense budget $=$ [Δ defense budget$_{t-1}$] $+$ [Δ defense budget of rivals$_{t-1}$] $+$ [Δ expansion of self] $+$ [Δ intersections] $+ u$
EXTERNAL VIOLENCE	Increasing thresholds of prevailing violence resulting from intersections, military competition and international alignments.	Variables indicating level of violence in international behavior (level and rate), military and alliance variables.	Violence variable computed on the basis of action data, casualties, "deathly quarrels," alliance commitments, military expenditures (rates and level of self and others).	Δ violence $=$ [Δ defense of self] $+$ [Δ defense of others] $+$ [Δ intersections] $+$ [Δ alliance commitments] $+ u$

* See the *Research Note* for operational details and theoretical justification. The use of delta variables already assumes the choice of the underlying. Alternatively level, percentage change, or ratio could be employed, as well as different data specifications for the indicator values.
** For other time periods and other situations different indicator variables are more appropriate. These four equations are *highly tentative*. (able reformulations are currently underway.

operations to derive precise analytical solutions can be solved by numerical operations to obtain specific numerical solutions.[46] Simulation allows us to determine the implications of a model, the consequences of various combinations of initial conditions. We can determine the implications of specific policy actions or sequences of policy actions (such as increases or decreases in defense expenditures, entering into novel alignment commitments, and modifying budgetary appropriations) and the effects of alternative values and rates of increases in the givens or in the less readily manipulable variables.[47] Such efforts offer the national leaders an opportunity to develop a feel for a proposed policy (and its alternatives) without entering into any commitment. They provide insights into the risks and costs of a particular policy or a particular decision-rule. For long-range as well as short-range purposes what is needed is an explicit estimate of coefficients for the most important policy instruments available to the decision-maker. By manipulating these coefficients it is then possible to begin raising questions about the cost-benefit calculus of policy choices. The model must also provide for the effect of a policy on other countries in the international system and anticipate their probable responses to the initiative being considered.

We have attempted to develop a model which includes both national and international effects while resolving the basic problems of estimation and identifiability. In theoretical terms different types of variables are more appropriate at some stages in the development of a conflict situation than at others. For example, dynamics internal to the nation-state (demands and lateral pressure) tend to dominate early stages. As nations extend their activities outside national boundaries and come into direct contact with other states, other sets of dynamics are likely to operate (such as intersections among spheres of influence). Mechanisms of competition in these later stages may become expressed in terms of armaments (military competition). In many cases our explanation of military competition will depend more upon external factors than upon internal factors, although a combination would probably be more likely. In this manner it should be possible to identify the "breakpoints" where external dynamics become more important than internal dynamics. A correct specification of these shifts could provide useful guidelines to the policy-maker. For example, insights would be

---

[46] An excellent illustration of this kind of procedure is provided by James S. Duesenberry and others, eds., *The Brookings Quarterly Econometric Model of the United States* (Chicago 1965).

[47] Charles C. Holt, "Validation and Application of Macroeconomic Models Using Computer Simulation," in Duesenberry and others, *ibid.*, 640.

provided into the payoff for minimizing the importance of internal constraints at times when international considerations appear to bear more directly on the issues. Break-points are very real, and their relevance for theory-building or empirical analysis should not be minimized. So far we have been able to isolate empirically some critical break-points in the progression of a conflict situation (Europe, 1870–1914).[48] The problem is to be able to *predict to* a break-point. This amounts to a major challenge. It is not difficult to specify in theoretical terms conditions under which critical shifts are likely to occur. It is not at all an easy matter to operationalize those conditions in quantitative and empirical terms. What we are suggesting, therefore, is that optimum specifications would, by necessity, include both internal and external variables. A "mixed" model of this sort is likely to yield greater payoffs in the long run; and the potential implications for policy purposes should not be minimized.

IV

Much of our empirical work to date has focused on major powers in Europe between 1870 and 1914. This is a period of considerable change and turmoil for which empirical data and documentation are readily available.[49] The four equations in the last column of Table 1 provided the bases for a first attempt at a mixed model, one including both internal and external variables. Indicators of lateral pressure, intersections among spheres of influence, military preparedness, and external violence served as the dependent variables to be explained by a combination of domestic and international considerations. Much of the statistical and methodological detail is discussed elsewhere.[50] We shall confine ourselves here to some results and implications.

Throughout the forty years or so prior to World War I all the major powers were generating more and more demands and improving their specialized capabilities—but from different bases and at unequal rates of change.[51] All were generating some amount of lateral pressure, and

[48] In this context sensitivity analysis would be extremely useful: that is, systematically altering the parameters and observing changes in the system and the extent of stability among basic relationships. See the *Research Note* at the end of the present article for some data on break-points.

[49] North and Choucri, *Nations in Conflict: Prelude to World War I* (in preparation).

[50] Choucri and North, 1968 (fn. 44), and North and Choucri (fn. 49). The specific nature of the empirical formulations providing the basis for the findings discussed in the following is described in the *Research Note* below and in the last column of Table 1.

[51] Because of the difficulties involved in measuring "demands" this statement is purely inferential.

most of them tended to express it in terms of colonial expansion. Those powers that expanded most widely were also those that were growing most rapidly in domestic population and/or technology and production. Between 1870 and 1900 the colonial populations under British control more than doubled in size (accompanied by a slightly larger increase in territory). Seventy-five per cent of the variance in this expansion can be accounted for: mainly by the differential between domestic population growth in relation to national (home) territory, by technological advancement, by the combined effects of population and technology, and by military preparedness.[52] The remainder of the variance—the unexplained 25 per cent—may well be accounted for by conscious decisions on the part of the national leadership, by policy calculations, and the like. But with so much of the variance accounted for by relatively non-manipulable variables, decision latitudes appear to have been considerably reduced.[53] This tendency stands in sharp contrast to the patterns in Sweden and other Scandinavian countries. The Scandinavian countries were inclined to rely upon trade, rather than colonial expansion, for the satisfaction of demands.[54]

Eighty-five per cent of the variance in the colonial population under French control from 1902 to 1914 can be accounted for: mainly by technological advancement, by the combined effects of population and technology, and by increases in military capability.[55] These variables were even more significant during the earlier years when French colo-

[52] Standardized regression (or path) coefficients for Britain are as follows: Population: —.40 (.17); technology; 13.13 (.29); the interactive effect of population and technology: 12.80 (.29); commerce: —.06 (.10); and military capability: —.43 (.11). Parentheses refer to standard errors. See Table 1 and the *Research Note* at the end of this article for operational definitions. The interactive term adds little to the information contained in the technology variable. There are some instabilities which are currently being ironed out.

[53] In the context of a stationary national area during the 1870–1914 period, Britain's domestic population growth averaged .89 per cent annually, increases in iron averaged .33 per cent and in steel 2.80 per cent annually, and national income per capita 1.4 per cent. These percentages are based on our data files for this period.

[54] See Nazli Choucri (with the collaboration of Robert C. North), "In Search of Peace Systems: Scandinavia and the Netherlands," in Bruce M. Russett, ed., *War, Peace, and Numbers* [forthcoming, 1972]. In 1960 the combined population of the Scandinavian countries was almost ten million lower than Great Britain's population one century earlier. The rates of growth for Sweden and Norway during the 1870–1914 period held annual averages of .65 per cent and .80 per cent respectively. Further comparisons are presented in this paper. Because of probable measurement error in the data series, these and following percentages are approximations at best.

[55] French domestic population growth averaged approximately .13 per cent annually, while growth in per capita income averaged 2.8 per cent—one of the highest among the powers—and industrial production (steel) almost as high (2.5%). In the French case it was the combination of low population growth and high technological achievement that contributed to lateral expansion. By 1914 the French empire extended to over twenty times its size in 1870.

nial expansion was at its height. The remainder of the variance, though unexplained by these variables, is nonetheless constrained by one basic relatively non-manipulable master variable (population) and one more readily manipulable variable (defense capability). But, as has been pointed out, severe constraints can sometimes seriously limit the decision latitude of national leadership.[56]

By 1892 well over 60 per cent of the variance in German expansion can be accounted for: in terms of gains in home population (relative to home territory), technological advancement, and the interactive effect of population growth and industrial production.[57] These are relatively non-manipulable variables on a day-to-day basis—variables difficult to change at the discretion of the political leadership. As will become apparent, however, even the more readily manipulable variables, such as military capability, are subject to serious constraints. It is true that the unexplained variance—37 per cent or so—might well be accounted for by variables that could be more easily manipulated. But the considerable constraints imposed by relatively non-manipulable variables cannot be ignored.[58]

Territorial expansion (and accompanying expansions of national interest) helped cause two major types of violent conflict. The first category consists of colonial wars which involved the subduing or policing of local bands, tribes, chiefdoms, and petty states lying in the path of great-power expansion. Great Britain became engaged in 14 such

[56] For a discussion of empirical data, methodological issues, and statistical results see Choucri and North, "Causes of World War I: A Quantitative Analysis of Longer-Range Dynamics," in Klaus Jurgen Gantzel and others, eds., *Grossmachtrivalität und Weltkrieg: Sozialwissenschaftliche Studien zum Ausbruch des Ersten Weltkrieges und Historikerkommentare* (Gütersloh, forthcoming, 1972). The problems associated with a logarithm transform of the first and third terms of the expansion equation are discussed in Choucri and North, above, as are modifications of the results. We have been able to determine the relative importance of the main effects of population and technology rather than the interaction effects. The implications of interaction, in terms of high collinearity with main effects, are also discussed. These coefficients pertain to analysis with the logarithm transform in the first and third terms.

[57] Standardized regression (or path) coefficients for Germany are as follows. Population: .77 (.40); technology: .71 (.28); the interactive effect of population and technology: .44 (.20); commerce: .20 (.02); and military preparedness: .08 (.17). In this case there is a distinct interactive effect.

[58] The average annual rate of population growth of Germany during this period stood at 1.14 per cent approximately; the rate of growth in steel, 5.28 per cent; in iron, 4.36 per cent. The rate of increase in national income averaged 2.3 per cent per year and in per capita income at 1.2 per cent (in comparison with 1.4 per cent for Great Britain, the difference being accounted for in large part by the higher rates of growth in the German population). It should be pointed out that the German rate of growth was not particularly high *per se*, but *in comparison with the other powers* (especially Britain and France) and in combination with German technology, it could be considered a potent variable.

wars, involving somewhere around three thousand casualties or less; France, nine wars; and Germany, Russia, Austria-Hungary, and Italy, one war each at that casualty level. The other category consists of wars between major powers themselves, or wars between the client states of major powers. These wars tended to come about somewhat indirectly. Great Britain became involved in nine wars of this nature, incurring between three thousand and thirty-one thousand casualties in each; Russia and Austria-Hungary, four wars each; and France, Germany, and Italy, three wars respectively.[59]

With all this expansion taking place, it is not surprising that the colonial territories, and the "perimeters of interests" of major powers tended to collide or intersect. These confrontations, many taking place at distant frontiers in Africa, the Middle East, and Asia, gave rise to further competitions in specialized capabilities, and for territory and resources. Thus the way was prepared for arms races, crises, and war.

The intersection equation in Table 1 accounts for more than 80 per cent of the variance in the intersections of each major power.[60] It becomes apparent that changes in prevailing levels of conflict [$\triangle$ violence of self and $\triangle$ violence of others] contributed significantly to intersections, as did each power's own military establishment. From this it could be inferred that a critical variable—defense capability—might have been manipulated in such a way as to decrease the intensity of intersection. For example, between 1872 and 1892 Great Britain's own defense capability provided considerable impetus to the intensification of her intersections with other powers. This means that the larger the increases in the defense budget, the more intense were her intersections with other powers. It suggests that measures taken in part, at least, to enhance national security contributed to conflict and sometimes to violence. This comes about because, as the international system operates, one nation's security tends to become another nation's insecurity.[61] It would follow, somewhat paradoxically, that decreases in the defense budget *might* have resulted in lowering the intensity of such intersections, although such a reduction might also be interpreted as compromising security.

From this limited and somewhat tentative evidence, we could argue that manipulating a variable such as the defense budget is likely to have important consequences in terms of intersections among spheres of

[59] Lewis F. Richardson, *Statistics of Deadly Quarrels* (Chicago 1960), 52-69.

[60] High R^2 are due, in part, to the loss of degrees of freedom. These, however, are taken into account when computing coefficients and related standard errors.

[61] J. David Singer, "The Political Science of Human Conflict," in Elton McNeil, ed., *The Nature of Human Conflict* (Englewood Cliffs, N.J. 1965), 144.

influence. But the probabilities of outcome are difficult for the policy-maker to assess. Since nations do not operate in a vacuum, their defense calculations are normally influenced, and sometimes set, by standards exterior to the nation-state itself. The policies of country *A* are both impelled and constrained by some of the policies of countries *B*, *C*, and *D*. During the 1870–1914 period, for example, each power predicated its naval policy on the naval policies of its perceived "adversaries." For Great Britain the Three-Power, Two-Power, and eventually the "twice-Germany" standards provided the basic decision rules.[62] By the turn of the century Germany's decision rule was to attain—and maintain—a strength within a margin of .6 of Britain's own defense increases. Such calculations were based on specific projections of their respective rates of change and variable performance. This essentially reciprocal arrangement amounted to a loss, or self-denial, of decision latitude on the part of both (but especially the British) leaderships. France, too, seemed to base her own policies on those of her "adversaries." Russia did also.

The linkages between increasing defense preparedness and intersections of spheres of influence to increasing levels of conflict behavior are yet to be made explicit, although in narrative fashion diplomatic history is rich with such linkages. In simple terms we found that expansion leads to intersections. These contribute in turn to increasing military preparedness on all sides. From this it would naturally follow that increasing military budgets would raise the probability of external violence. But the effects are more complex. It is the combined impact of intersections and defense preparedness that contributes most strongly to an intensification of conflict behavior.

The single most significant determinant of external violence is the *intensity* of intersections among respective spheres of influence. And intersections, it will be recalled, were highly conditioned by variable rates of lateral expansion and variable rates of military preparedness. On the other hand, we found that at least in this case changes in the number of each power's alliance commitments had very little effect on a nation's external violence. In the context of the 1870–1914 situation (a classical case of the conflict spiral) alignment commitments *per se* contributed only minimally to the intensification of conflict behavior.[63] The determinant variables were intersections and increasing military competition, as indicated by the military budget. Both these variables

---

[62] Kendall M. Moll, *The Influence of History Upon Seapower, 1865–1914* (Stanford 1968); Robert C. North and Richard P. Lagerstrom, "An Anticipated Gap, Mathematical Model of International Dynamics" (Stanford 1969).

[63] This finding refers to long-term trends and not to crisis confrontations where alliance commitments may be more influential.

were potentially manipulable, but as pointed out earlier, highly constrained by basic master variables. The critical link in the long-term conflict spiral seems to be the point at which a nation extends its behavior outside national boundaries. Intersections (and violence) are often outcomes of growth, generally considered highly desirable, along dimensions of population, technology, production, and military capability. The contrast between the great powers and the Scandinavian countries during the 1870–1914 period serves to underscore the range of variability in external behavior. The initial mode of behavior undertaken beyond national boundaries tends to condition eventual outcomes. In this sense the leadership of nations involved in arms races (presumably undertaken to optimize national security and decision latitude) may in effect abdicate (or deprive itself of) decision freedom at some later point of choice.

After World War II colonial expansion was no longer a feasible mode for the expression of lateral pressure. There is often a tendency, however, for leaders and some of the populace of a country to feel that overseas interests (of whatever mode) ought to be defended. Also, high capability, high lateral-pressure countries, are inclined to attempt to deny their rivals the possibility of economic, political, or military penetration into low-capability areas. This suggests that some of the processes of competition and conflict characteristic of the pre-World War I period may have analogues in the postcolonial system following World War II. We might expect to find lateral pressure expressed in terms of trade, aid, investment, military assistance, troops overseas, military bases on foreign soil, and control of political parties in foreign countries.

Recent Japanese trends illustrate some of the problems that appear to be just around the corner for other major powers. From 1870 through 1941 Japan—in terms of population growth, rapid technological advancement, limited home territory and resources, territorial expansion, and international conflict—presents a clear-cut, extreme example of increasing demands, the development of specialized (including military) capability, and the generation of strong lateral pressure. In retrospect, the concept of a Greater East Asia Co-Prosperity Sphere may be viewed as a crude measure of Japanese demands. The acquisition of control over Taiwan, Korea, Manchuria, large sectors of China, Indochina, the Dutch East Indies, and so forth serves as a rough indicator of lateral pressure. Japanese expansion was counteracted by the expansionist activities of western powers as they expressed their own lateral pressure in various ways.

After World War II Japan reduced her birth rate considerably. The annual percentage increase in the 1950's was about .9. During the late 1960's it increased slightly to 1.1 per cent. By then, however, the level of population was sufficiently high so that each increment—approximately one million per year—added to an already large base. Writing in 1946, Warren Thompson presented two predictions for the Japanese population in 1970: (1) 88 million or (2) 105 million, as estimated by the Population Institute of Japan. Thompson inclined toward the lower estimate. It is now evident that the higher estimate was more nearly correct. Thus, in spite of Japan's lower population growth rate after the war, the outcome so far has been somewhat above Thompson's personal expectation.[64] The population of Tokyo, currently approaching 16 million, is projected to reach 40 million by the year 2000.[65]

The probable magnitude of future demands (as we have defined the term) is further suggested by post-World War II trends in primary energy consumption and GNP. Between 1950 and 1964 the consumption of solid fuels, natural gas, oil, and hydroelectric power nearly quadrupled. At the beginning of that period "indigenous resources supplied 90 per cent of the total requirements"; by 1964, on the other hand, "imports represented more than 60 per cent of the total."[66] Around 1980 Japan's total requirements may be twelve or thirteen times what they were in 1950.[67] These figures are only illustrative. Obviously a wide range of other resources will be demanded in larger quantities and supplied largely through imports. Between 1958 and 1967 the GNP increased at an average rate of about 10 per cent. Chemicals and heavy industry accounted for nearly 70 per cent of this growth. Tendencies toward urbanization were strong. Over the next ten to twenty years, moreover, the Japanese Islands will be plagued with many of the same problems of pollution, ecological imbalance, and extensive urbanization that will increasingly trouble other highly industrialized countries. Other problems will be added to the extent that Japan confronts limitations and constraints on her access to materials and markets.

The combination of the demands of a rapidly growing technology with those generated by a relatively moderate population growth makes it highly probable that access to resources and markets will remain one of the basic underpinnings of a stable and peaceful Japan in the foreseeable future. To the extent that our findings for the major European powers (1870–1914) are suggestive for the analysis of the Japanese case

[64] Warren S. Thompson, *Population and Peace in the Pacific* (Chicago 1940), 99.
[65] Ehrlich and Ehrlich (fn. 10), 48.
[66] *Energy Policy: Problems and Objectives*, Organization for Economic Co-Operation and Development (Paris 1955), 91.
[67] *Energy Policy: Problems and Objectives, ibid.*, 94.

in the present and immediate future, we would expect Japanese leaders to be increasingly confronted by the implications of longer-term, relatively non-manipulable variables. And, so far as the foreign affairs of Japan are of interest and consequence to other countries (the United States, Canada, U.S.S.R., the People's Republic of China, Taiwan, Australia), leaders in these countries also will be increasingly concerned with the same long-term, relatively non-manipulable variables. These variables, especially population and technology, are at least in considerable part the aggregation of millions of private, individual decisions (or their side effects). Or they are the accumulation of small, disjointed incremental decisions by leaders, bureaucrats, and at least some of the citizenry. For these reasons these long-term variables are frequently difficult for even the far-sighted leader to influence or plan for without sophisticated forecasting techniques.

Among the more easily manipulable variables are diplomatic negotiations of various sorts, the administration of trade, technical assistance, and military aid programs, and troop movements and mobilizations. The problems of Japanese trade, for example, are susceptible to, and sometimes dependent upon, manipulation by the leadership of many other countries interacting with Japan. Such manipulations are limited, however, by such medium-range variables (which become parameters for day-to-day operations) as military budgets, draft quotas, men-under-arms, alliance commitments, trade treaties, tariff arrangements, and the like. Between the relatively non-manipulable long-range variables and the day-to-day responses of other national leaders, a considerable amount of decision latitude and control over the course of events is lost, putting the nation at the "mercy" of earlier developments.

Given present levels and rates of population growth, technological advances, and the depletion of basic resources—together with the high risks of conflict in an age of massively destructive weaponry—national leaders might begin to undertake longer-range studies of these "non-manipulable" variables. To what extent can they be controlled by careful planning, by the introduction of incentives, penalties or other countervailing forces, by educational programs affecting externalities, and by disjointed incremental drifts? Possibly business and industrial leaders, small investors, entrepreneurs, and private citizens in all trades and professions might be shown some of the ways in which their legitimate (and sometimes personal and intimate) decisions, or the side effects of these decisions, may constrain a whole society or contribute to disjointed incremental drifts.

As suggested earlier, the constraints and impulsions affecting heads of state or other high-level decision-makers are not the outcome of an ironclad determinism. They emerge from decisions made by predecessors, from the polities of other countries, from bureaucratic decisions made at least partially in pursuit of personal or narrowly departmental goals, and from millions of private decisions made by individual citizens in terms of normally legitimate personal, family, or professional values and goals. The national leader or policy-maker will remain seriously boxed in—caught in the interstices of the larger international system and its component subsystems (including wide sectors within his own country). To the extent that he shapes policy, it is largely within a narrow, day-to-day context without careful thought for middle- and longer-range consequences, and to the extent that he accepts the constraints and impulsions as givens.[68]

We recognize that national policy-makers cannot easily escape from these day-to-day concerns, nor free themselves from the responsibility for tomorrow morning's decision. Yet the implications of our findings, if projected to the future, are in no sense encouraging. The prospect of states and super-states carrying their leaders along in response to dynamics of which few people are aware, and over which no one seems to have adequate control, is somewhat chilling in a nuclear world. We believe that such conditions ought to be monitored on a systematic basis—not in terms of the usual intelligence operations—but in terms of (a) how the international system has been operating over the last two or three decades (in terms of impulsions and drifts); (b) projections of what the world is likely to look like if recent and current impulsions and drifts continue; (c) alternative courses of action and the identification of variables that can and should be altered; and (d) specification of the means for changing these variables and the probable benefits and costs associated with such means.

With these tools at hand, the head of state and his advisers would have a more systematic and professionally-based opportunity to balance immediate or short-term benefits against probable medium- or long-range costs. He would be in a better position to perceive each potential

[68] Otto A. Davis and others, "A Theory of the Budgetary Process," *American Political Science Review*, LX (September 1966), 529-47. Also see J. David Singer, ed., *Quantitative International Politics, Insights and Evidence* (New York 1968), Part I. Relevant also are N. B. McEachron, "Modelling Macro-Social Tension and Change in American Society," presented at the Fourth Hawaii International Conference on Social Science, Stanford Research Institute, 1970; and Kenneth E. F. Watt, "State Planning Failures: What to Do About It," *Cry California* (Winter 1969-70).

as a stimulus reverberating through the system, so to speak, and affecting the future in a large number of ways. With some reasonable assessments of both benefits and costs he would find himself in a stronger position for undertaking long-term policies which are in the interests of the more distant future. Moreover, he would be able to present to his constituents the rationale of his actions. And possibly he would be able to elicit public support that otherwise would not be available.

The idea of using more readily manipulable variables, such as budget allocations, as leverage for altering less readily manipulable, longer-range variables is not new. The post-World War II Marshall Plan offers a well-known example. What the evidence of this paper suggests is that the network of interdependencies may be more intricate, more pervasive, more extensive—and yet potentially more susceptible to planning—than is sometimes assumed. Conceivably, a more unified strategy of long-term/short-term policy-making might emerge. While undertaking whatever feasible to minimize the immediate outcome of a population-technology-resource imbalance, for example, a head of state might also make effective use of more easily manipulable variables in order to achieve leverage for bringing about a preferable technology-resource balance in the future.

If a larger body of theory and experience had been available in recent years, it would have been feasible for a President of the United States to initiate a massive shift from defense allocations into sustained, ecologically-oriented investments and projects, a shift of resources from "high-pollution" sectors of the economy into research and development for "low-pollution" (and relatively high demand-satisfying) production and services. As another illustration, in the sphere of international relations a President might have commissioned a half-decade ago a set of thirty-year projections of Pacific Basin trends so that countries around the ocean periphery could cooperate to meet future needs and demands. The intent would be to alter undesirable probabilities by acting earlier to encourage more universally favorable outcomes farther down the road.

Conceivably, too, such undertakings might have been systematically monitored so that negative information secured at one point in time could be used with long-range criteria as a basis for operational correction at a subsequent point in time.

These observations suggest the utility, in other words, of *long-range* trend analyses and alternative projections by components of a national leadership. They point out the desirability of setting early priorities in terms of long-range variables and middle-range variables, and the desirability of establishing parameters that have some possibility of widening the alternatives in day-to-day decision-making.[69]

RESEARCH NOTE

This note includes a brief discussion of some basic methodological issues, a summary of our statistical work to date, a description of the operational measures employed, and some empirical evidence for the occurrence of breakpoints in the development of conflict systems between 1870 and 1914.

Perhaps the most basic issue in making the transition from a theoretical structure, stated verbally, to a model amenable to empirical verification is specification of the causal ordering. In the most general sense "causation" refers to hierarchies of influences or effects, most readily characterized by asymmetrical relations within a specified system. The two dominant views on this issue can be summarized as follows. On the one hand there is the argument that because causal models approximate "reality" only to a limited degree, variables are by necessity excluded from each equation in the system. Therefore the real number of variables is always understated, and to consider only the explicitly stated variables is to run the risk of treating truly endogenous variables as exogenous. For these reasons it is not possible to unravel causal dependencies among complicated sets of interrelated variables.[1] The opposing position is based on the argument that the real world is not composed of simultaneous dependencies, but that hierarchies characterize relationships, and that true systems are always of a recursive, hierarchical nature.[2] It is therefore possible to determine causal relations.

The adoption of either position results, of necessity, in the construction of vastly different systems of equations.[3] A plausible reconciliation of these very real concerns suggests that simultaneity is present within some localized domain; that at a more general level simultaneity, though present, is probably not overriding; and that the world outside is more nearly block recursive than it is completely simultaneous or completely hierarchical.[4] And it is this middle position that has provided the basis for our model-building efforts. Its theoretical justification lies in the theorem that if a system is clearly decomposable it is plausible to proceed *as if* it were completely decomposable.[5] In the short run the costs of such an assumption will be minor.

---

[69] For an elaboration of the implications of both theoretical framework and empirical data presented in this paper see Robert C. North and Nazli Choucri, "Population and the International System: Some Implications for United States Policy and Planning," prepared for the National Commission on Population Growth and the Future of America, August 1971.

[1] T. C. Liu, "A Simple Forecasting Model for the U.S. Economy," International Monetary Fund, *Staff Papers* (August 1955), 434-66.

[2] H. Wold, in association with L. Jureen, *Demand Analysis* (New York 1953).

[3] In one case single equation estimation methods for recursive systems are called for, in the second simultaneous estimation techniques are appropriate.

[4] Franklin M. Fisher, "On the Cost of Approximate Specification in Simultaneous Equation Estimation," in Albert Ando and others, *Essays on the Structure of Social Sciences* (Cambridge, Mass. 1963), 32-63.

[5] *Ibid.*, 92-106.

A further complication arises in that causation is not necessarily implied by a particular time sequence, nor does a particular sequence of events necessarily imply causation. In a persuasive argument Herbert Simon has suggested that causal orderings can best be determined by the appearance of zero coefficients in a system of equations.[6] This *a priori* specification of zero coefficients thus raises the issue of identifiability. For operational purposes causation is closely related to identifiability. And the requirements of identifiability impose certain constraints on the process of model-building.[7]

With these considerations in mind, the comments that follow are in the nature of a progress report regarding the development of the model presented in Table 1. The equations in the last column are still *highly* tentative, and considerable experimentation is yet to be undertaken. Nonetheless, a brief survey of the research plan that has led to this model may highlight some of the difficulties encountered.

The first attempt to operationalize aspects of our partial theory involved two different, and fairly artificial, sets of hypotheses with different, and equally artificial, implications for the policy-maker. The first set was based on the proposition that a nation's behavior is, in large part, determined by *internal* processes—population growth, technological advancement, the development of specialized capabilities, such as a defense establishment, and so forth. Thus, actions could be accounted for by a model specifying only *national* considerations. The second set of hypotheses, proceeding from different assumptions, argued that national behavior is determined first and foremost by the capabilities and behavior of *other* nations. In the gap or distance between one's own capabilities and those of others (often the closest rival) is to be found much of the explanation for a nation's actions in the international system.[8]

The major policy guidelines provided by the first model are that national leaders explicitly recognize both the limited effects of other nations in conditioning outcomes and the importance of internal dynamics and internal considerations when evaluating competing constraints on their freedom of action. The implications of the second model are almost the reverse: that greater attention should be paid to external variables, and internal considerations be relegated to secondary importance. Obviously these different guidelines or implications give rise, by necessity, to different assessments of priorities and different policy alternatives.

The artificial nature of these hypotheses was further reinforced by the consideration that a model focusing either on national *or* on international

---

[6] *Ibid.*

[7] Here we are again indebted to recent econometric literature on problems of model-building. See especially J. Johnston, *Econometric Methods* (New York 1963), and Arthur S. Goldberger, *Econometric Theory* (New York 1964).

[8] Two variants of this model were developed. In one the independent variables were defined in terms of the rival's attributes and capabilities. And in the second the independent variables were defined as the distance or gap between a state's capabilities and those of the rival. See Choucri and North (fn. 44 of text), 43-61. We are grateful to Raymond Tanter for assisting us in spelling out the implications of these models.

effects is likely to be vulnerable on theoretical terms (by reducing everything to internal factors or to considerations external to the system) and incomplete in operational terms (by allowing for large serial correlation reflecting incomplete specification). Certain features of both models yielded fairly good "fits" with empirical data for the 1870–1914 period. But because national and international hypotheses were not included *in the same model* it is difficult to compare their respective explanatory power and, by extension, the accompanying assumptions and implications. Of course, problems related to identifiability compound when estimating the parameters of a model which includes level as well as gap or distance variables. And estimation problems increase as larger numbers of independent variables are included in each equation.

The next step, therefore, was the development of a model comprising internal *as well as* external considerations without violating the requisites of identifiability. The four equations in Table 1 represent an initial operational statement within which more explicit structures could then be derived. For example, the equation combining both demands and lateral pressure is clearly a summary statement of more intricate processes which need be made explicit. Furthermore, uni-directional effects estimated by ordinary least squares do not adequately represent a system in which mutual dependencies are known to operate. It therefore becomes necessary to model these dependencies as clearly as possible employing appropriate techniques for simultaneous estimation. A related, and equally important, problem involves the isolation of break-points (shifts in dynamics). If unnoticed, these may give rise to poor "fits" and misleading inferences.[9]

Many alternative formulations may be empirically consistent with the same set of data. Identifying the most valid equations is seldom an easy task. Statistical criteria for evaluating an equation or model include (1) proportion of variance explained, R^2, (2) magnitude of standard errors, and (3) sign of the coefficients. Misspecifications may give rise to bad fits and to severe serial correlation. Corrective procedures such as a re-specification of the model or the application of iterative methods to reduce autoregressive effects are often necessary.

We have attempted to incorporate the element of change by expressing each variable in terms of its delta value $(x_t - x_{t-1})$, although we recognize that other specifications such as relative or percentage change are also valid.[10] Our selection of this measure is exploratory, subject to further experimentation with alternative values.

[9] On empirical grounds alone it is difficult, if not impossible, to determine exactly when a break-point has occurred. It is also as difficult to predict break-points as it is to predict the behavior of the system beyond the break. On the other hand it is possible to test for the existence of a break-point and for the significance of the break. We are grateful to Professor Franklin Fisher of the Economics Department, M.I.T., for a clarification of this problem and for suggesting means of redefining the issues in ways that can be amenable to empirical inquiry.

[10] Theoretically, at least, we postulate that, in the long run, changes are more important than absolute levels, but in terms of short-range day-to-day decision-making levels are probably more important. We have conducted parallel analyses with level variables as well.

The first equation representing the process of lateral pressure summarizes the combined effects of internal demands and specialized capabilities on a state's external expansion. The effects of population, technology, commerce and military capability are depicted as follows:[11]

$$\Delta \text{ col. pop.} = a + B_1 \Delta [\text{home pop./home area}] + B_2 \Delta [\text{steel production per capita}] + B_3 \Delta [\text{home pop./home area}] . \Delta [\text{steel per capita}] - B_4 \Delta [\text{total trade per capita}] + B_5 \Delta [\text{defense budget per capita}] + u.$$

The dependent variable represents only a first order approximation of expansion (since colonial population is subject to a natural growth component independent of dynamics internal to the major powers) but at the same time it depicts the extent of external involvement. The effect of home population is summarized in the first term Δ (pop./area) where the denominator reflects internal constraints on the demands generated by the population.[12] Technology is represented by change in the production of steel per capita.[13] And the combined effect of population and technology, so central to our theoretical framework, is summarized in an interactive variable composed of the product of the first and second terms. Trade (imports and exports per capita) is included in this equation to indicate attempts to meet internal demands through commerce. The negative sign relating this term to the others signifies a hypothesized inverse effect. That is, high rates of increase in per capita trade are likely to contribute to lower rates of expansion, although a certain simultaneity or feedback effect is likely to operate. The next term in the equation represents a specialized capability that may enable a society to translate demands into actions or behavior. Again, the defense budget on a per capita basis is only a first order approximation of specialized capability. And finally, the error or disturbance term, u, represents random factors as well as deterministic effects that should have been explicitly modelled.[14] The greater the serial correlation among the u's (and the greater the deterministic component), the more extensive are the effects of those unmodelled factors. It then becomes necessary to incorporate these in the equation (or to expand

[11] Estimation was undertaken with the use of the TROLL interactive computer system for the analysis of non-linear models developed by the Econometrics Project at M.I.T. We are grateful to the supervising staff for their assistance.

[12] See Choucri and North (fn. 56 of text) for the rationale underlying the use of logarithm transform in the first and third terms and comparison of results obtained without the transform and without the interactive term.

[13] Steel per capita can be considered only as a rough indicator of industrial production, and, by extension, of technology. The unavailability of data for other, more appropriate, indicators necessitates the use of this variable for the 1870–1914 period. A critique of our choice of indicators is provided by Joseph M. Firestone, "Remarks on Concept Formation: Theory Building and Theory Testing," Prepared for Delivery at the 66th Annual Meeting of the American Political Science Association, Los Angeles 1970.

[14] We have employed the Hildreth-Lu iterative procedure for estimating the autocorrelation parameter and specifying the needed adjustments. See Clifford Hildreth and John Y. Lu, "Demand Relations with Autocorrelated Disturbances," *Technical Bulletin*, No. 276 (Michigan 1960).

the equation into a larger number of relationships involving more than one equation).

An alternative and comparable (though not identical) formulation of the lateral pressure equation employs colonial area as the expansion term, national income as the technology term, and navy budget as the defense or specialized capability term:

$$\Delta \text{ colonial area} = a + B_1 \, \Delta \, [\text{home pop./home area}] +$$
$$B_2 \, [\Delta \text{ national income}] +$$
$$B_3 \, \Delta \, [\text{home pop./home area}]. \, \Delta \, [\text{national}$$
$$\text{income per capita}] -$$
$$B_4 \, [\Delta \text{ total trade per capita}] +$$
$$B_5 \, [\Delta \text{ navy budget per capita}] + u$$

The second equation in the model is considerably more straightforward and represents the effects of expanding spheres of influence as follows:[15]

$$\Delta \text{ intersections} = a + B_1 \, [\Delta \text{ expansion of self}] +$$
$$B_2 \, [\Delta \text{ expansion of others}] +$$
$$B_3 \, [\Delta \text{ defense budget of self}] +$$
$$B_4 \, [\Delta \text{ violence toward others}] +$$
$$B_5 \, [\Delta \text{ violence of others}] + u$$

The dependent variable summarizes changes in the intensity of intersections among the major powers. The independent variables include expansionist activities, indicators of capability, and variables denoting prevailing conflict and violence in interactions among nations. Again, the operational definition of the variables approximates the conceptual terms only to an approximate degree. The [Δ expansion of others] term was operationalized as five separate variables denoting the expansionist activities of each power. Intersection and violence variables were derived from the same data base, but the coding rules which yielded each variable differ considerably. Extensive care was taken not to create (theoretically and operationally) redundant indicators.[16]

The military budget equation has perhaps been the subject of greatest experimentation—with gap variables, with internal variables, and with external variables.[17] It gradually became possible to incorporate break-points

[15] Operationalizing intersections involved first, isolating those instances in which major powers interactions revolved around disagreements, disputes, conflicts, etc. over colonial territories or potential colonial territories or spheres of influence in Europe and overseas; second, noting the intensity of the intersection on a conflict-cooperation scale designed specifically for purposes of inter-nation and inter-situation comparisons; and third, isolating the most intense intersection variable. (Some index or aggregation would yield a more representative value, but serious methodological problems are involved in the construction of such a measure.) For the interaction scale, see Lincoln E. Moses and others, "Scaling Data on Inter-Nation Action," *Science*, 156, 3778 (July 1967), 1054-59, and Edward Azar and others, "Methodological Developments in the Quantification of Events Data," paper presented at the 1970 Michigan State University Events Data Conference, April 15-16, 1970, for a more intensive discussion of operational issues.
[16] See North and Choucri (fn. 49 of text), for operational definition of violence, and Moses and others (fn. 15), for coding rules.
[17] Moll (fn. 62 of text); North and Lagerstrom (fn. 62 of text).

explicitly in the equation (in terms of a redefinition of rivals and adversaries, perceived or actual), and thus account for some shifts over the period in question. Of the many equations we have examined the following functional form seems to be the most valid:[18]

$$\Delta \text{ navy budget} = a + B_1 \left[\Delta \text{ navy budget}_{t-1}\right] +$$
$$B_2 \left[\Delta \text{ navy budget of adversary}_{t-1}\right] +$$
$$B_3 \left[\Delta \text{ expansion of self}\right] +$$
$$B_4 \left[\Delta \text{ intersections}\right] + u$$

The first term is an internal variable representing bureaucratic and organizational effects (approximating habit patterns or bureaucratic constraints), the second is the adversary allocations, and the third and fourth refer to dynamics of an international nature. We should emphasize, however, the tentative nature of this analysis by noting that further work is necessary before accepting this formulation as a valid statement of the dynamics in question.

The fourth equation in the model seeks to depict the intensity of violence among the major powers as follows:

$$\Delta \text{ violence} = a + B_1 \left[\Delta \text{ defense budget of self}\right] +$$
$$B_2 \left[\Delta \text{ defense budget of others}\right] +$$
$$B_3 \left[\Delta \text{ intersections}\right] +$$
$$B_4 \left[\Delta \text{ alliance commitments}\right] + u$$

The first term represents an internal variable, and the other three refer to external considerations.[19] Operationally [Δ defense budget of others] was defined as five separate terms, one for each major power. It is still an open question whether gap or distance variables need to be included in this final stage.

Shifts in underlying dynamics became apparent in light of the fact that the explanatory power of each equation changes considerably for different periods between 1870 and 1914. In general, best "fits" were obtained not for the forty-five years as a whole but for shorter periods.[20] As an example, the best fits for the lateral pressure equation were during the earlier years, whereas the intersection equation best fit the intermediary and later years. The best fits for the violence equation were also obtained in later years. But because break-points were explicitly included in our analysis of armament competition, extremely good fits were obtained for the period as a whole as well as for sub-periods. Knowledge of these shifts was based on the historical and documentary record. Without this information, however, it would have been very difficult to take into account breaks and estimate the relation-

---

[18] We have also experimented with gap variables, but have encountered severe identification problems. The same equation was examined employing army budget and total defense budget as alternative measures of the endogenous and exogenous budget variables.

[19] The last term was operationalized as the *number* of alliance commitments based on the Singer-Small data. See J. David Singer and Melvin Small, "Alliance Aggregation and the Onset of War, 1815–1945," in Singer, ed. (fn. 68 of text), 247-86.

[20] Sub-periods were selected somewhat arbitrarily by trial and error. The possibilities are limited, however, with only 45 years.

ships successfully beyond the break. Comparative R^2 for all four equations, presented in Table 2, are illustrative of shifts in underlying processes.[21] And it is then a relatively straightforward exercise to test for break-joints.[22]

TABLE 2

SOME INFERENTIAL EVIDENCE FOR THE OCCURRENCE OF BREAK-POINTS[1]

Period and Equation	Britain	France	Germany	Russia	Austria-Hungary	Italy
LATERAL PRESSURE						
1872–1914	.06	.05	.02	.04	.08	.03
1872–1892	.05	.19	.03	.15	.11	.14
1892–1902	.24	.50	.75	.79	.73	.20
1902–1914	.28	.21	.16	.07	.25	.48
1872–1900	.48	.06	—	.11	.11	.05
INTERSECTIONS						
1872–1914	.43	.56	.26	.55	.46	.43
1872–1892	.84	.50	.40	.56	.83	.70
1892–1902	.49	.96†	—	.98‡	.92	—
1892–1914	.11	.87	.45	.75	.57	.62
1902–1914	.85†	—	.97	.85	.76	—
MILITARY COMPETITION[2]						
1870–1914	.03	.34	.11	.21	.56	.30
1872–1892	.28	.47	.55	.19	.26	.58
1892–1902	.27	.56	.88	.79	.55	.65
1902–1914	.21	.76	.34	.34	.68	.60
1906–1914	.41	.81	.62	.50	.46	.79
VIOLENCE						
1872–1914	.25	.17	.36	.30	.31	.30
1872–1892	.43	.35	.63	.69	.20	.43
1892–1914	.73	.61	.49	.27	.45	.55
1892–1904	.89	.73	.67	.30	.63	.60
1904–1914	.96†	.85	.49	.98†	.92§	.96†

[1] Empty cells arise as a result of missing observations or problems in matrix inversion due to low variance in the independent variables.

[2] These results represent navy budget competition. See Choucri and North (fn. 56 of text) for additional comments on methodology, regression coefficients, and empirical data, and for a comparison of results for army, navy, and total defense budgets. In general, the same patterns persisted across the three operational measures.

† Significant coefficients and high R^2 despite the loss of degrees of freedom due to the inclusion of a large number of variables in relation to the number of observations.

‡ High R^2 and 5 significant coefficients.

§ High R^2 but only 1 significant coefficient.

These results pertain to analysis of rates of change and not absolute values. Because of the degrees of freedom problem, results pertaining to longer time periods are likely to be more stable than those for progressively shorter periods.

[21] These data are presented for illustrative purposes only. The magnitude of R^2 *alone* is not an adequate indication of fit. The progressive loss of degrees of freedom effects R^2, but not the significance of individual coefficients (since this loss is taken into account when computing the F ratio or t statistic).

[22] See Gregory C. Chow, "Tests of Inequality Between Sets of Coefficients in Two Linear Regressions," *Econometrica*, XXVIII (July 1960), 591-605.

When this is done it becomes possible to employ this model for simulation and forecasting.[23]

From these (tentative) results we infer partial (and equally tentative) validation of the change-in-dynamics thesis and of the particular sequence postulated. Considerable extensions of this analysis (and of the equations) need be undertaken before adequate validation can be achieved. None of the operational or methodological issues raised in this note are trivial. They can be resolved only by experimentation, trial and error, and further analysis. At the very least, alternative formulations of the underlying theoretical specification need be undertaken along with the use of alternative data series for different countries and different time periods.

Finally, we should point out once more that a theory (or set of hypotheses) cannot be "tested" adequately against the same set of data which has provided at least a partial basis for the development of the theory. Our analysis of the 1870–1914 period should be considered illustrative of the dynamics postulated and not as an empirical "test" of the partial theory in the strict sense of the term. Altogether different sets of data and empirical referents are needed to provide the systematic test. In this respect also, much is still to be done.

[23] For an extended discussion, illustrations, and empirical results see Nazli Choucri, "Applications of Experimental Econometrics to Forecasting in Political Analysis," prepared for the Conference on International Relations Forecasting, December 1970; revised August 1971.

CRISIS DIPLOMACY, INTERDEPENDENCE, AND THE POLITICS OF INTERNATIONAL ECONOMIC RELATIONS

By EDWARD L. MORSE

DURING the past decade policy makers and academic observers have become increasingly aware of the political importance of economic relations, especially among the advanced industrialized states. Some of this awareness came precipitously when monetary crises threatened not only individual currencies such as sterling, the franc, or the dollar, but also the basic structure of the international monetary system. Some of this awareness was more incremental, as with the growing fear that neomercantilist trade policies might result in a reversal of the postwar policies of trade liberalization pursued by the Western industrialized states.

Two aspects of these phenomena have become particularly salient. On the one hand, international economic relations have assumed a central political importance as the "welfare effects" associated with them have become requisite policy goals.[1] On the other hand, theoretical knowledge concerning the relationship between political and economic aspects of statecraft, or concerning the dynamics of interdependent relations, has remained rudimentary. Policy implications are less clear than they must be if these relations are to be consciously managed by central political authorities.

This essay is concerned with exploring both of these issues, through an examination of the sources and significance of crisis diplomacy in international economic relationships among the Western industrialized states. In particular it is addressed to the following series of questions:[2]

1. Why have crises become characteristic political features of international economic affairs in the West? How recent a set of political phenomena are they? Is the management of international economic

---

[1] For a more detailed analysis of the reasons for which foreign economic policy has assumed a new political significance, see my essay, "The Transformation of Foreign Policies: Modernization, Interdependence, and Externalization," *World Politics*, XXII (April 1970), esp. 379-83.

[2] These questions will not be taken up in this essay in the order in which they are posed here. Rather, it is hoped that the exposition of the *argument* in this essay will clarify answers to them.

crises likely to remain a salient feature of international politics in the future?

2. In what ways has economic statecraft been characterized by deliberate efforts to provoke and to manipulate crises in order to achieve political objectives? What factors have made crisis manipulation an effective form of statecraft? What is the nature of the constraints which can limit its effectiveness?

3. How does the diplomacy of economic "crisis management" and of economic "crisis manipulation" reflect the growth of economic interdependencies, especially among the highly industrialized Western states? What other forms of interdependence can we identify? How might these widen the range of issues which enter diplomacy at different levels?

4. What new advances are likely to be forthcoming in our ability to theorize about international interdependence in the next decade? How might such advances in knowledge serve policy makers who are concerned with controlling such effects of interdependence as monetary crises?

5. Finally, in the absence of fully developed theories, how might policy makers become more sensitive to the political implications of international interdependence? And, how might the current state of theory serve policy makers and allow them to act more effectively in the face of uncertainty?

Crisis Diplomacy in the 1960's

The foreign policies of the United States, Britain, France and the other highly industrialized Western states had to cope with a series of monetary crises whose frequency appeared to accelerate during the 1960's and 1970's. These crises threatened to alter significantly the structure of the international monetary system and the gold exchange standard upon which it and the international position of the dollar were based. At the same time, some governments, particularly those of France, Italy and Germany, and, most recently, the United States, consciously provoked crises in the Common Market (especially in the formulation of a Common Agricultural Policy), in matters of transportation (airline routes), or in monetary relations, in order to increase the benefits which could be gained in forthcoming negotiations. Thus, for example, the French threatened several times to withdraw from the European Economic Community unless the Common Agricultural Policy was settled, and, by setting arbitrary deadlines, instituted a form of marathon multilateral diplomacy. This tactic of negotiation created an aura of crisis so that decisions could be precipitated which would benefit French farmers and enhance the economic position of the French in Europe vis-à-vis Germany.

Sometimes these crises were even more complex, for they involved not only predominantly economic affairs, but a mix of economic and security matters. This has characterized, for example, recent tensions and crises between the United States and Japan. Japanese foreign policy toward the United States in the early 1970's was predicated upon a conscious attempt to link the renewal of the Japanese-American Security Treaty to access to the American market for Japanese products, including steel and textiles. And, to an equal degree it has characterized U.S. relations with the countries of Western Europe where changing security relations have been complemented by a shifting balance in economic power marked by the monetary crisis of the summer of 1971.

Most of these crises were not anticipated by political decision-makers who generally did not have a conceptual understanding of the changes in the structure of international relations which made the crises more likely.[3] Indeed, much had been written in the early 1960's about crisis management in matters of security or "high politics." And there had been a flourishing of strategic thinking which drew political implications from the development and spread of nuclear weapons.[4] The "new diplomacy of crisis management" was to cope with crises over Berlin, those which might develop from the accidental use of nuclear weapons, or from miscalculation.[5] The Cuban missile crisis supposedly bore out

[3] Certain economists had, by 1960, begun to predict a series of future crises in the international monetary system. These predictions were, by and large, focused upon a presumed insufficiency of liquidity to meet the needs of a burgeoning level of global trade. They failed to predict either the *political* significance of the crises which did occur, or the form they would assume due to the relatively free floating market of short-term capital that later emerged. See, for example, Robert Triffin, *Gold and the Dollar Crisis* (New Haven 1960).

[4] The distinction between *Grosspolitik*, or "high politics," and "low politics" belongs to the Saint-Simonian tradition of meliorism as it was embodied in the "functionalist" school of thought on supranational integration. Areas of "low politics" were assumed in this tradition to be amenable to non-political and technical manipulation by experts. When combined with the assumption that the growth and the survival of industrialized societies is dependent upon the coordination internationally of national policies related to these "technical" issues, this argument produced a powerful prescription for functional integration. Theorists who argued this position profoundly overestimated both the urgency of the task and the degree to which "technical" problems could remain out of politics. For a succinct statement of this position, see Ernst Haas, "Technocracy, Pluralism and the New Europe," in Stephen R. Graubard, *A New Europe* (Boston 1964), 62-88.

[5] See, for example, the outline of this argument in Alastair Buchan, *Crisis Management: The New Diplomacy* (Paris 1966). An analysis of the political science literature on crises can be found in Charles F. Hermann, "International Crisis as a Situational Variable," in James N. Rosenau, ed., *International Politics and Foreign Policy* (rev. ed., New York 1969), 409-21.

the proof of these predictions. Ironically, however, the new notion of "crisis management" was soon rendered inconsequential for two principal reasons. First, crisis management as originally conceived was contradicted by new issues which arose in the late 1960's, such as possibilities of detente in Europe and the negotiation of common concerns between the United States and the Soviet Union. Crises of the sort envisaged never arose. Second, the theory implied a need for centralizing control over NATO military forces by the United States. This could never be achieved given the unwillingness of other NATO members to accept the loss of autonomy entailed.

The crises which did occur did not pertain, as had been expected, to high political and strategic matters. Rather, they occurred in the realm of low political and economic affairs. They nonetheless bore the same political significance that was anticipated for high political crises. In order to investigate why this was the case, it is important to explore the following: first, what has been meant by the term "crisis"; second, reasons for which *economic* crises became highly politicized; and, third, what is meant by a "growth in international interdependence" as a reason for the occurrence of these economic crises.

"CRISIS"—THE DEFINITIONAL QUESTION

"Crisis" usually bears the connotation of its etymological origin. It is a medical term (derived from the Greek) describing a decisive and sudden change which can lead to *either* recovery or death. From this definition, political crises usually are understood as circumstances involving the survival of a political system, or an intensive political interaction carrying implications for the *stability* of some pattern of interactions. When crises are so understood, their analysis is likely to be cast in some form of "systemic" framework. This is the case whether such analyses are predominantly political or predominantly economic.[6]

Theories cast in a systemic framework usually assume that crises can be understood in terms of conditions which give rise to disequilibria or instabilities. These theories also typically involve etiological analysis of the causes of crises and the various stages they go through before resolution (i.e. before the return to equilibrium conditions).[7] These efforts

[6] For a forcefully argued example of a systemic analysis of crises involving the use of force, see Oran R. Young, *The Politics of Force* (Princeton 1968). An economic conceptualization of the same sort can be found in Robert A. Mundell, "The Crisis Problem," in Robert A. Mundell and Alexander K. Swoboda, eds., *Monetary Problems of the International Economy* (Chicago 1969), 343-49.

[7] This pattern of analysis is typical of the work of Charles A. McClelland, but can also be found in a variety of other writings. See, for example, McClelland, "The Acute International Crisis," *World Politics,* xiv (June 1961), 182-204, and his "Access to Ber-

to theorize have by and large failed to live up to expectations or to yield fruitful generalizations. Many reasons might explain this failing, including the relative lack of quantifiable data. To me these efforts were bound to be weak because of fundamental conceptual problems inherent in equilibrium and etiological analyses, rather than because of lack of data. A major emphasis is placed on behavioral traits which can be measured in terms of changes in one or more systemic variable, or variables, requisite to a system's "pattern-maintenance."[8] Mundell, for example, has identified these as changes in "boundary conditions" or in "control mechanisms."[9] Such analyses inevitably turn the attention of an observer away from the central political focus of crises—namely the confrontation of different, if not mutually incompatible objectives which can be identified with the states involved in a crisis. Through the emphasis of behavioral traits, such as "intensity" or "duration," or of equilibrium conditions, the conflicting goals involved tend to be ignored.[10]

It seems to me that more fruitful conceptualizations of crises would be developed if the crisis were objectified in a form that was more amenable to deductive analysis. Such a conceptualization would focus upon state objectives whose achievability could be translated into terms such as those associated with economic models, terms such as opportunity costs and possibility functions. This would also clearly point out the interdependent relations of different governments in crises situations. It would, therefore, lead logically to an analysis of those sources of crises traceable to the growing interdependence of states. I will define a "crisis" for these purposes as the sudden emergence (whether or not anticipated) of a situation requiring a policy choice by one or more states within a relatively short period of time, a situation requiring a choice between mutually incompatible but highly valued objectives.

In a simplified model, a crisis can then be understood as a situation in which two highly valued objectives—call one the *status quo* in Berlin

---

lin: The Quantity and Variety of Events, 1948–1963," in J. David Singer, ed., *Quantitative International Politics: Insights and Evidence* (New York 1968), 159-86.

[8] For a fuller but more sympathetic exposition of systemic analysis of crises, see Hermann (fn. 5), 411-13.

[9] Mundell (fn. 6), 343.

[10] There is a set of additional problems associated with etiological or "stage" analysis of crises which can be identified, but the full exposition of them is beyond the scope of this essay. For example, such analyses assume that a class of crisis situations can be identified which bear similarities in the way they begin or terminate. These assumptions frequently are not warranted. They, therefore, assume that the dynamics of crises tend to be similar and that generalizations about them can be fruitful. This assumption has never been fully tested empirically. Moreover, as a premise it has not yielded notably powerful propositions.

and another the avoidance of risking war in Europe—seem to become suddenly mutually incompatible, when they were earlier held to be mutually compatible. Given the new circumstances, regardless of how they come about, in order to maintain peace in Europe, concessions must be made to the Soviet Union over Berlin. Or, in order to maintain the *status quo* in Berlin, the risk of war in Europe is substantially increased.

It is precisely this type of choice between highly valued but incompatible objectives which has increasingly characterized international economic relationships. This is another way of saying that economic relations have become more politicized. Two sets of questions must be asked with regard to this politicization of international economic relationships. One is factual and the other theoretical: When did this politicization occur? What processes were responsible for it?

International economic crises, of course, are not in themselves recent phenomena. The history of international economic crises extends as far back as the beginnings of international trade. But the political consequences, even as recently as the mid-nineteenth century, were negligible. For example, in 1862–1866 the domestic crisis in the British textile industry clearly resulted from the supply of cotton being cut off during the American Civil War. But this was perceived as an inevitable fact of economic life and not as having important international or domestic political significance.[11] The recent politicization of economic relations seems to have arisen in the period between the two world wars. French financial policy in the 1920's, and Roosevelt's devaluation of the dollar in 1933, for example, were manipulative efforts to achieve political ends. In the French case, artificial currency depreciation policies were implemented in order to increase the French gold stock, to help France regain coequal stature with Britain as one of the two leading global powers. Roosevelt's devaluation was apparently motivated by similar, but not coincidental, aims. It seems to have been the first such act taken for primarily domestic political purposes.[12] With the French policies of the 1920's Roosevelt's devaluation foreshadowed much of the political manipulation of economic policies which began to occur with accelerating momentum and became widespread after World War II.

It might be objected that such policies are not in fact so novel, that they represent a reversion to the mercantilist tendencies which domi-

[11] For a short descriptive history of this and other economic crises in the nineteenth and twentieth centuries, see Maurice Flamant and Jeanne Singer-Kerel, *Modern Economic Crises and Recessions*, translated by Pat Wardroper (New York 1968).

[12] For a fuller account of both policies, see Fred Hirsch, *Money International: Economics and Politics of World Money* (Garden City 1969), 250-59.

nated international affairs in the seventeenth and eighteenth centuries. To the degree that such an objection holds, arguments about the development of "neomercantilism" after World War II are significant. But important differences between mercantilist policies and *soi-disant* neomercantilism should be examined.[13]

For mercantilist doctrine, economic and political matters were virtually inseparable. An increase or decrease in relative national wealth (e.g., state gold holdings) was, for most purposes equivalent to a similar change in power. Even when separated distinctly in policy, power and plenty were generally regarded as harmonious.[14] This was the case because economic policies under mercantilism were designed "not to promote the welfare of the community and its members, but to augment the power of the state."[15] In addition, mercantilism had postulated that wealth and power were finite and, at least in the long run, constant. Consequently increases in the power or wealth of one state resulted in an actual or potential loss of either for others. As Viner has argued, "The significance of such doctrine [mercantilism] is not that those who adhered to it placed power before plenty, but that they grossly misunderstood the true means to and nature of plenty. What they were lacking in was not economic motivation, but economic understanding."[16]

"Economic understanding" under liberalism is predicated upon a reversal of the major assumption of mercantilism: namely, the separability of economic and political variables. In this sense liberalism represented a frontal attack on mercantilist ideas. For Adam Smith, Ricardo, and other founders of economic liberalism, the world of wealth was not only viewed as separate from that of political power, but wealth was also understood to be expandable. This was supported by the political versions of liberalism, from which can be traced the separation of "low" policies from "high" policies as discussed above. The political version of liberalism is usually exemplified by the Cobdenite perspec-

[13] Arguments about neomercantilism can be found in Joan Robinson, *The New Mercantilism* (Cambridge 1966), and in Harold B. Malmgren, *Trade Wars or Trade Negotiations? Non-Tariff Barriers and Economic Peacekeeping* (New York 1971).

[14] In Jacob Viner's paradigm of the policy of mercantilism, the following more accurate relationships are postulated between power and plenty: "(1) wealth is an absolutely essential means to power, whether for security or for aggression; (2) power is essential or valuable as a means to the acquisition or retention of wealth; (3) wealth and power are each proper ultimate ends of national policy; (4) there is a long-run harmony between these ends, although in particular circumstances it may be necessary for a time to make economic sacrifices in the interest of military security and therefore also of long-run prosperity." See "Power Versus Plenty as Objectives of Foreign Policy in the Seventeenth and Eighteenth Centuries," *World Politics*, 1 (October 1948), 10.

[15] Edward Hallett Carr, *Nationalism and After* (London 1967), 5.

[16] Viner (fn. 14), 10.

tive on international trade as a guarantor of peace. Emphasis on low politics through the creation of a laissez-faire international economy would permit under liberal doctrine the growth of the "natural harmony of interests"—a harmony which was perverted by the dynastic claims to increased power associated with the ruling groups of mercantilist Europe.[17]

Liberalism, like mercantilism, has similarly come under attack. Leaving aside Marxist criticisms of liberal doctrine, it has been argued that inherent in the basic assumptions of liberalism is the illusion that predominantly economic and predominantly political affairs are separable. However true it may be theoretically that free trade increases the wealth of all trading partners, the liberal vision of international economic and political relations could never be implemented. Not only are industrialized states unwilling to institute laissez-faire trade policies, but even if they are, conflicts would exist among trading powers which would politicize economic relations. This failure to achieve a liberal international system, where economic and political matters could be separated, is a direct result of changes in the structure of governments in virtually all societies, and specifically a result in a change in *domestic* policies. Joan Robinson states the case clearly:

> Ever since the war [World War II], partly by good luck, partly by good management and partly by the arms race, overall effective demand has been kept from serious relapses. Nowadays governments are concerned not just to maintain employment, but to make national income grow. Nevertheless, the capitalist world is still always somewhat of a buyer's market, in the sense that capacity to produce exceeds what can be sold at a profitable price. . . . The chronic condition for industrial enterprise is to be looking round anxiously for prospects of sales. Since the total market does not grow fast enough to make room for all, each government feels it a worthy and commendable aim to increase its own share in world activity for the benefit of its own people.
> This is the new mercantilism.
>
>   * * *
>
> [Outside the Communist camp] everyone is keen to sell and wary of buying. Every nation wants to have a surplus in its balance of trade. This is a game where the total scores add up to zero.[18]

[17] For elaborations of the political and economic arguments associated with liberalism, see Carr (fn. 15), 11-17, and *The Twenty Years' Crisis, 1919–1939* (London 1939), chap. 4. The origins of liberal doctrine in the eighteenth century are traced in Felix Gilbert, *To the Farewell Address: Ideas of Early American Foreign Policy* (Princeton 1961), 44-75.

[18] Robinson (fn. 13), 9-10. Richard N. Cooper presents a different but complementary argument for the political tensions which characterize international commercial and financial interactions. See "Introduction" to Hirsch (fn. 12), xiv-xvii.

Whether this represents, as Robinson claims, a reversion to the finite world of mercantilism (which may have always lurked behind liberalism), or whether it presents a new set of tensions in international economic relations, stemming from the collectively incompatible goals of all states pursuing balance of payments surpluses, the outcome is the same: economic interactions have become politicized in a significant way since World War II. Five general arguments may be offered to help explain this politicization of economic diplomacy, and therefore of economic crises. One of these has already been briefly alluded to.

First, at the level of high politics, the policy-making elite of the superpowers have been socialized into the world of nuclear weaponry and have, for practical purposes, accepted stalemate at the nuclear level. The crises anticipated in that realm either have not emerged; or, when they have, as in Cuba in 1962, they seemed to reinforce the stalemate.[19] One result of the stalemate has been the diminished utility of the realm of high politics for achieving foreign policy objectives. Second, welfare type policy objectives have, under the influence of the nuclear stalemate and the dynamics of domestic industrialization, gained a more equal footing with the classical foreign policy goal of military security. As welfare, in the sense of material well-being for the citizens of the advanced industrialized states, has become increasingly attached to the phenomenal growth in world trade after World War II, so attention to the politics of economic affairs has become increasingly important to their governments. Consequently, when crises of adjustment, or crises inherent in the nature of these new relationships emerged, these crises seemed to overshadow to some degree the anticipation of crises in the other realm.

Third, the need to create a well-integrated and regulated international financial system is a direct result of dramatic changes in the structure of national economies during this century. So long as such a system has not been created, crises are inevitable in international economic affairs and have a necessary political cast. As Hirsch has argued, "To a real degree, the pre-1914 standard avoided external financial crises at the expense of internal financial and economic instability. Of the modern triangle of conflicting economic objectives, stable exchanges—stable prices—domestic growth at full employment, the pre-1914 system aimed only at the first."[20] Today, all three are stated goals, as governments have assumed

[19] For a compatible view on this which relates to the declining value of territorial conquest in international affairs, see Klaus Knorr, *On the Uses of Military Power in the Nuclear Age* (Princeton 1966), 21-34.

[20] Hirsch (fn. 12), 56.

increased responsibility for maintaining and creating minimum standards of welfare. So long as the international monetary system remains unintegrated, and so long as domestic growth at full employment is requisite for democratic regimes to stay in power (to paraphrase Hirsch), internal financial and economic stability can be maintained only at the cost of external financial crisis.

Fourth, international economic affairs became a substitute for high politics for all but the great powers in East and West Europe because they presented the only area where foreign policy action could be effective. If diplomacy is less effective in terms of the classical alliance politics of coalition-building, given the asymmetries of the NATO and Warsaw Pacts and the logic of control over weapons delivery systems, diplomatic action in economic affairs can appear attractive for the political pay-offs. The marathon sessions which in the latter part of 1967 characterized the negotiations for both a Common Agricultural Policy in the European Communities and a community position in the Kennedy Round, assumed the transcendental significance which once characterized the politics of grandeur. In this sense, the fact that negotiations *could occur* assumed the same significance as the results which might be gained, especially within Europe itself.

Fifth, and finally, economic relations became a focus of crisis politics not only because of their newly acquired intrinsic political significance, but especially because of the forms of interdependence assumed in these relationships. As will be argued below, advanced industrialized societies have become significantly interdependent over the past two decades. At the same time, the objectives of the various societies have become more and more incompatible. And this incompatibility, together with a high level of interdependence, has served to provoke crises in the relationships among advanced industrialized states.

INTERNATIONAL INTERDEPENDENCE AND THE SOURCES OF CRISIS DIPLOMACY

The hypothesis suggested above, that the occurrence of crises in international affairs is related to the growth in the levels and types of interdependence in international society, touches upon a controversy in the theoretical literature on international politics. It rests on the empirical generalization that international interdependencies have, in fact, increased in scope over the last century. Some observers of international politics have argued the opposite.[21] Specifically, they have taken the

[21] The outstanding example of this position may be found in Kenneth Waltz, "The Myth of National Interdependence," in Charles P. Kindleberger, ed., *The International*

position that since there is no central structure of political authority in international society, i.e. no supranational government, it is rather useless to discuss interdependence at the international level. It is further argued that even if one could have once profitably discussed international interdependence, levels of international interdependence are much lower now than at the turn of the century.

It seems to me that this perspective, which depreciates the value of conceptualizing international politics in terms of interdependent relationships, is misleading.[22] Even if levels of interdependence characterizing various types of political or economic goods are lower among nations than within them, this does not mean that an examination of interdependencies in international society has no value. That would depend on the definition offered for understanding interdependence. In the absence of a definition, no judgment can be made on the empirical utility of the concept. For the purposes of this essay I will define interdependent behavior in terms of the outcome of specified actions taken by two or more parties (individuals, governments, corporations, etc.) when such actions are mutually contingent. These parties, then, are interdependent with respect to specific issue areas and not with respect to the whole spectrum of their activities. None of the actions involved are fixed. Nor need they be consciously perceived as being mutually contingent or dependent, although such perception would be necessary if interdependence is to be manipulated. I intend now to develop more fully this definition of interdependence, to illustrate by example and analysis the new diplomacy of crisis management in international economic relations, and to draw certain implications for foreign policy decision-making.

Two sets of questions about international interdependence are important. As in our discussion of crises, one set is empirical and the other theoretical. First, are levels of interdependence in international society increasing? If they are, how can such increases be measured? In what domains or issue-areas ought we to look for increased interdependence? Secondly, how might we explain these increases? How would such explanations or theories serve policy makers?

Neither set of questions has yet received satisfactory attention. In fact, if there were adequate theoretical explanations for increases in

---

Corporation (Cambridge, Mass. 1970), 205-23. The argument, however, is shared by a large number of political scientists.

[22] I have critically examined this literature elsewhere and will only summarize my argument here. For a more detailed analysis, see my essay, "Transnational Economic Processes in the Twentieth Century," *International Organization*, xxv (Summer 1971).

international interdependence, the empirical question of whether there had been increases in international interdependence would not be as controversial as it apparently now is. Theory would have settled it by explaining changes in the levels of interdependence by means of deductively linked propositions with empirical referents. I have assumed here that interdependencies have risen dramatically in recent years. I shall now briefly sketch the lines of theoretical development which seem likely to lead to future theoretical payoffs.

In the definition of "interdependence" offered earlier, I suggested that interdependent behavior may be understood in terms of the outcome of specified actions of two or more parties, when such actions are mutually contingent. I also argued that interdependence is better understood as a phenomenon which refers to specific issue-areas, rather than to the whole spectrum of relationship between the parties. For example, two states can be interdependent more with respect to security than with respect to trade. The strategic relationship between the United States and the Soviet Union illustrated this. These interdependent actions need not be consciously perceived as being mutually contingent for an interdependent relation to exist. The perception of contingency is, however, requisite for the successful manipulation of the relationship by one or the other party.

These interdependent relations can be divided into several categories. One subset would distinguish parties aware of the mutual contingency of their actions from those who are not. A second division would differentiate interdependent relations according to the issue-areas involved.

When interdependencies are perceived by the parties involved, behavior is more than likely to be strategic.[23] In strategic interaction, bargaining becomes a means of dealing with interdependence. In such situations one can, for theoretical purposes, apply the axioms of rationality models. It is possible to symbolize such interdependent relationships in mathematical form. Theorizing then, proceeds through deductive logical analysis on specified assumptions and hypothesized relationships.

This sort of analysis ought to prove useful in situations where real world conditions parallel the assumptions of rationality. Those assumptions include the following:

> The first assumption is that of connexity. . . . It is assumed that for each pair of alternatives, either one is preferred to the other or the two

[23] For a more formal definition of strategic behavior and of rationality models, see the essay by Norman Frohlich and Joe A. Oppenheimer, "Entrepreneurial Politics and Foreign Policy," in this volume.

are indifferent. The second assumption is that of transitivity . . . if *A* is preferred to *B*, and *B* is preferred to *C*, we assume that *A* is preferred to *C*. . . .

Finally, and perhaps most important, it is assumed that the choice from any environment is determined by the ordering, in the sense that if there is an alternative that is preferred to every other alternative in the environment, then it is the chosen element.[24]

Each of these assumptions is predicated upon a more basic assumption: namely, that the actors involved are purposive and rational in their behavior. By and large, classical assumptions about international politics, and especially about the security relations among states, smack of these assumptions. First, states have been conceived of as relatively autonomous. Borders are normally thought of as relatively impermeable, and statesmen who formulate policies are seen to be motivated by the desire to maximize security. Societies have not until recently been interpenetrated by mass communications, or by substantial interchanges in populations. This has meant that foreign policy could be pursued relatively independently of domestic concerns. The two spheres could be maintained separately. Secondly, the classical instruments of statecraft involved the actual or potential use of force, even between allies, in order to achieve objectives. Third, and as a result of the first two, foreign policy could be pursued through the rational maximization of external objectives, usually the "security" of the polity.

It is not surprising, therefore, to see the development of strategic bargaining models based on rationality assumptions which utilize formal logical techniques. These assumptions are particularly implied in the models of strategic interdependence which deal with the relationship between the two nuclear superpowers.

The economic crises, and the crisis diplomacy in the 1960's to which I referred earlier, cannot always be treated satisfactorily by such models. The empirical referents, or real world conditions, involved are quite different from the conditions which were the basis of the classical diplomatic accounts, or more formal accounts of strategic interaction. Either by "accident" or by design, radical changes in the structure of international politics—especially among the Western industrialized states—have emerged during the twentieth century. They have resulted from several factors: from the geographical configuration of forces which occupied Europe at the close of World War II; from attempts to institutionalize free trade in both Europe and the North

[24] Kenneth Arrow, "Public and Private Values," in Sidney Hook, ed., *Human Values and Economic Policy* (New York 1967), 5.

Atlantic region through the progressive dismantling of trade barriers; and from the renunciation of the use of force among these states. Consequently, the once impermeable borders have become highly permeable by both governmental and nongovernmental groups through certain sets of activities (trade, investments in industrial production, the creation of the gold-exchange standard, etc.). And, domestic politics has increasingly restricted foreign policy decisions (and vice versa). In addition, the onset of the Cold War and the emergence of a common external enemy brought about conscious efforts to put an end to internecine warfare in Europe. The use of force among the Western industrialized states was virtually renounced. Thus the classical instrument of statecraft was eliminated for a large set of countries. Finally, the notion of rational calculation built into classical diplomacy is severely weakened by the breakdown in the separation of foreign and domestic affairs, by the influence of pressure group politics on national policy making, and by the increased bureaucratization of politics within the governments involved.

These structural changes in classical patterns strengthened the interdependencies among the advanced industrialized states of the West and were reinforced by two additional changes. Technological changes served to reduce transportation costs and thereby facilitated additional trade interactions among these societies. Also, these governments became increasingly responsible for a panoply of activities associated with the maintenance of minimal standards of well-being. Governments fostered centrally directed economic growth and dealt with the difficulties of maintaining viable urban habitats. The increased multifunctionality of the governments of all highly modernized societies was made all the more necessary by the increased politicization of their citizens and the consequent increase in their demands upon government.[25]

A paradox has characterized the growth of these phenomena: as governments have added to their domestic and foreign responsibilities, their autonomy, and, therefore, their ability to control these additional policy outcomes, has been *reduced* by a concomitant growth in international interdependence.

It is at this point that recent theoretical developments concerning international interdependence and based on economic models of public policy ought to be introduced into the discussion, for these changes in international relationships and in foreign policy are illuminated by the theoretical models which have been recently developed. Especially

---

[25] This argument is more fully developed in Morse (fn. 1), 383-86.

illuminating are policy models based upon an examination of the relationship between policy targets, or goals, and the requisite number and type of instruments, or procedures, needed to achieve them. These models range from the general one constructed originally by Jan Tinbergen[26] to more specific ones such as those associated with J. E. Meade[27] which relate policies of full employment and balance of payments equilibrium. Without going into the details of these models,[28] some conclusions important to the present discussion can be examined. According to Tinbergen's model, which is a general and well-accepted model of economic policy analysis, an ideal policy situation exists when the number of policy instruments (e.g. tax incentives, subsidies and the like) exceeds the number of policy targets. "In the general case where the number of instruments surpasses the number of targets, it will always be possible to find one among the infinity of solutions . . . for which welfare, however defined, is a maximum. This would be the optimum solution."[29]

In such a case there exists, ideally, an infinite number of solutions for implementing policy goals. Some instruments can supplement others and thereby resolve conflict between otherwise incompatible goals. A major problem exists, however, when the number of goals surpasses the number of policy instruments. In such a case, not all goals can be simultaneously attained. This is the case *even if* it is assumed that different instruments can be used for achieving more than one goal. This state of affairs traditionally enters into budgetary politics. Unless the economy is rapidly expanding, a government cannot support a high level of welfare spending (including subsidies, grants and social overhead capital) and a high level of defense expenditure while simultaneously maintaining a low level of taxation, since taxation is the main vehicle for financing both. Either the number of policy objectives will have to be reduced and their scope narrowed, or the number of policy instruments increased, if all goals are to be satisfied. Given the increased level of demands on all governments, the former is less likely than the latter. With new sources of tax revenue shrinking, it is likely governments will turn to international policy coordination effectively to increase the number of available policy instruments.

This unbalanced relationship between policy objectives and policy

[26] Jan Tinbergen, *On the Theory of Economic Policy* (Amsterdam 1963 [1952]), and *Economic Policy, Principles and Design* (Amsterdam 1956).

[27] J. E. Meade, *The Theory of International Economic Policy*, 1 (London 1951).

[28] For a lucid exposition, see Leif Johansen, *Public Economics* (Amsterdam 1965), 9-17.

[29] Tinbergen, *On the Theory of Economic Policy* (fn. 26), 37-38.

instruments is a key to the policy dilemmas confronting all governments in contemporary international society. Recently in the industrialized states, there has developed a significant expansion of policy
objectives—both external and domestic—as governments have assumed
increased responsibility in various domestic spheres. At the same time,
governments have developed a wide panoply of policy instruments to
obtain these objectives—especially through government expenditure.
However, as international conditions have approached the model of
interdependence outlined above, the available number of effective instruments has inevitably decreased. As a result of these interdependencies, activities "outside" the states—such as monetary flows from abroad
—are less easily controlled by national policies alone. The result has
been a *de facto* decrease in the available number of policy instruments.[30] Efforts to rectify this have led to international coordination
among the advanced industrialized countries in matters of economic
affairs. The multilateral negotiations in a number of formally institutionalized organizations, as well as in less formal groups, are an example of this. Whether one looks at the GATT, the Group of Ten
monetary countries, or the smaller Council of Ministers of the European Economic Communities, multilateral diplomacy has been the
only way to gain the requisite level of policy coordination in either
long range planning or in short-term, *ad hoc* crisis management or
manipulation. As the need for multilateral coordination has increased,
so have the occasions for sudden crisis and the opportunities for certain
states to create crisis situations in the pursuit of idiosyncratic policy ends.

The Range of the Diplomacy of Interdependence

In defining "interdependence" earlier, I suggested that it is more
fruitful to look at the specific terms in which two or more parties are
interdependent than to consider interdependence as a general characteristic of the relationship between parties. In this section, I will sketch
some of the issue-areas which may be involved in those relations.[31] The
importance of these issue-areas is due to growth in the range of issues
which have entered diplomacy at different levels over the past century,
and to the kinds of different situations evoked in interdependent relationships.

First, interdependence can be of a *strategic*, or security, nature. The
development of intercontinental ballistic missiles, and the consequent

[30] See Richard N. Cooper, *The Economics of Interdependence* (New York 1968),
153-59.
[31] I am indebted to Harold Sprout for the definition of this range.

effective shortening of the "distance" between the societies of the world (when distance is measured in terms of time needed to deliver nuclear weapons) has served to increase the strategic interdependence of all societies. The security of most states, but especially of the two super-power states, the United States and the Soviet Union, has become highly interdependent in the years following World War II. Given these new conditions, neither state can effectively move toward isolation or increase its own autonomy so far as security is concerned.

Interdependence can also be thought of in *psychological* terms. Revolutionary developments in communication and transportation have facilitated the virtually instantaneous transmittal of information and ideas from one society to another. Some of these ideas serve to broaden horizons and increase the development of economic growth and material well being. Other ideas, especially when predominantly ideological in nature, serve to increase tensions. In both cases, the interrelatedness of global life has, in psychological terms, become an important, if indirect, feature of diplomacy.

A third form of interdependence involves *economic* relationships and the set of phenomena discussed above in terms of the politicization of economic affairs in the past century. This has been especially significant in relations among the Western industrialized states. But it can be found in other forms in the relations between the lesser developed and the highly industrialized societies. There, interdependence is far more asymmetrical than among the highly industrialized societies. But these asymmetrical interdependencies also illustrate the differential nature of increased vulnerability as well as the benefits which can be derived from economic interdependence.

Finally, a fourth form of interdependence can be seen in the increasing significance of *migratory pollutants* which disregard international jurisdictions. These have recently become significant issues in diplomacy concerned with international waterways and in the drafting of treaties aimed at controlling the effects of atmospheric pollutants. These migratory pollutants are likely to be even more salient issues of diplomacy in the coming decades.

As statesmen become aware of the increased range of issues which have entered diplomacy at different levels, they also become aware of the trade-offs between different sorts of interdependence. These trade-off effects have given rise to what I will call the opportunities of interdependence. They also, however, give rise to a more general set of political problems associated with the costs of interdependence. For the trade-off effects point up the interrelatedness of each type of interdependence, and this has resulted in the more general problem of controlling various interdependence effects. Both sorts of problems will be illustrated by briefly described cases from recent history.

The Opportunities of Interdependence: France and the Politics of Crisis Manipulation

French statecraft in the 1960's provides the most illuminating example of the manipulation of interdependent relationships to maximize policy objectives. Whether one turns to the diplomatic maneuverings involved in the preparations for reform of the international monetary system (where French statecraft was not particularly successful) or to the elaboration of a Common Agricultural Policy (CAP) and a common E.E.C. negotiating position for the GATT Kennedy Round (where French policy was highly successful) crisis manipulation was the key tactic employed by the French. So salient did this tactic become that more than one writer has asserted that crisis diplomacy is the essence of diplomacy within the Common Market.[32]

The French tactic of crisis manipulation involved forcing its Common Market partners to choose between incompatible and contradictory policy objectives. They did this in the elaboration of the CAP by threatening to leave the Common Market unless that policy was formulated. Other countries, particularly Germany, were unwilling to accept either alternative. Without France, the political and economic benefits of the Common Market could not be secured, and with a CAP, Germany would pay disproportionately to enrich French farmers.[33] The French backed up their threats by imposing deadlines for the various stages of implementing the E.E.C. These deadlines resulted in marathon procedures for Council of Ministers meetings in December/January 1961–62, December 1963, May–June 1965, and May–July 1966. The marathon procedures have been described as

a typical decision-making process for a system in permanent crisis. It develops under the pressure of time limits agreed upon beforehand, or imposed under a threat by one member state. Its style is one of intergovernmental negotiation on ministerial level with the participation of

[32] See F.A.M. Alting von Geusau, *Beyond the European Community* (Leyden 1969), 41, and Leon N. Lindberg, "Integration as a Source of Stress on the European Community System," *International Organization*, xx (Spring 1966), 233-65.

[33] It can be argued that this may involve a rather special case where a government is actually willing to pay the price of opting out of the community. However, de Gaulle always cast his threats ambiguously which led to their being taken seriously by the other Five. For a classical discussion of this sort of threat, see Thomas C. Schelling, *Arms and Influence* (New Haven 1966), esp. chap. 2.

several ministers from each member state. The Commission takes part in the sessions as institutionalized mediator with the task of suggesting compromises and choosing the appropriate moment for tabling a package deal. The procedure excludes the European parliaments from participating in the decision-making process. . . . To avoid the risk of provoking an immediate crisis, ministers must reach a package of concrete arrangements and/or restrict themselves to vague declarations of intent and the fixing of new time limits. In this way, one Marathon session tends to lead to another thus keeping the system in a state of permanent crisis.[34]

Given the range and interrelatedness of issues involved in interdependent relationships, crises provoked in one political or economic sphere inevitably generate effects in other spheres. This can be seen in the relationship between the CAP and two other related policies—the common negotiating position of the Six in the Kennedy Round and the common monetary policy in the E.E.C. In the first case success for the E.E.C. members was contingent upon the elaboration of the CAP. In the second case, the fact that the French and their European partners would not accept the logic of a customs union in Europe, and that they would not create a common monetary policy, led to the eventual collapse of the CAP and its later renegotiation.

In the first case, the E.E.C. had five years to negotiate the Kennedy Round of trade negotiations before the 1962 U.S. Trade Expansion Act expired. The French refused to negotiate a common trade policy until the CAP was fully worked out. This served to stall GATT negotiations. When the French position is juxtaposed to the American position (which linked progress in industrial sectors to progress in agriculture, lest the U.S. be cut off from its European markets by common high agricultural tariffs), no serious negotiation could take place until January, 1967, six months before the Trade Expansion Act expired. Those negotiations inevitably took place in the same atmosphere of Marathon crisis which characterized the sessions involved in the elaboration of the CAP.[35] The success of the Six in preventing the U.S. from gaining trade-offs between agricultural and industrial sectors was in no small measure a result of the French tactic. By 1967 the American negotiators were eager to come to an agreement at almost any cost.

In the second case, as a result of the currency crisis which had been developing over a year-long period and the French devaluation in August, 1969, the entire CAP had to be suspended temporarily. This

---

[34] Alting von Geusau (fn. 32), 59.
[35] For a description of crisis diplomacy in the GATT and an elaboration of these points, see Ernest H. Preeg, *Traders and Diplomats* (Washington, D.C. 1970), 178-95.

was because the complicated price levels involved in the CAP were pegged to a unit of account equal to the dollar. The common policy assumed the equivalent of fixed exchange rates or a common currency among the Six. Once the franc was devalued, the fixed base upon which the agricultural policy had been built was shattered. The devaluation and the current CAP arrangements were incompatible. Thus, a renegotiation was required of the policy whose creation had been a central focus of French diplomacy during the previous decade.

If the second case demonstrates the potentially costly effects of interdependence, the first one exemplifies the potential use of crisis manipulation for diplomacy. The French were successful crisis manipulators in that field and in the short-run for several reasons. First, Gaullist foreign policy, more than that of any of the other Six or of the United States, was relatively insulated from domestic pressures, given the Constitutional framework of the Fifth Republic and the "reserved powers" of the President (at least until the Paris Spring of 1968). This enabled de Gaulle to implement a "rational strategy" relatively free of domestic pressures for what may be called consummatory external purposes.

Secondly, the French had the support of the E.E.C. Commission which saw in the development of a CAP an important step to the building of a politically united Europe.[36]

A third reason is often given for autonomous and precipitous action in such interdependent relationships. This is the "free-rider" effect of collective goods. When a policy exists for the members of a group, its benefits can be withheld from any single member at only a very high cost. This gives an individual member considerable freedom of action in other fields, while continuing to receive the benefits of that good.[37] In this case, however, French diplomacy had less to do with the free-rider situation than it did with the nature of interdependent relationships. In such relationships there is always the possibility that one state will have an incentive to manipulate the dependency to obtain increased benefits. Since there inevitably are trade-offs, the leadership of any one state, large or small, can always threaten "agonizing reappraisals" which are designed to precipitate change under the threat of destroying some common activity. Such a policy, however, cannot be

[36] Indeed, the Commission's proposals for sweeping changes in the structure of the Community which led to the French boycott of 1965 was predicated on the stake of the French in the CAP. See John Newhouse, *Collision in Brussels, The Common Market Crisis of 30 June 1965* (New York 1967).

[37] For a discussion and reformulation of the "free rider problem," see Norman Frohlich and Joe A. Oppenheimer, "I Get By With a Little Help From My Friends," *World Politics*, xxiii (October 1970), 104-20.

attempted too frequently because of domestic reactions[38] and because of the potential reactions of other international participants.[39] An example of this is the case of the Paris Spring where workers joined in a student-led protest in order to extract benefits withheld by a government which wanted to spend more on defense and maintain a foreign policy of independence.

THE COSTS OF INTERDEPENDENCE: THE U.S. AND THE POLITICS OF CRISIS MANAGEMENT

French politics in the E.E.C. illustrate the opportunities for crisis manipulation in an interdependent world. The American position during the set of monetary crises which has occurred since the late 1960's illustrates the loss of U.S. control over foreign and domestic policies which has accompanied the growth of international interdependence. This loss of control also leads to a politics of "crisis management."

The recent currency crises can be viewed from several perspectives. First, for some, especially economists, the crises have represented a series of inevitable adjustments in the search for new sources of international liquidity.[40] Second, they can be seen as the result of the progressively declining ability of the U.S. government to meet its obligations to foreign holders of dollars. Third, they represent an attack on the United States and the role of the dollar. European governments have been increasingly unwilling to accept the trade-off between the efficiency of the gold-exchange standard and the status of the dollar as the major international currency on the one hand, and the injustice of the American government running a seemingly perpetual balance of payments deficit and the resulting "imposition" of inflation, unemployment, or economic stagnation on her trading partners on the other hand.[41] This attack has also reflected a shift in the balance of

[38] The role of domestic factors in crises cannot, in the present state of knowledge, be precisely determined. Governments can manipulate domestic opinion to a degree, especially in the short term, but the extent of manipulability is dependent upon many factors, including the political saliency of the issues involved. Moreover, once an interdependence is identified between some domestic factors and some external factors, a government may provoke an institutional crisis in order to achieve predominantly domestic ends. This is often the case, for example, when a government's legitimacy is at stake.

[39] A fourth reason, independent of the French case, might be given. This has to do with the bargaining position of "small" or "weak" parties over "larger" or "stronger" parties.

[40] For a review of this literature in predominantly economic terms, see M. O. Clement and others, *Theoretical Issues in International Economics* (New York 1967), 213-48.

[41] This is the view presented by Valery Giscard D'Estaing when he first was Finance Minister of France (1962–1966). It is summarized in Serge-Christophe Kolm, "La

economic power in the Atlantic world over the past twenty-five years.

A fourth and most important explanation is that these crises were a result of structural changes in the international monetary system related to the rapid growth of interdependence. In particular, these crises resulted from the increased mobility of capital in recent years and the growth in the Eurodollar market which could escape the jurisdiction of any of the Western governments. This increase in capital mobility represented more than a balancing between American long-term investments in Europe and short-term European loans to the United States. It represented a type of transnational interaction which served to break down governmental control over the foreign activities of citizens. It illustrates a type of interaction, carried out by citizens across international boundaries, which brings about situations in which governments are forced to act while their freedom to maneuver is restricted. This is especially the case in matters affecting the stability of currencies. As private transnational interactions have increased, the possibilities of affecting decision-making within a purely national setting, of isolation or encapsulation have become less likely. Therefore, control has become a more difficult problem, especially insofar as knowledge of the effects of interdependence is still limited.

In American and West European diplomacy crisis management in monetary matters involved the creation of new policy instruments. These instruments were usually created in *ad hoc* fashion when the "managers" of the international monetary system—central bankers, finance ministers and their deputies—met to patch up the crisis-prone system. New sources of credit were developed to cope with the loss of control over foreign exchange markets (which stemmed from the interdependency described above) and also to deal with a predicted slackening in the sources of international liquidity which were inadequate to meet the demands of the accelerating pace of global trade. The creation of these new instruments of control were directly related to the six currency crises which characterized the monetary system between November 1967, when sterling was devalued, and August 1969, when the franc was devalued. The problem of short-term capital flows, which are very difficult to control through the mechanisms of any national market, is crystallized in the Eurodollar market. This market of free-floating capital made up principally of the liquid assets of international banks and multinational corporations, expanded enormously

monétisation américaine du capital français," *Revue economique*, xviii (November 1967), 1038-57.

in the 1960's, especially during the last five years when volume rose from $13 billion to $60 billion.

Two sorts of arrangements were worked out to meet these crises by means of crisis diplomacy before the major crisis of summer 1971. On the one hand, there were special arrangements among the major mone-tary countries to lend capital to a country whose currency was in crisis. These were largely *ad hoc*. They included the Basle Arrangements created after the 1961 sterling crisis, the General Agreements to Borrow creating the Group of Ten monetary countries, and special bilateral swap arrangements and credits among central bankers. On the other hand, there were long-term plans negotiated throughout the 1960's which resulted, in 1967, in the creation of Special Drawing Rights (SDR's) in the International Monetary Fund. These were to supplement if not to supplant the dollar as a form of reserve asset or credit facility (depending on the political view of the country involved).

The international monetary system was made manageable by the coincidence of several factors. Most important was the preponderant strength of the United States which was able to provide the necessary material wherewithal and political leadership to enable all of the major Western industrialized states to overcome unanticipated crises. In addition, the U.S. government was able to occupy a pivotal position in the management of monetary crises because it consistently sacrificed domestic policy options in order to meet its international responsibility. The U.S. therefore was able to be the central arbiter and manager of the monetary system while other governments assumed a more passive stance in the system's management.

By summer 1971, however, the preponderant strength of the American position was significantly reduced. First, the U.S. was no longer in a position to provide the wherewithal to permit the system to function since it was no longer able to meet its outstanding obligations to the central banks of other states. Second, for the first time since Roosevelt's decision in 1933 to leave the gold standard, the U.S. took a major step affecting the stability of the international monetary system for primarily domestic economic and political reasons. American international obligations—including treaty commitments in the GATT—were sacrificed in the imposition of an import surcharge in order to help redress imbalances in the domestic economy and to secure the President's political position in the election campaign of 1972. Third, the U.S. began to relinquish the leadership role it had occupied for a generation as the most significant participant in the management and reform of the international monetary system. The government in fact asked the other industrialized states to take actions to rescue the system and, therefore, to come up with plans for its reform.

The crisis of the summer of 1971 therefore also reveals a basic paradox in the contemporary international monetary system. It first demonstrates the degree to which the U.S. government was forced to surrender control of the process of reform it had maintained during the previous decade. It also provides an index of the changing balance in economic power between the United States and the other advanced industrialized states. Third, it illustrates the way a government's decisional latitude may be reduced by external events—but also the way it may make decisions affecting the entire international monetary system for predominantly domestic political considerations. Finally, however, it demonstrates the central problem for crisis management at the present time. Even if the U.S. can no longer make decisions for the whole system, the system's operation depends upon the central role of the dollar. The system is also in need of leadership once provided by the U.S. and now apparently provided by no one. The paralysis of the U.S., in short, is now reflected in a paralysis elsewhere. While all of the major states in the system have become so interdependent that they cannot afford to see a dramatic change in it, such a change is needed if the growth in trade which it supports is to continue as it has since World War II.

SUMMARY AND POLICY IMPLICATIONS

I have argued that international economic interdependencies have increased in scope and significance, especially in the years after World War II. Although the result of a series of converging factors, these interdependencies stemmed especially from two sets of factors: from the increased sensitivity to external phenomena on the part of societies which have become highly industrialized and at the same time witnessed a radical centralization in international organization;[42] and, second, from conscious efforts on the part of decision-makers, especially in the industrialized states, to lower the barriers to international interchanges.

These interdependencies have been accompanied by benefits and costs to the citizens and governments of the societies involved. They

[42] This sensitivity has been exacerbated by technological changes which have increased the mobility of persons, of ideas, of goods and services, of monies, and of patents.

have facilitated an increased awareness on the part of individuals of the peoples and habits of other cultures and societies. And these changes have brought new opportunities for satisfying material wants that have, themselves, been part of the expectations of individuals in all modernized societies. But this increased interdependence has also brought new problems—problems associated not only with the regulation of interdependencies and the crises associated with them, but also problems associated with the loss of political autonomy. For, with interdependence has come a decreased latitude for governments to act to achieve domestic social goals, international goals, or even to regulate their interdependent relationships.

The importance of these interdependent relationships, especially in economic affairs, is that they have become highly political matters. They have been politicized not only for reasons already specified but also because economic affairs present possibilities for manipulation which are less dramatically costly than manipulation in military and security matters. This, in itself, has served to broaden the range of issues which have entered diplomacy in the industrialized states. Unlike security affairs where the stakes have been traditionally perceived as too high, governments have begun to use their new leverage over other societies to create a variety of effects, including some aimed directly at home.

Crises have occurred in international economic relationships in part as a result of these new opportunities for political payoff. But they would have occurred even had there been no de Gaulle on the scene to see the possibilities inherent in them. For at least in the contemporary international system, new forms of interdependence have arisen without the appropriate mechanisms needed to control them. Crises have arisen because national goals tend to conflict, especially as international interdependence has increased the contacts among societies. So long as there is no integrated supranational government, transnational or interdependent interactions serve to break down government control over the foreign activities of citizens. As transnational interactions increase, the possibilities of affecting decision-making in a purely national setting become less likely. And so long as governments will not relinquish their "sovereign" rights to autonomy, control remains even more difficult.

Increased control over interdependence effects is, however, only in part a function of new international agreements. The reform of the international monetary system brought about by the two-tier gold system and the creation of Special Drawing Rights only bought time—witness the most recent crisis.[43] *Ad hoc* arrangements have not yet served to centralize the international monetary system and thereby bring it under control. Increased control through new institutional arrangements is also a function of the recognition of interdependence and its various effects. This sort of knowledge will have to await further theoretical developments before its practical effect will become obvious.

Officials responsible for formulating and implementing governmental policies cannot, of course, postpone their actions until the day when new knowledge of interdependence is at hand. They must act to meet crises and to head off potential disruptions caused by international interdependence. But they need not face situations of uncertainty in a complete theoretical void. Some of the knowledge of interdependence already at hand can serve them well. Such knowledge, however uncertain and weak, is real knowledge. It can serve to sensitize officials to the reasons for which choices between incompatible goals must be made and the reasons for which a new range of issues has become politicized. And it can help them to understand why they will be unable to achieve an increasing number of objectives through independent actions.

Some of the actions which governments might consider undertaking in order to curtail the destabilizing effects of interdependence might be deduced from theoretical assumptions such as those outlined above. The central focus of those assumptions pertained to the relationship between policy objectives, or targets, and policy instruments needed to attain them. Interdependence, it was suggested, results in a significant loss of policy instruments relative to policy targets, at a time when the number and types of policy objectives have substantially increased. Two major types of choices are then available. The major political decisions to be made involve the appropriate mix of the two. On the one hand, new efforts, such as the creation of SDR's in the late 1960's, can be made to marshal new policy instruments for the attainment of existing objectives. Since these new instruments are likely to result from multinational diplomacy, and to involve some loss of national autonomy, they ought to be created from a perspective which takes into account long-term benefits and costs. On the other hand, a new, prudential statecraft is called for, one which establishes priorities among existing objectives and depreciates a few so that governmental control at the national level can be reasserted. This may involve the reimposi-

---

[43] See Robert Triffin, "The International Monetary Scene Today and Tomorrow," *Lo Spettatore Internazionale* [English Edition], v (July-December 1970), 375-90.

tion of barriers to international interchange, as governments adjust to the phenomenal rate at which such barriers have been removed in recent years. (For example, quotas might be imposed on particular items in order to protect domestic industry or import controls, along the lines of the quotas imposed by the British in the 1960's in order to head off the collapse of sterling.)

Since policy regulation of this sort must be directed toward a wide range of issues related to both international and domestic affairs, and to both economic and security matters, success will hinge upon the degree to which various kinds of efforts can be coordinated within governments. In recognition of the need for such coordination President Nixon established a cabinet-level Council on International Economic Policy early in 1971. It is this sort of agency which the governments of all the highly industrialized states ought to create. Such agencies should be responsible for long-range planning in foreign affairs related to the political economy of international relations. They should draw up both projections and contingency plans to meet crises stemming from international interdependencies and clarify those changes which affect the society's "political economy." In the American government, for example, the new Council should concern itself with projections concerning the future of U.S.-European relations following the enlargement of the Common Market, and to the question of what linkages between security and trade arrangements in Europe might exist after British entry into the EC. It also ought to concern itself with projecting shifts in European trade, or a U.S. trade shift toward Eastern Europe that might result from efforts at detente in Europe. What might, for example, be the economic and security consequences of a major reorientation of the Federal Republic in Europe? The political motivations and implications of such change are momentous enough to warrant long-term consideration.

Planning efforts are requisite to the reassertion of central national political control over the destiny of the industrialized societies. That they are needed can be deduced from the theoretical perspective discussed above. Their exact nature will depend upon the specific issues confronting governments, since our ability to theorize is not yet well enough advanced to isolate the relationships among particular variables. But no amount of political engineering through the creation of cabinet-level planning agencies will substitute for an understanding of the degree to which governments are able to manipulate different variables. To date, theory has advanced only far enough to offer a new perspective on international affairs. It is from that perspective that the crisis of national sovereignty seems to me to be most satisfactorily explained. It is likewise from the perspective of international interdependence that certain policy decisions can be taken. Depending on the values of the decision makers in office, it can be decided to maintain the status quo; to take steps toward increased international integration with the concomitant trade off between greater stability, greater wealth and less national control; or to reassert autonomy at the loss, in terms of national wealth, which such a move might entail.

ENTREPRENEURIAL POLITICS AND FOREIGN POLICY

By NORMAN FROHLICH and JOE A. OPPENHEIMER*

WHILE engineers, economists, and doctors can often prescribe a remedy for an undesirable situation by inference from a general theoretical construct, the architects of foreign policies rarely, if ever, have had such an advantage. Yet, the availability of a general theoretical construct could yield numerous benefits. To the degree that the theory were reliable and general, the foreign-policy maker would be able to deal with a wide range of concerns with confidence, at a minimum cost. For such a theory would allow him to know precisely what information would be needed to analyze the situation and how the information could be used to infer a prescription which would, with a high probability, get the desired results.

In what follows we will sketch a theory of politics based on the behavioral assumptions of economics. This theory treats political interactions as the relations between political entrepreneurs, who supply goods for gain, and their publics. The purpose here is not to formally derive hypotheses which will be of immediate application to the policy maker, but rather to indicate how this theory might be applied to situations of interest to the policy maker. We hope to show how the theory draws attention to a number of variables and to interactions which may prove important in specific applications.

The theory itself may be viewed as a further development within a family of theories which have in the past been applied to international politics. Theories about political phenomena, based on the assumptions used in economics, recently culminated in models treating strategic interaction. Indeed, the 1961 volume of *World Politics, The International System*, was largely concerned with the reporting and application of game theoretic models of strategic interaction to international politics.[1] The game-theoretic mode of analysis proved to be a useful basis for the construction of deterrence theory and policies. Thus, Bernard Brodie, Thomas Schelling and others quickly applied strategic

* We should like to thank Oran Young and Richard Ullman for reading and offering constructive criticisms of early drafts. We should also like to thank Carol Oppenheimer and Roberta Frohlich for evaluating and offering suggestions regarding revision of the situations treated. And finally our thanks are owed one anonymous critic for one good point.
[1] Klaus Knorr and Sidney Verba, eds., *The International System* (Princeton 1961).

analysis to the policy problems of deterrence, civil defense, disarmament negotiations, etc.[2] Along a different dimension, but within this general family of theories, another development took place. Mancur Olson, among others, advanced the theory of collective goods by applying it to the analysis of political behavior in general.[3] Our theory is related to the constructs of Olson, but differs in a number of ways.[4] Thus, what follows is best seen as a development within a larger, recognized theoretical approach, even though much of it will be reported so as to emphasize the unique findings and elements of the current theory.

In its present formulation, the theory is most applicable to international relations when the foreign policy objectives involve changing, or influencing, behavior internal to another state. Indeed, foreign-policy makers are most often concerned with the manipulation of behavior within other societies, and seldom, in practice, think of the international system as such. Thus, the perspective presented here is consonant with the orientation of practitioners and addresses itself directly to a number of policy concerns. To illustrate how the construct can be applied, we will sketch three rather specific situations, and then analyze each situation using this "entrepreneurial" theory of political behavior. In these applications we will try to illustrate the sorts of insights which the fully developed theory would be capable of yielding.

I. The Situations

Each of the illustrative situations which follows is simplified. Since the purpose here is to indicate the theoretical importance of some aspects of situations of interest to policy makers, such simplification is necessary. The examples are also specific. The specificity, however, should not be construed as implying that the theory is limited in application to such situations. Rather it should be viewed as a result of an attempt to treat cases which involve specific problems for the policy maker. For different purposes the theory can be applied to more general situations.

The first situation we will treat is one in which a number of societies could conceivably share the protection afforded by a single defense establishment. Such situations can and often do lead to the establish-

[2] In particular, see Bernard Brodie's *Strategy in the Missile Age* (Princeton 1959) and Thomas Schelling's *Strategy of Conflict* (Cambridge, Mass. 1960) for some of the more theoretical discussions. On the other hand, Thomas Schelling and Morton Halperin, *Strategy and Arms Control* (New York 1961) is a good example of applied theory of strategic interactions.

[3] Mancur Olson, Jr., *The Logic of Collective Action* (Cambridge, Mass. 1965).

[4] Differences in formulation between ourselves and Olson, *ibid.*, will be discussed in Sections II and III.

ment of a defensive alliance among nations. If the defense arrangements are to be realized, and maintained at reasonable levels, sufficient contributions from the alliance members must be received. There are, however, theoretical reasons which make the obtaining of such contributions problematic. What conditions are needed to insure that these contributions will be sufficient for the defense to be maintained at levels representing the needs of the citizens of the member societies?

Second, we will analyze a situation in which the political leaders of one country give aid to the government of a second country to increase its capacity to coercively mobilize resources. That is, foreign aid is being given to increase the recipient's capacity to collect taxes, to draft men into an army, or to extract payment of any kind.[5] What will be the secondary effects of such an attempt to increase the recipient's effective powers? How and when will such policies tend to change the stability of the recipient government? What factors might allow for prediction of these effects?

Finally, we will analyze a situation in which one country's leaders undertake a military intervention in another country to remove an unwanted opposition movement. Historically, such operations have often led to unforeseen difficulties and disastrous consequences for all parties involved. Is it possible to increase the foresight of the policy maker in such situations? What factors will increase the probability that such an operation will fail? Can one predict under what conditions the side effects are likely to prove most costly?

In the next section, we sketch a theoretical argument which can be used to show how certain general laws of behavior are common to all three situations. And we suggest how these laws may be used to infer policy prescriptions which would achieve the specific goals of the policy maker. But bear in mind that these are only a few examples of the range of phenomena amenable to such analysis.

II. A Sketch of the Theory

What follows is a sketch of an "entrepreneurial" theory of politics. Political leaders of states, and political sub-leaders inside states, are here viewed as individuals who provide goods outside of a market context for gain and profit. Such individuals, or political entrepreneurs, gain resources from other individuals, who are often, but not always, the citizens of the state. In talking about political entrepreneurs, it is

---

[5] Increasing tax collections, after all, was one of the major policy objectives in the Alliance for Progress and is a standard policy prescription given by the International Monetary Fund.

necessary to specify what motivates other individuals to give resources to the entrepreneur. Therefore, we begin our discussion by specifying our assumptions about the behavior of individuals in interactions with the political leader. This is followed by a sketch of the structure of the relationships between the leader and other individuals, showing how the leader obtains rewards from these relationships. We will then illustrate how these constructs may be used to analyze the situations described above.

The theory proposed for application to the above problems is based on a number of the behavioral assumptions used in theories of economic behavior.[6] Chief among these is the assumption that individuals behave rationally. For our purposes, rational behavior may be summarized as choosing the preferred alternative from the set of available alternatives.[7] It is assumed that individuals always choose in this way. To increase the explanatory power of this assumption, a number of further restrictions are made concerning individual behavior in situations of choice.

It is assumed that individuals are self-interested. That is, they do not make sacrifices to enable others to achieve preferred positions, unless such a sacrifice enables the sacrificing individual to realize preferred positions he otherwise could not obtain. That is, the individual is assumed to help others only instrumentally.[8]

We will be concerned with individual choice among alternatives

[6] Space does not permit anything approaching a full presentation of the theory which will be employed in deducing the specific hypotheses. Fuller treatment of the model appears in Norman Frohlich, Joe Oppenheimer, and Oran Young, *Political Leadership and Collective Goods* (Princeton 1971) and Frohlich and Oppenheimer, *An Entrepreneurial Theory of Politics*, unpubl. Ph.D. diss. (Princeton University 1971) [hereafter cited as *Entrepreneurial Theory*]. Here only a brief descriptive sketch of some of the assumptions and relevant variables is presented. The description of the theory presented here is done in a relatively non-technical fashion and all mathematical manipulations and symbolization have been omitted. Although the authors feel that the basic model can be applied to numerous political situations, not very many specific applications have yet been constructed. And in no case have the results yet been subject to empirical test. Such situations, of course, are not rare. For example, the models of deterrence and strategic interaction were not subject to great empirical testing until after their initial adoption for policy purposes. But such testing, we feel, is important and should have relatively high priority in future empirical work.

[7] More technically, an individual behaves rationally if he conforms to the following three conditions in choosing among alternatives: 1) the individual evaluates alternatives in his environment on the basis of his preferences, 2) his preference-ordering is transitive, and 3) he always chooses the alternative he prefers.

[8] The interested reader, who wishes to see how alternative assumptions might be used to construct choice models, is referred to Stefan Valavanis, "The Resolution of Conflict When Utilities Interact," *Journal of Conflict Resolution*, II (June 1958) 156-69. The article is suggestive of some of the difficulties which can be encountered through the employment of such assumptions.

involving risky or probabilistic outcomes. Thus, in evaluating alternatives, individuals will be concerned with taking into account probabilities associated with each of the possible outcomes. We assume that
individuals evaluate alternatives in an expected value fashion. That is,
the expected value of a risky outcome is the value placed on the occurrence of the outcome multiplied by the probability that it will occur.
The value of an alternative is the sum of the expected values of the
outcomes associated with the alternative.[9] These assumptions can be
used to derive hypotheses regarding the behavior of individuals in a
wide variety of situations involving choice. But to fully predict the
choices individuals will make in political situations, a few characteristics of these situations must be specified.

In general the political decisions of rational individuals involve giving
up something to gain something else. If the individual is rational, he
must feel that what he is going to receive is more highly valued than
what he is giving up. If this were not the case, the individual would
not choose to undertake the action.[10] We are primarily interested in
the behavior of individuals in groups: in their dealing with each other.
In these situations, rational individual behavior involves "exchanges."
That is, individuals give up things to others in exchange for things
which they prefer. In exchanges with political and economic entrepreneurs, individuals give up things to the entrepreneur in the expectation
that this will result in their receipt of a unit or object of utility. We
define this object as a *consumption unit*. In other words, what the
"consumer" receives, or expects to receive, in exchange for what he
gives up is a consumption unit. On the other hand, the object held by
the entrepreneur in the exchange relationship is defined as a *production unit*. The consumption of a good may entail the actual transference
of a production unit to a consumer. On the other hand, this need not be
the case. It may well be that providing consumption units merely en-
tails the granting of access to a production unit for a period of time.
Such access need not even preclude the simultaneous granting of access
to others to the same production unit. Thus, *granting consumption
units need not involve the transferring of production units*. What the

[9] The derivation of a cardinal utility scale with these characteristics was performed
by John von Neumann and Oskar Morgenstern, *Theory of Games and Economic Behavior* (2nd ed., Princeton 1946), and was summarized in Duncan Luce and Howard
Raiffa, *Games and Decisions* (New York 1957), chap. 2.
[10] The choice may be from among the lesser of two evils. Thus, for example, it is
conceivable that the rational individual in a prison chooses suicide rather than torture.
In *Leviathan*, Thomas Hobbes discusses rational choice under coercion at length in
chap. 21.

supplier is expected to grant, therefore, is a consumption unit. A consumer demands consumption units which are equal to or derived from production units.[11]

To analyze the "mechanics" of exchanges the theory employs an assumption regarding the behavior of the holders of the production units. It is assumed that these individuals are entering into the exchanges as profit-seeking entrepreneurs. Both economic and political entrepreneurs (or leaders) are described as having similar motivational patterns. They differ from one another due to differences in certain structural features of the exchanges in which they deal. Before analyzing these differences, however, it should be noted that the notion of entrepreneurial political leaders is not foreign to political analysis. Thus, a number of analysts, such as Edward Banfield, Richard H. Wagner, and others have utilized the concept in the informal treatment of political situations.[12] Recently, Albert and Raymond Breton and Robert Salisbury have utilized the concept in more formal constructions regarding political behavior.[13] Empirically, there is considerable primary and secondary literature to suggest that such a concept may not be inaccurate, and not culturally specific. Thus, for example, Karl Wittvogel, in *Oriental Despotism* utilizes (at least implicitly) such a notion of profit-seeking political leaders to analyze politics in ancient China.[14] Further evidence can be found in the studies of African tribes by Schapera[15] or in the analysis of big-city politics by Sayre and Kaufman.[16] To understand how and why the political enterpreneur differs from the economic entrepreneur, let us examine the structural characteristics of each type of exchange relationships. In general there can

---

[11] Paul Samuelson makes a similar distinction in "A Diagrammatic Exposition of a Theory of Public Expenditure," *Review of Economics and Statistics*, XLVII (November 1955) 350-56.

[12] Edward C. Banfield, *Political Influence* (New York 1961), chap. 8, and Richard H. Wagner, "Pressure Groups and Political Entrepreneurs," *Papers on Non-Market Decision Making*, 1 (1966), 161-70 (a review of Olson, fn. 3).

[13] Albert and Raymond Breton, "An Economic Theory of Social Movements," *American Economic Review*, LIX (May 1969), 196-205; also Robert H. Salisbury, "An Exchange Theory of Interest Groups," *Midwest Journal of Political Science*, XIII (February 1969), 1-32.

[14] Karl Wittvogel, *Oriental Despotism* (New Haven 1957), especially pp. 25-27 and 34-43.

[15] Isaac Schapera, *Government and Politics in Tribal Society* (New York 1956). (Pages are cited from the Schocken paperback edition, 1967.) An interesting comparison between tribal chiefs and Plunkitt of Tammany Hall may be made in this regard: see p. 75 of Schapera and p. 28 of William L. Riordon, *Plunkitt of Tammany Hall* (New York 1963).

[16] Wallace Sayre and Herbert Kaufman, *Governing New York City* (New York 1960). Here also, the modern-day entrepreneur can be compared with Plunkitt. See p. 542.

be shown to be two dimensions along which such exchange relationships can be differentiated. Both have important theoretical consequences.

First, one can differentiate exchanges with respect to the number of consumption units a given production unit supports. Whenever a production unit supports only one consumption unit, it will be referred to as a *private good* for the recipient of that consumption unit. If the production unit supports more than one consumption unit, more than one consumer can share the same production unit of the good. Whenever each of the consumers in a given group receives a consumption unit derived from the same production unit, that production unit will be defined as a *public good* for that group.[17] Whether or not a particular production unit, *capable* of supporting more than one consumption unit, actually is *used* to do so will be a function of the exchange relationships entered into by the entrepreneur who holds the production unit. Both economic and political entrepreneurs can supply public goods. Thus, for example, the economic entrepreneur who owns a movie theater can make money by selling tickets to the performance of a movie. As such, the performance is a public good to which consumers purchase access. Political leaders also can supply public goods. Thus, political leaders often engineer the supply of such public goods as defense, highways, and the like. But often these goods are not supplied in a manner such that each consumer can gain access to the good as an individual. This leads directly to our second line of analysis.

Exchanges can vary regarding the degree to which the consumption units are granted on an "individualistic" (or exclusionary) basis. If granting a consumption unit to one individual does not *ipso facto* change the probability that other individuals in a specified group will obtain other consumption units, then the exchange relationship is defined by us to be an individualistic one relative to that group. The good is (or goods are) *individualistically supplied*. If, on the other hand, granting a consumption unit to one individual directly results in granting a consumption unit to the other individuals in a specified group, the exchange is defined as a collective exchange for that group. The good is *collectively supplied*.[18] Economic entrepreneurs, those that

[17] The original distinction between public and private goods was implicit in the definitions made by Samuelson (fn. 11). There, and in an earlier article, "The Pure Theory of Public Expenditure," *Review of Economics and Statistics*, XLVI (November 1954), 387-89, he laid the ground work for the development of collective good theory.
[18] A far more detailed discussion of these distinctions is found in *Entrepreneurial Theory* (fn. 6), chap. 2. There the problem of mixed cases, and the nature of the dimensions are discussed. The collective-individualistic distinction was also introduced in Samuelson's articles (fns. 11 and 17). The distinction was first developed

derive their profits from the supply of goods in market contexts, never specialize in the supply of goods collectively. Such activity is characteristic of political entrepreneurs.

These two dimensions of variation yield four polar types of exchange relationships, two of which involve collective, and two of which involve individualistic supply of valuables. They are: the collective supply of private or public goods, and the individualistic supply of private or public goods. Perhaps the distinctions can be clarified by illustrating each of the forms of the exchange relationships.

An example of the collective supply of private goods is a foreign aid program (such as UNICEF or CARE), in which all individuals in a certain group are given food and medical treatment. The goods given to each individual require the transfer of substantive production units by the supplier. And the program is offered collectively to members of groups so that if one individual in a group, such as a tribe, or income stratum, receives consumption units so do the others. In the analysis of the illustrative situations we will use these structural characteristics to analyze taxation situations. A tax will be conceptualized as a payment made to avoid a private-good punishment which is collectively supplied to individuals who refuse to comply with the tax programs of the political leader.

An example of another polar case, the collective supply of a public good, is the supply of national defense. In the analysis which follows, military defense capability will be conceived as a public good collectively supplied to alliance members. Similarly, the alternative programs offered by a political competitor will be conceptualized as a public good, in terms of which all "citizens" receive consumption units.

Examples of the individualistic supply of public or private goods (the third and fourth polar cases) are given by the activities of economic entrepreneurs. These exchanges are illustrated by "market" transactions in which the individuals each give up something to receive a consumption unit for himself. Thus, for example, the individual who buys food

---

into a broad theoretical work of importance to political scientists by Mancur Olson (fn. 3). But it is clear that in his work, Olson was aware that the distinctions made by Samuelson needed further refinement. Olson was able to deal with the four types of exchanges by differentiating between what he called "exclusive" and "inclusive" groups. Exclusive groups are groups which in our terminology receive private goods collectively, while inclusive groups receive public goods collectively. The first attempts to improve upon the Samuelson definitions are by J. G. Head, "Public Goods and Public Policy," *Public Finance*, xvii (November 1962), 197-219. A fuller discussion of the relevant literature can be found in *Entrepreneurial Theory* (fn. 6), and in Carl S. Shoup, *Public Finance* (Chicago 1969).

for himself in a market is involved in an exchange relationship characterized by the individualistic supply of private goods. And as indicated in the earlier example of the movie house, the supply of public goods may also involve individualistic supply in a market context.

We would contend that the political process can be better understood by utilizing such a four-fold distinction of exchange relationships. The behavior of individuals in such a process is, in many ways, predictable, once the mechanics of each exchange type have been specified.

In the analysis of exchanges, and indeed, in defining the types of exchanges, we distinguished between the *role* of an entrepreneur and that of a consumer. A role can be defined as the set of costs, and benefits, that an individual can expect to incur by undertaking a specific activity. Thus for example, the rewards and costs that could be logically expected from undertaking to climb mountains define mountain climber roles. In certain roles, individuals may be expected to maximize the payoffs which can be associated with the role.[19] In the theory which we have developed we assume that individuals who occupy the particular roles which we analyze will maximize the payoffs associated with those roles. Although elsewhere we develop the analysis of exchanges without such role assumptions,[20] the notions of entrepreneurial and consumer roles are employed in the analysis which follows.

An entrepreneurial role can be conceptualized as the set of rewards and costs which an individual can expect to incur by supplying consumption units in exchanges. Combining this definition with the assumption that individuals in such roles behave to maximize the associated payoffs leads to considerable theoretical power. In economics, entrepreneurs have long been assumed to be profit maximizers. Economic entrepreneurial activity consists of supplying what usually are private goods in individualistic exchanges and receiving revenue through market sales. In economics, the entrepreneur is assumed to maximize the difference between the revenues he so obtains and the costs imposed as he acquires or manufactures his product. His revenues can be computed as the number of consumption units which are sold at each price times that price. Costs, in the private good case, can also be readily calculated as the total fixed costs of the business plus the costs associated with the actual production and delivery of the consumption units. In private good situations, the number of units which can be

---

[19] A discussion of the types of cases in which such an assumption is most likely to be successful would lead us too far astray for the purposes at hand.

[20] *Entrepreneurial Theory* (fn. 6).

sold will equal the number which are "produced." As may by now be apparent, entrepreneurial roles will look quite different in political, or collective exchanges. These differences are manifested in two ways.

First, in collective exchanges the entrepreneur must be concerned with the establishment of a mechanism by which the costs of supply can be shared by the consumers. If there is no arrangement for the beneficiaries to share the costs of these acquisitions, rational, self-interested behavior will lead to a sub-optimal level of supply.[21] As long as such arrangements do not exist, the maximum attainable level of supply will be that level at which the cost of an additional unit is greater than the value of the unit *to any one individual*. Even if the aggregate valuation by all the beneficiaries of the additional unit greatly exceeds the cost, without some cost-sharing arrangement, the additional unit will not be supplied.[22] This, quite obviously need not be a problem with regard to the individualistic supply of goods.[23] The political entrepreneur, then, can fulfill a necessary function, by providing a pooling mechanism for the resources to be applied toward the supply of consumption units.

Second, in political exchanges the revenues which an entrepreneur can receive will not be a simple multiple of price and quantity. It is the collective characteristic of the exchange undertaken by the political entrepreneur which changes the structure of his revenues. Rather than collecting a fixed price for each consumption unit delivered, the political entrepreneur would receive revenue in a very different fashion. If consumption units are being supplied collectively, then an individual can gain such units by the efforts of others: he can be a free-rider.[24] Since individuals can receive the consumption units without paying a "price" (indeed, at times without making any effort at all) the revenue of the entrepreneur must be collected independently of the delivery of the consumption units. These revenues can be in the form of a sum of contributions from individuals who feel that their contributions can make a difference with regard to the consumption units they

[21] Suboptimality (and therefore optimality) are defined in terms of Pareto's familiar criterion. An optimal situation is one in which no individuals can be made better off without at least one individual being made worse off (side payments included).

[22] For a particularly lucid, and brief, formal discussion of this problem, the reader can consult Mancur Olson, Jr. and Richard Zeckhauser, "An Economic Theory of Alliances," *The Review of Economics and Statistics*, XLVIII (August 1966), 266-79, reprinted in Bruce M. Russett, ed., *Economic Theories of International Relations* (Chicago 1968) 25-45. Page references are to the Russett volume.

[23] Note however that this problem can arise in situations involving externalities.

[24] For a fuller analysis of free-rider problems see Frohlich and Oppenheimer, "I Get By with a Little Help from My Friends," *World Politics*, XXIII (October 1970) 104-20.

expect to receive collectively, or in the form of payments made for other reasons.

Thus, to the extent that the political entrepreneur is relying on voluntary contributions made to fund the collective good, his revenues are not guaranteed, even if they are to be applied toward the supply of consumption units which the consumers desire. In calculating his revenue raising strategies, he must take into account the free-rider potentials of the group. His revenue stream will be jeopardized whenever individuals feel that their contributions cannot make a difference. But the individual's estimation of the difference he may be able to make in securing the supply of the good collectively will be a function of his expectations of the aggregate behavior of others.[25] The entrepreneur must try to so coordinate these expectations that he is able to raise sufficient revenue to make a profit, regardless of his program.

Revenue may also be raised by the threat to collectively supply a set of private goods which are negatively valued. Thus, for example, taxation can take on the characteristics of a collective exchange. The option chosen by the taxpayer determines the characteristics of taxation relations. If he chooses to evade his taxes he subjects himself to punishment. This punishment would be one of a set of negatively valued private goods collectively supplied to evaders. The political leader who supplies negatively valued consumption units collectively, attempts to receive revenue in exchange for alleviating the undesirable situation for the threatened individuals. Thus, the individual who chooses to pay his tax and avoid punishment enters into an individualistic exchange. He purchases egress from a group slated for punishment (i.e., he buys access to the public good of "safety"). Such taxation relations will share the characteristics of each of the exchange relationships involved.[26]

In summary, the revenues of the political entrepreneur will consist of donations and taxes. His costs are made up of the costs involved in collecting the revenues, co-ordinating individuals' expectations, and supplying the consumption units which make up his program. It is assumed that the entrepreneurial political leader maximizes the expected value of his profits (the difference of his revenues and his costs).

Consumer roles, which have been introduced in the description of entrepreneurs, are equally important theoretical constructs for the purposes of the theory. Such roles have long been analyzed in economics,

[25] *Ibid.*

[26] For a fuller discussion, see Frohlich and Oppenheimer, "Governmental Violence and Revenues," in Herbert Hirsch and David Perry, eds., *Political Microviolence* (New York, forthcoming).

but as might be expected, the political consumer differs considerably from his economic counterpart. From our analysis of the free-rider problem, it follows that the consumer need not spend his own resources to receive a consumption unit. Thus, the individual is faced with calculating what difference his contribution will make. His costs, as a political consumer, are the taxes he pays and the donations he makes. His benefits (which may be negative) are the consumption units which he receives.

This overly simplified portrayal of political behavior can be made considerably more realistic by introducing the possibility of political competition. The political entrepreneur faced with competition must now ask himself how the supply of consumption units, and the raising of revenue, relate to his chances of occupying the role in the future. On the other hand, given competition the political consumer must ask himself how he can best improve his situation. In these calculations, the consumer must decide how to affect the outcome of the competition, and hence what is the probability of his receiving the alternative consumption units constituting the programs of the competitors.

Other theorists have used similar, even if somewhat more restrictive, role constructs in the analysis of social behavior. Judging from those constructs, there appear to be no compelling reasons to believe that the political roles we have defined are likely to be less useful for theoretical analysis than the traditional roles posited in economic theory. After all, the traditional economic roles have already been shown to be special cases of a more general family of roles. Indeed, the analysis of other analytic role constructs employed to analyze political behavior can be derived as special cases of the roles we have defined. For example, the roles hypothesized by Anthony Downs in *An Economic Theory of Democracy* have been shown to be a special case of the more general political entrepreneurial role in Frohlich, Oppenheimer, and Young, *op. cit.*

Thus, the two dimensions of variation in exchanges which we have identified determine the structure of the relationships between the recipients, or consumers, of the goods and the suppliers of the goods. These constructs are translatable into models with wide applicability to political interactions. At this point, the reader may wonder how the above theory can be expanded to deal with international relations. To generate models which can be applied to the analysis of international politics there must be a number of leaders delivering programs to different sets of individuals. Relations between the leaders and their groups depend upon whether individuals can receive programs from more than one leader. Such cross-cutting membership can generate demands for program expansions to service the "customers" of other leaders. Such demands will often take the form of asking the leader of one group to introduce incentives for program changes within another political group.

Elsewhere, this theory has been developed to deal with a number of particular political phenomena.[27] Except for the illustrations found in this essay, the bulk of these analyses have been directed toward the explanation of political phenomena internal to a given society. We first analyzed the generation of political leadership roles and opposition roles as discussed in the context of the collective supply of public goods.[28] Other applications to internal politics have dealt with the organization of profitable coercive structures, the generation of political sub-leaders and sub-groups, and in a preliminary discussion the development of constitutional rules governing political processes. Preliminary applications to international politics have dealt with the generation of independent political structures, political migration, and arms races.

Having discussed in considerable detail the nature of the theory, it now remains to give some indication of the kind of theoretical leverage one might get over the illustrative situations, were the consequences of the theory fully worked out. The reader should keep in mind, however, that not all of the steps have been formalized. The illustrative "applications" which follow are best understood as "progress reports." As such, however, they should show that the theoretical models are not so abstract as to have no application to international relations. Indeed, we would predict that the theory will be able to be manipulated so as to yield guidelines for policymakers dealing with similar situations. However, at the current stage the illustrations merely show factors which the theory would point out for consideration by the policymaker as he plans to achieve his objectives.

III. Analyzing the Situations

A. alliance establishment and maintenance

In one of the first formal applications of "public-collective goods" theory, Mancur Olson, Jr. and Richard Zeckhauser analyzed the problem of cost sharing in alliances.[29] Their application is relatively straight-

[27] These applications can be found in Frohlich, Oppenheimer and Young (fn. 6), and in *Entrepreneurial Theory* (fn. 6).

[28] This analysis which antedates the current four-fold typology of exchange relationships can be found in Frohlich, Oppenheimer and Young (fn. 6), chap. 3.

[29] Other discussion of some of the points developed in Olson and Zeckhauser's work include Jacques van Ypersele de Strihon, "Sharing the Defense Burden Among West-

forward. After all, the purpose of many alliances is the collective provision of the public good of a defense establishment against some real or imagined foe. Ideally, in military alliances the military capacity of the partners is pooled against potential enemies. The common force of the group is thus expected to provide a higher level of security at a lower cost than each of the partners could secure individualistically.

Empirically Olson and Zeckhauser describe the NATO alliance mechanism as one in which changes in the military expenditures of the alliance are paid for by members individually. That is, costs of changes in defense levels (as opposed to benefits) are not shared by alliance members. Rather, the alliance's military expenditure is merely the sum of each individual partner's military budget. If the alliance obtains another unit of defense capacity, therefore, it must be that some one government has paid for it. More technically, the nations never share the marginal costs of changing force levels. The collective supply of defense, and the absence of marginal cost sharing, lead to two major difficulties regarding the supply of defense to the alliance.

First, there is potential for free-rider behavior on the part of alliance partners. Each partner may have a strong temptation to limit his contributions, hoping that the pooled contributions by the other alliance members will be sufficient to furnish an adequate defense for all. Because the defense is to be collectively provided, he would get a free-ride and be protected without paying a portion of the burden. This type of free-rider behavior could appear in any alliance designed to provide a common defense. Thus, the interactions in SEATO, the Warsaw Pact, NATO, etc., offer potential scope for such behavior.

Second, without some arrangement to share any costs of changes in the level (i.e. marginal costs) of defense, then the level of defense supplied will always be suboptimal. Once the member with the highest valuation of defense provides force levels consonant with its valuation, other members would have greatly reduced incentives (in terms of the desire for a common defense) to provide additional force levels.

These characteristics are used to derive a number of consequences for alliance maintenance. Two of the most important are:

1) Those nations which most value the goods being supplied collectively by the alliance will have to bear a disproportionate burden of the costs of the alliance.

ern Allies," *Review of Economics and Statistics*, XLIX (November 1967), 527-36, and "Explaining the Difference in the Relative Defense Burdens Borne by the NATO Allies," *International Studies Quarterly*, XII (No. 4, 1968). Also see Olson and Zeckhauser's "Collective Goods, Comparative Advantage, and Alliance Efficiency," in R. N. McKean, ed., *Issues in Defense Economics* (New York 1967).

2) The goods being supplied by the alliance will be suboptimally supplied.

But, as is pointed out, this mechanism for furnishing the requirements of an alliance does not extend to all physical needs. In particular, Olson and Zeckhauser found that in NATO expenditures for infrastructure (i.e., physical plant, common bases, etc.) marginal costs of additional units are shared, according to negotiated percentages.[30] Under this type of cost-sharing arrangement, the disproportionality and suboptimality associated with other types of expenditures appears to be constrained. With regard to infrastructure payments, the smaller members do not exhibit a disproportionate shirking of payments. This leads Olson and Zeckhauser to conclude that the suboptimal supply and disproportionate burden problems of other expenditure can be remedied by the extension of the institutional arrangements which govern the cost sharing of NATO infrastructure to other sectors of the alliance.[31]

As would be expected given the basic similarity of approach, many of our conclusions are similar to theirs. In particular, we would agree that the free-rider problem is central to the analysis. The sharing of the costs of additional units of defense capability is necessary to overcome this problem. However, if one adds the entrepreneurial element discussed above, it is possible to extend the analysis.

Indeed, the existence of political entrepreneurs in our theory leads us to identify the changing factors in terms of which the leader will calculate costs and benefits. It also leads to an identification of additional necessary conditions for the eradication of suboptimality in the supply of defense capability to NATO in particular, and in the supply of benefits through alliances in general. The leaders of nations may be conceptualized as political entrepreneurs who supply goods to their populace for their own gain. Defense is only one of the goods provided by the leadership. If our assumptions are valid, the primary concern of leaders is the overall size, and security of, their own private gain. Their valuation of defense in these instrumental terms will differ from any overall societal valuation of defense.

It is true by definition that if "suboptimality is typical of international organizations (and alliances in particular), it is possible to design policy changes which would leave everyone better off, and which accordingly may have some chance of adoption."[32] But, if the supply of goods, is in fact, so suboptimal as to cover transaction and institutional "start-up" costs, our theory would indicate that some entrepreneur would capi-

---

[30] Olson and Zeckhauser (fn. 22), 41.
[31] *Ibid.*, 43-45.   [32] *Ibid.*, 45.

talize on this situation. New arrangements to decrease the suboptimality (including marginal cost sharing) should, after all, hold a profit. All would theoretically gain from such an enterprise. It is at this point that the overall concerns of the political leader might allow us to identify the referents in terms of which the leader makes his cost-benefit calculations. The suboptimality in international alliances is calculated by Olson and Zeckhauser in terms of the value of a collectively supplied public good to each society as an aggregate, and to the defense community as a whole. The persistence of the "suboptimality" indicates that these suboptimal arrangements may be optimally profitable to the political leaders in terms of their overall concerns in maximizing their surplus over a whole range of activities. Insofar as the overall profitability of each leader's operation causes his valuation of defense to diverge from that of the society, and from that of other leaders, we would expect many foreign policies to exhibit great resistance to changes (in alliances and organizations in general) directed toward the attainment of societal optima.

In their analysis, Olson and Zeckhauser assume a utility function for the public good in terms of which decisions are made. They then argue that *without* marginal cost sharing the state acts to have such expenditures on defense as are needed for the marginal utility given by this function. We would argue that the cost-benefit calculations are *never* made with direct reference to the issue of societal optimality. Given that the leader's major revenue sources are coerced (i.e., taxation), his programs will reflect the means by which he is able to hold down competitive challenges to his position. Furthermore, his programs will reflect the interests of those individuals who make supplementary donations. In general, the *aggregated* social benefits enter into the leader's calculations only in terms of the threats of competitors and the threat of massive rebellions which would disrupt his tax mechanisms (i.e., only in terms of threats to his utility income stream). If we consider that the start-up costs of competition vary from society to society, the possibility of any particular issue being raised will be a function of whether the programs of the opposition can be so constructed to solicit sufficient support to cover the entry costs of the opponent. Thus, if an issue (such as defense) became salient amongst the citizenry, we would expect the increased profitability of the issue eventually to motivate the leadership to remedial action.

At times of great military threats, therefore, we would expect that the suboptimality reflected in alliances would tend to be overcome. At such times it would likely become profitable to institute cost-sharing arrangements, and the leadership would respond.

Three factors emerge out of this analysis. First, if "good alliance partners" are those who will help shoulder the burden when the need is greatest, states in which there is potential for political competition at relatively low cost would make the best allies. Second, although Olson and Zeckhauser's recommendations are necessary for optimality, structural changes must be made with regard to the incentives faced by the domestic political leaders if a social optimum is to be approached. And finally, because the political leader can find the military useful also for the maintenance of tax revenues and the suppression of opposition, we would expect that the total defense budget would more often reflect these interests than the defense needs of the citizenry. Thus, from the point of view of the citizenry, there may be supraoptimal supply of military capacity. Pulling these together: insofar as the alliance can meet its objectives by the maintenance of conventional multi-purpose forces in times of peace, then partners who can be expected to maintain high force levels, for whatever reason, would be useful to an alliance. (Three NATO countries whose defense budget, as a percentage of GNP, were higher than predicted by Olson and Zeckhauser, were Turkey, Greece, and Portugal.) On the other hand, to the extent that the alliance requires mobilization of forces in times of common threat, then those countries in which the costs of competition are low are the more useful partners.

From this we can conclude that any policy which is designed to increase the supply of goods in alliances in general must take careful cognizance of the effects of such changes on the overall activities of the political leaders and their competitors. Policies designed to reach some sort of optimal supply in terms of overall alliance needs must structure recommendations so that the changes suggested give the leaders incentives to have the good supplied in line with societal valuations and alliance needs.

But the divergence between societal valuation of defense and the value placed on defense by leadership in the context of its overall profit structure, is only one type of potential disagreement between entrepreneurs and consumers. Where the leadership coercively extracts resources from individuals other areas of tension are introduced. An international input in this area is likely to have significant consequences for the relationship of the leadership to the public. These consequences are analyzed in the next illustrative "application."

B. FOREIGN AID FOR RESOURCE MOBILIZATION

The second situation is one in which aid is given to the leadership of a country to increase its capacity to coercively mobilize resources. Before analyzing this situation in detail, it might be useful to indicate the range of phenomena which can be subsumed under this general rubric. Any exchange which involves the use of coercion to extract resources of any kind from individuals may be defined as a form of taxation.[33] Thus, forced conscription of manpower, whether for military service, cutting cane, working on roads, or whatever, may be viewed as taxation. In this section we will be concerned with showing the internal effects on a government's likelihood of staying in office after outside aid increases the government's capacity to tax (broadly defined). What, for example, might be the long-range effects on support for the Saigon regime of their increased capacity to enforce military conscription? And what are the likely reactions of the population to the outside power which made this possible?

To examine these questions, however, taxation must first be formulated as an exchange. And political opposition must be analyzed in terms of entrepreneurial behavior. As was discussed earlier, a tax may be conceptualized as an exchange. The entrepreneur can impose a sanction (or punishment) on an individual if he fails to surrender a specified set of resources (the "tax") to the leader. To tax, therefore, the entrepreneur, or leader, needs a coercive apparatus capable of inflicting punishments on individuals who fail to pay the tax. If the leader has a coercive capacity (the ability to deliver a set of punishments which can be viewed as a stock of negatively valued private goods) which is larger than the number of individuals from whom he is demanding a tax, the interaction between the taxer and the individual subject to the tax is relatively straightforward. If the punishment threatened is more disliked than the payment of the tax, the individual will pay the tax. If not, he will withhold payment and suffer the punishment. But when a leader demands tax payments from more individuals than he can punish, the situation is more complex. In such a situation if enough people refused to pay, some persons would escape punishment. The evading individual would not necessarily be punished. From his perspective, the leader would only be able to deliver the punishment on a probabilistic basis. Thus, the payment of taxes could be viewed as the individualistic purchase of access out of (or egress from) a group of evaders who would receive a sanction probabilistically. The leader would have a set of

[33] Frohlich and Oppenheimer (fn. 26).

private goods (sanctions) which would be probabilistically supplied on a collective basis to the individuals who did not purchase egress.[34]

For any individual, the expected valuation of the sanctions would be a function of how many individuals he thinks will evade the taxes. That is, the individual evaluates the severity of the leader's threat by estimating the probable behavior of others subject to the tax program. If the individual felt that the number of others likely to refuse payment would be greater than the coercive capacity of the leader, the threat of expected punishment would be diminished. Evading taxes, therefore, can contribute to a decrease in the probabilty of punishing each evader. Such a deterioration of the value of the leader's threat is collectively supplied to everyone who evades. If the leader is forced to revise his tax demands, even those who pay may be future beneficiaries of the others' evasion. Thus, the leader who attempts to tax more individuals than he could conceivably punish may face a situation involving potential evaders. Indeed, it is important for him to coordinate the expectations of the individuals from whom he demands taxes so that they do not contribute to his demise as a tax collector. His subjects must be led to believe that their fellows are likely to pay, and that consequently each is likely to be punished if he refuses payment.

The leader who wishes to tax more individuals than he can punish may use a variety of devices to persuade the citizenry not to evade *en masse*. For example, he may use tax revenues to supply a number of positively valued programs. This would increase the expected utility of paying taxes. And if he supplies such programs he can further increase the incentives to pay taxes by including the denial of access to positively valued programs in the punishment threatening evaders. Since the leader is usually trying to tax a larger number of individuals than he is capable of punishing, such incentives are likely to be quite common.[35]

But before we can specify the relationship between outside aid which increases a government's coercive capacity, and the government's likelihood of remaining in office, we must also analyze how a government loses its position to a competitor.

Examining opposition it is clear that political competitions are won and lost, at least in part, as a function of the relative strengths of the

[34] In *Entrepreneurial Theory* (fn. 6), we have shown that the price set by the leader for egress will be such that each individual will either buy guaranteed egress, or none at all. Chapters 8 and 9 deal extensively with taxation.

[35] Here our formulation diverges from Olson's in *The Logic of Collective Action* (fn. 3). Rather than viewing taxation solely as a mechanism used to engineer the collective supply of valuables, we view the supply of valuables as a potential buttress to a profitable taxation apparatus. Both directions in the relationship are possible.

competitors (in terms of arms, money, votes, and other resources). Therefore, any opponent of the leadership will need to collect resources. One way to do this is to promise alternative programs to the citizens, programs which at least *some* prefer to those of the government. Such a preferred alternative can be used to motivate individuals to contribute resources to help their preferred competitor win.[36] These programmatic promises can be conceptualized as public goods collectively supplied to members of the society if and when the competitor becomes leader. As such, the exchanges in which the opponent participates are analytically similar to those of the established leadership. Both engage in exchanges centered around the supply of political programs, i.e. collective supply of consumption units to subsets of the population in exchange for contributions. The motivation is profit from the exchange.

Citizens contribute to the entrepreneur of their choice with much the same motivation as they contribute toward the supply of a collective good. They contribute to the competitor to make a difference. Moreover, the difference which they hope to make can be of two types. First, the contributing citizen may make a donation to affect the probability of the outcome in the competition. Thus, if the citizen prefers one competitor's program, he may contribute to increase the preferred competitor's chances of victory. Second, the citizen may contribute to have a competitor remove, or avoid, potentially onerous programs, or to have him add programmatic promises which are particularly desirable from the individual's standpoint.[37] When the citizen contributes in this fashion, the contribution may even go to the less "preferred" competitor. For example, a landlord in a rural hamlet in South East Asia may donate to a pro-land reform faction in order to receive special treatment, although he prefers the government. He might do this even though the contribution would help the faction in its competition with the government.[38]

[36] The discussion of opposition and political competition here is necessarily abbreviated. For a fuller discussion of the mechanisms and relationships which obtain, the reader may refer to chapters 3 and 4 of Frohlich, Oppenheimer, and Young (fn. 6) and chapter 11 of *Entrepreneurial Theory* (fn. 6). The sketch above, at least superficially, resembles the analysis by Anthony Downs, *An Economic Theory of Democracy* (New York 1957). There he described the motivation of the politician as vote maximizing. Our formulations are quite different. The politician is assumed to maximize expected profits. This means, for example, that an opponent may well find permanent installation as an opponent to the established leadership a profitable venture, even if he never wins the leadership position. Other differences are discussed in Frohlich, Oppenheimer and Young (fn. 6).

[37] Interest groups are infamous for their donations to political parties to have certain issues avoided or taken up.

[38] Such a donation may be analytically similar to a tax payment where the pro-

The analysis can be summarized by noting that contributors enter into exchanges with political competitors. They give up valuable resources to gain valued changes in programs and changes in the outcomes of the competition.[39]

When an outside power attempts to increase the leadership's capacity to coercively extract resources a number of consequences for the internal politics of the country follow. Some of these consequences will buttress the government's base of support in the country, others will damage it.

One of the sources of revenue to the competitors which might bear on the outcome of the competition will be the tax revenues collected by the government (and in some cases the opposition also). To the extent that this is true, one immediate and obvious consequence of increasing the government's ability to coercively extract resources would appear to be an increase in the government's likelihood of holding office. But such a simple conclusion is somewhat premature.

True, the value of "taxes" extracted by the government will rise in the short run. But if the leadership's ability to punish tax evaders is increased, and no supplementary programs of positive value are added to augment those already provided, potential support for the government will be eroded among some groups and *among all other groups there will be no counterbalancing increase of support.*

Individuals who, before the increases in the punishment capacity were content to evade and take their chances at being punished, would now find the government's new capacity threatening. If the leader's new level of threat leads them to place an overall negative valuation on the government, they would be increasingly willing to expend some resources to remove the government. This would be true also of those who became taxpayers because of the added threat of punishment. Those who were taxpayers before the government increased its coercive capacity would not be directly affected.

But the disaffection among those who had heretofore been evaders has certain implications regarding the potential organization of an opposition. The more the tax collection mechanism has been improved, the more individuals would be willing to donate to have the leadership .

---

grammatic purchase by the individual is the avoidance of a negatively valued private good.

[39] Note that we here assume the competition is a two-way struggle between the faction and the government. This is done to simplify the analysis and the presentation. Of course, although we are discussing donations here the members may also be taxed by the leadership and the opposition. In this analysis, however, we will focus on the basis for voluntary support for the competitors.

removed. And remember, many of these are individuals who could have been counted on to support the leadership before it increased its tax capacity. Thus, a program which increases the leader's potential to tax without requiring other changes in the overall programs of the leadership runs the risk of generating whole new classes of potential opposition supporters.[40]

The opponent, however, like any political entrepreneur must be able to overcome the free-rider tendencies in the population if he is to take advantage of this improved situation. Thus, he must be able to make individuals feel that he is likely to obtain sufficient support to make a contribution from them worthwhile. In this matter, the improvement of the leader's coercive mechanism helps him in one way and hinders him in another. These improvements help the opponent if individuals perceive that their fellows will be more inclined to support a movement to displace the leadership. However, given the leader's increased level of revenue and the decreased level of evasion, individuals may be less sanguine regarding the opposition's ability to effectively utilize whatever resources it can obtain in the competition with the leadership.

But regardless of the outcome of these cross-cutting tendencies, such an aid program, if unaccompanied by concomitant changes in other government programs, will increase the potential resource base for opposition. Consequently, if the coercive capacity of the leadership in a country is to be increased by aid, precautions must be taken. The increase in coercive capacity should be tied to increased programmatic incentives for those who would be affected by the tax, or there will be potentially a generation of support for opponents to the regime. Moreover, in the absence of government programmatic incentives and to the extent that the increased coercive capacity is directly related to outside aid, those who seek support from the populace against the government have incentives to include, in their programs, policies antipathetic to those outside interests. Thus, the opponents can be expected to attempt to agitate the populace against the outside source of aid.

Finally, it should be noted that such unwanted effects are most likely in precisely those cases where outside aid may appear to be most useful: namely in situations involving high levels of evasion and low levels of valued governmental programs. For the larger the level of tax eva-

---

[40] In a similar fashion, an outside power attempting to increase the disposable resources available to the government by ending "petty graft and corruption" in the machinery of the state runs the risk of alienating the lower level operatives of the state from the leadership. Some compensating support may be generated among those who bear the cost of the "graft," however.

sion, the larger the proportion of the population to be affected by such increases in the government's efficiency of tax collection. Furthermore, the fewer the positively valued programs of the government, the more potential there is for this change to turn former evaders into an active opposition.

It is precisely in cases in which governments have been weak, inefficient, and unresponsive, that foreign aid programs have been directed towards these objectives. Thus, aid programs in these situations would do well to insure the supply of supplementary positively valued programs if the foreign policy objective is to support extant governmental structures.

C. INTERVENTION TO REMOVE AN OPPOSITION MOVEMENT IN ANOTHER STATE

The final case to be analyzed is concerned with outside military intervention to remove the opposition movement to an incumbent government, when that opposition has programs which are viewed as undesirable. Given the view of political competition sketched above, we can examine the likely effects of a military intervention to remove an opposition viewed as undesirable by the intervening country's leadership. How might such interventions affect the domestic political system? Historical experience regarding United States military interventions in Latin America (Cuba, Dominican Republic) and recent interventions in South East Asia indicate that a variety of problems for domestic political life are raised by such interventions. Here we will try to identify some relationships between outside interventions and changes in the internal political climates of the intervened state, and how these changes might subsequently affect the intervening power itself.[41] Let us examine the sources of revenue for the faction, analyze under what circumstances the military intervention can decrease, and can increase, that flow of resources; and analyze how this will affect the competition[42] between the government and its besieged opposition.

Consider first the effects of the intervention on the general citizen. Insofar as the competition between the government and the opposition

---

[41] Military interventions in one particular state may be undertaken in part for their effect on other interests of the intervening power. We will not treat these effects here. Rather we will concentrate on internal consequences of the intervention and how these might affect future interactions between intervenee and intervenor.

[42] Here we will discuss the potential revenue which the leadership of the faction's replacement could command were it successful in coordinating the expectations of potential followers. Later we will discuss some of the problems that the leaders must overcome to realize this revenue potential.

utilized resources which the population would prefer turned to other purposes, and insofar as this competition decreased the probability that either side would be able to deliver the programs promised, the population might welcome the demise of opposition. But this is only one side of the coin. Although the removal of the opposition may appear to place the government in a better position to deliver the programs promised, it may actually decrease the government's incentives to deliver them. The reasons for this are not hard to find.

Insofar as the government relied on voluntary contributions for some of the resources needed for competition they might be expected to make programmatic promises to individuals to obtain resources from them. And if the competition were to extend over time, they might be expected to deliver some of the promises. The removal of the opposition, however, will remove some of the government's immediate incentive to actually deliver the programs promised.

Even if the government is aware of the potential consequences of its own unresponsiveness for potential opponents it will find policies of exploitative unresponsiveness profitable under specifiable conditions. Insofar as intervention does not impose great costs to the leadership of the intervened state, reliance on such outside aid for continued tenure of office could be an extremely lucrative mode of operation.

The main factor working in this direction will be the overall change in the government's constituency due to the intervention. Having militarily intervened in the internal affairs of the society, and having eliminated the opposition, the intervening power presents the government with a potentially cheap source of support in future competitions. Insofar as the government is able to convince the intervening power that future opposition movements have the same undesirability as the one just eliminated, they might rely on continued outside aid to secure their tenure in office. Indeed, they will have incentives to reassure the outside power that such oppositions are present. If successful, they can rely on outside aid for continued tenure of office, and continue to be less responsive to programmatic demands placed on them by their domestic constituency. Some citizens may find such decreases in governmental responsiveness more than offset by the insurance of the continuity of the government secured by the intervention. But decreases in the value of programs provided by the government will lose the government the support of others. To the degree that their interests are damaged by the government's lack of responsiveness, these citizens would identify their former higher level of benefit with the existence of an opposition. Such individuals will have increased incentives to support a replacement movement. Moreover, since the deterioration of their position can be traced to the actions of the intervening power, they have increased incentives to support programs opposing future intervention. Thus, the intervention could result in an increased pool of support for oppositions. If, on the other hand, the government were not to renege on its previous promises, if it continued to deliver the programs, new support for opposition would not be generated in the society. Thus, if the intervening power is unable to preserve governmental responsiveness to programmatic demands, then the intervention will increase the potential pool of support for future opposition movements.

But shifts in preferences due to possible changes in programs will not, by themselves, guarantee an increased profit to the leader of a potential replacement opposition movement. As already discussed one problem faced by an entrepreneur who wishes to supply any good collectively (e.g. a set of alternative policy promises) will be overcoming the potential free-rider effect. He must insure that enough individuals feel sufficiently effective to contribute to achieve the supply of the good. If the potential resources available to a would-be leader of a new movement were shown to be increased, he would have an added incentive to coordinate the expectations of potential followers. However, the intervention also places a number of obstacles in his path. He must, for example, lead the people to believe that future interventions are not likely to succeed.

To the extent that government responsiveness to citizen demands is not decreased by the intervention, an increased support for oppositions will be avoided. But as indicated above, the government apprised of the willingness of the outside power to intervene, and remove certain undesirable oppositions, would have incentives to cut back on program expenditures and rely on the outside assistance to remain in office. And the government would have an incentive to insure that any opposition which did appear be viewed as undesirable by the outside power. Indeed, the government might even indirectly tolerate and encourage undesirable oppositions to insure the continuance of outside support. In this regard their desires become antithetical to those of the outside power which is interested in eliminating all such oppositions.

Thus if undesirable opposition movements are to be eliminated, some method of preserving government responsiveness to citizen demands must be found. Any threat by the outside power to withdraw support from the government (unless suitable programs are instituted) is likely to lack credibility in the absence of other factors. That is, the government would not believe such threats if the only alternative government which might be placed in office by the institution of the threat is an undesirable opposition.

Thus if the outside power is to exercise leverage over the policies of the government a credible alternative must exist to the incumbent government. Thus the policymaker in the outside power interested in reducing future support for undesirable opposition movements would find himself in a seemingly paradoxical position after a military intervention. In order to maintain the responsiveness of a government on whose behalf the intervention took place, some form of acceptable opposition movement is needed. Indeed, it may be necessary to fashion such an opposition movement. For only if the government's responsiveness is maintained can the outside power be reassured that additional support for an undesirable opposition is not being generated.[43]

There are, however, some conditions under which the considerations sketched here will not be crucial. For example, it is sometimes the case that one's objectives in intervening are transitory. That is, it may be that the removal of a faction is done only for temporary gain. In such cases, intervention by the military can assure the attainment of the objective. And the potential political shifts in the intervened country need not be considered as important. Rarely, however, is intervention posited only on such narrowly defined and transitory goals.

The costs may also be low if the present government is extremely popular among survivors, and if there is reason to believe that it will remain responsive to its citizenry. This is most likely to occur when the faction being considered for elimination is extremely unpopular. In such situations, however, it is usually not necessary to intervene unless there is considerable external support for the faction.

Finally, as was suggested above, the possibility of future difficulty may be avoided even if the preferences of the people shift radically against intervention, so long as the population views itself as being unable to affect the situation. Logically, it is possible for this to occur. But with increasing communication, and decreasing costs of transportation throughout the world, it is hard to imagine a country which could not form an alliance with a second outside state to prevent sub-

---

[43] The difficulties of instituting such a policy should not go unnoticed. Chief among these is the difficulty of insuring that the opposition supported by the outside power does not attempt to capture the support of those in the society who favored the movement removed by the intervention by including its undesirable policy stances in its programs. And of course the difficulty of supporting an opposition movement to a government which is being supported, in itself, is a nice feat.

sequent interventions. Were this done, maintaining the potential to intervene is likely to prove ever more costly.

IV. Conclusion

Having briefly discussed the theory employed in this essay, and having sketched how it might be applied to a few specific types of situations, we now summarize the implications of the analysis for the foreign policymaker.

First, it should be apparent that no specific policy recommendations can be derived from the relatively informal arguments regarding the situations treated. But it should also be apparent that a fuller and more formal application of the theory could produce interesting and valuable hypotheses. And indeed, there are strong reasons to believe that such results will be forthcoming. Economics is the only area of the social sciences in which large numbers of reasonably reliable predictions regarding social behavior have been accumulating. Economics, built on rationality models, offers a wealth of theory containing laws held with high levels of confidence. Any theory which attempts to explain political phenomena, which has predictions which overlap *in any particular* with the predictions of economic theory must, in those particulars, yield the same, or more accurate predictions. Political theory which yields predictions of an economic nature *must be consistent with verified economic theory*. In our discussion of exchange relationships we have indicated the interface and overlap of economic and political phenomena. And the theory sketched here proceeds in a direct fashion from that overlap.

Thus, as a first order of business we would urge further work on the completion of the formal theoretical model. Despite the apparently pedestrian nature of such an appeal for "further work," in the absence of formal theory which has been tested with some rigor, any attempt to derive quick and easy policy implications are premature.

But beyond a mere appeal for a further development of the theory, even at this stage there are indications of the sorts of data which need to be gathered to test the consequences of such a theory and to specify the relevant parameters needed for specific applications of the theory.

If political leaders obtain profit from the supply of sets of goods, then more data on these goods should be gathered. Of course, data does exist on goods such as education, health care, taxation, public facilities, and so on. But almost invariably these goods are recorded in terms of their costs of supply. Insofar as goods are supplied outside of market mechanisms, the costs of supply do not indicate the aggregate valuation placed on the goods provided. Particularly when a good is a public good, and many individuals get consumption units collectively from the same production unit, the cost of the production unit furnishes a poor measure of societal valuation of the good. Yet the degree of societal contentment with the government depends not necessarily on the amount of expenditure by the central government, but upon the valuations placed on the goods provided. More data are needed on both the valuations placed on, and the distributions of, goods provided outside market interactions.[44]

But even in the absence of hard data on these matters, the entrepreneurial approach presented here, with its emphasis on the entrepreneurial role in overcoming strategic interaction problems and furnishing goods for gain, is useful. Given that foreign policies are frequently concerned with changing the course of events in other countries, this perspective helps to identify the variables and the interrelationships which could determine the effects of such policies. By drawing the foreign policymaker's attention to these variables, we identify an area for inquiry, and a theoretical approach to that area, from which numerous predictions and prescriptions could be derived.

[44] Mancur Olson, Jr. discusses some of the factors bearing on such data in *Towards a Social Report* (Washington 1969). See also Raymond Jackson, "A 'Taxpayer's Revolution' and Economic Reality," *Public Choice*, x (Spring 1971), 93-96.

THE PERILS OF ODYSSEUS:

On Constructing Theories of International Relations

By ORAN R. YOUNG

CONFUSION and misconceptions about the state and nature of "theory" have reached monumental proportions in the field of international relations. This situation is debilitating both because it misleads academics and policymakers alike about the contributions that can be made by theorists of international relations and because it operates to set back serious efforts to pursue theory in the field. Accordingly, I write in an effort to cut through some of this confusion and to set the problems of constructing theories about international phenomena in perspective. Specifically, I wish to explicate the following theses in these pages:[1]

1. There is no viable theory in the field of international relations. The few logical models that do exist at this time fare very badly in terms of the criterion of predictive accuracy.

2. Most current efforts in the field (even those that are self-conscious about the *goal* of theory) are not moving toward the development of viable theory. And many of them may well be hampering the theoretical enterprise.

3. Policymakers should not expect to receive much help from theorists of international relations, at least not in the short run. Policymakers should probably take a friendly view of theoretical work in this field, however, on the same grounds that basic research is supported in other fields.

4. Those who wish to pursue the development of theories of international relations should forget about the problem of "relevance," at least in the short run. If their efforts should lead to major successes, there is little doubt that their products will find a receptive audience quickly enough.

---

[1] Most of the discussion in this essay is relevant, *mutatis mutandis*, to the whole field of political science. Since my principal concern here is international relations, however, I will not emphasize this point explicitly in my argument.

THE THEORIST'S GAME

The term "theory" has been used so imprecisely and indiscriminately by social scientists that it is in danger of losing any meaningful content.[2] In this essay, however, I wish to employ the term in a specific and precise sense. A theory is a set of general statements such that: (1) some of the statements (the assumptions or premises) logically imply the others (the theorems), and (2) the theorems can be cast in the form of falsifiable predictive statements about the real world.[3] Lest anyone be misled, let me emphasize immediately that there is an important and well-known distinction between the processes through which a theory is created and the statement of a theory in terms that make it possible to evaluate it for logical truth, predictive accuracy, and so forth. This is the distinction Karl Popper has made famous in the phrase "conjectures and refutations."[4] Scientific creativity is a process about which remarkably little is known, but it is of crucial importance in the selection and conceptualization of topics for research, the formulation of specific logical models, and the invention of theorems within the framework of any given model.[5] The statement of a theory in formal terms, on the other hand, is a process that has been analyzed in great detail and that has led to the formulation of elaborate rules of logical and empirical procedure.[6] This imbalance of knowledge about the evolution of theory may account for the widespread tendency (at least among social scientists) to overemphasize the formal rules of logical and empirical procedure at the expense of recognizing the central role of the creative process in the development of viable theory. In fact, however, what makes the scientific enterprise such a delicate one

[2] For a helpful discussion of some of the meanings associated with the term "theory" see Anatol Rapoport, "Various Meanings of 'Theory'," *American Political Science Review*, LII (1958), 972-88. And for an instructive discussion that includes comments on some of the meanings attached to the term "theory" by European writers see W. G. Runciman, *Social Science and Political Theory* (Cambridge 1965).

[3] For good introductory discussions of the formal implications of this definition of theory consult, *inter alia*, May Brodbeck, "Explanation, Prediction, and 'Imperfect' Knowledge," in May Brodbeck, ed., *Readings in the Philosophy of the Social Sciences* (New York 1968), 363-97, and Carl G. Hempel, *Philosophy of Natural Science* (Englewood Cliffs 1966).

[4] Karl R. Popper, *Conjectures and Refutations: The Growth of Scientific Knowledge* (New York 1963), esp. 33-65.

[5] For an account that stresses some of these subjective elements in the construction of theories see Michael Polanyi, *Science, Faith, and Society* (Chicago 1964).

[6] Any well-known text in philosophy of science will serve as an introduction to these rules, even though there are various significant issues on which the leading scholars in this field disagree. Consult, *inter alia*, Carl G. Hempel, *Aspects of Scientific Explanation* (New York 1965); Ernest Nagel, *The Structure of Science* (New York 1961), and Karl R. Popper, *The Logic of Scientific Discovery* (New York 1959).

is that it is based on a remarkable balance between highly unstructured creative processes and highly disciplined adherence to a variety of formal rules of logical and empirical procedure. Under the circumstances, it is hardly surprising that major theoretical advances are somewhat unpredictable in all fields and that they are major events in any area of scientific endeavor.[7]

In sharp contrast to other epistemological postures, the criteria in terms of which scientific theories should be judged, once they have been stated in formal terms, are distinct and relatively precise. The theorems of a scientific theory must be derivable as logical truths from the model upon which the theory is based.[8] The predictive statements derived from the theorems should correspond with empirical observations based on some identifiable universe of cases in the real world.[9] Naturally, this is a yardstick that allows for considerable variation. But, in general, the greater the correspondence, the better the theory. And in the case of theories that yield non-probabilistic theorems even a single counter example is sufficient for falsification.

Beyond this, theories are often judged in terms of the criterion of parsimony, or, the ability to explain the maximum number of phenomena with the minimum number of assumptions or premises. This is a measure of the power of a theory, as well as a critical practical issue from the point of view of facilitating logical manipulations. A single parsimonious theory may well yield the same amount of explanatory leverage as several theories that are less parsimonious.[10] Next, theories are often judged in terms of the notion of "heuristic fruitfulness."[11] Thus, a theory that does not itself yield accurate pre-

---

[7] This point is explicated in a particularly suggestive fashion by Kuhn. See Thomas S. Kuhn, *The Structure of Scientific Revolutions* (Chicago 1962).

[8] For an introductory discussion of modern logic see John G. Kemeny and others, *Introduction to Finite Mathematics* (2nd ed., Englewood Cliffs 1966), 1-57. Suggestions for additional readings in this area can be found on p. 57.

[9] Whether or not the logical model associated with a theory actually mirrors reality in some objective sense is a subject of considerable controversy, much of it metaphysical in nature, among philosophers. But this issue is not relevant to the argument set forth in this essay.

[10] Parsimony has two distinguishable manifestations. First, in the case of two theories designed to explain the same phenomenon, the one that requires the smallest number of assumptions and/or premises is superior in terms of parsimony. Second, all theories gain in parsimony to the extent that they are able to explain the maximum number of different phenomena in terms of the minimum number of assumptions and/or premises. In both cases, however, parsimony has to do with minimizing the formal apparatus of one's model while expanding explanatory leverage to the fullest extent possible.

[11] See, for example, Carl G. Hempel, "The Theoretician's Dilemma," in Hempel (fn. 6), 173-226.

dictions may nevertheless play a key role in facilitating intellectual progress by suggesting or precipitating the development of additional theories that do produce good predictions.[12] Finally, logical constructs are sometimes praised as sources of insight concerning complex problems even when they do not yield accurate predictions. This is obviously a less precise criterion than some of the others associated with the evaluation of theories. But the employment of logical constructs in the search for insights is of some importance in generating interest in the theoretical enterprise in fields that have not yet produced a corpus of viable theories.[13]

It is often pointed out that these criteria do not support a precise dichotomy between theory and non-theory and that theoretical efforts in all fields vary substantially in these terms. This is of course true. The field of biology, for example, has only recently begun to produce theories that stand up really well in terms of the criteria discussed in the preceding paragraph. And there is a great deal of interest in physics at the present time arising from the predictive failures of existing theoretical models. But it is important not to carry this line of thinking to extremes. It is exceedingly difficult to justify the term "theory" for a set of propositions that cannot be logically derived from the model (if any) with which they are associated, though there are many cases in which lengthy formal proofs are not needed. Similarly, a set of logically impeccable theorems which fail to predict anything is of little value as an end in itself, though it may play a role in stimulating further theoretical developments that do have predictive value.[14] In fact, the history of advanced scientific disciplines is littered with models of this type, many of which are never even recorded.[15] In short, the construction of theories that fail is easy to justify in terms of the apparent dynamics of the process of scientific creativity. There is, however, no point whatsoever in clinging to theories that obviously are not viable in terms of the criteria of logical truth or predictive accuracy.[16]

[12] For an argument along these lines that is particularly relevant to the social sciences see Anatol Rapoport, *Two-Person Game Theory* (Ann Arbor 1966), pp. 186-214.

[13] For clear statements of this view consult *ibid.*, chap. 12, and Rapoport (fn. 2).

[14] This is a key point of divergence between non-empirical disciplines such as logic and mathematics and all of the empirical disciplines.

[15] In some parts of physics, for example, theorists come up with sophisticated mathematical models on a day-to-day basis, but the great bulk of these models are discarded almost as quickly as they are formulated.

[16] There is some debate among scientists about the exact point at which a theory should be discarded for lack of predictive accuracy. It is sometimes argued, for example, that if a theory is sufficiently elegant and aesthetically pleasing, it should be pursued, at least for a while, even in the face of negative empirical evidence. And the example of the ultimate vindication of the Copernican system of astronomy is often

What can a viable theory do for the policymaker? The actual functions of theories are often grossly exaggerated, but even when treated
realistically they are of great importance. To begin with, the development of viable theories is the best procedure available for those who
wish to make accurate predictions, whether in the physical sciences or
in the social sciences.[17] And the ability to make accurate predictions
is often of obvious and critical importance in efforts to make policy
choices successfully. Even more important, viable theories often make
it possible for man to manipulate his environment by specifying what
he should do in order to achieve particular results. This is not of course
true of all theories. We have an excellent theory of the dynamics of
the solar system, for example, but very little ability to manipulate any
of the variables at the moment.[18] Moreover, it is possible to argue that
man's ability to manipulate his environment has led to more harm than
good in various substantive areas. This is obviously a matter deeply
affected by normative concerns, but it is an issue frequently raised with
respect to fields, such as nuclear physics, which have enjoyed great
theoretical successes in recent times. Nevertheless, the great *practical*
contribution of scientific theories derives from the fact that they constitute man's most important tool in manipulating his environment to
achieve his own ends, whatever those may be.

Given this somewhat lengthy introduction, let me comment upon
the development of theories concerning international phenomena. In
the field of international relations, no matter how broadly defined, very
few efforts have been made to construct formal theories,[19] and the few
efforts that have been made do not stand up well in terms of the criteria of evaluation discussed in the preceding paragraphs. In fact, the

---

cited in support of this position. In the context of the present discussion, however, this
is a nuance that should not be allowed to obscure the point that models which fail the
test of predictive accuracy should not be retained indefinitely.

[17] In accordance with the general orientation of my argument, this paragraph
stresses the potential functions of theory for policymakers. There are, of course, other
functions of theory which have little bearing on the problems of policymaking. The
very act of constructing theories, for example, is regarded by many theorists as a re-
warding process in itself. Moreover, many investigators pursue the development of
theories from an interest in explanation rather than prediction, even though the
logical status of explanation and prediction is treated as identical by most philosophers
of science.

[18] Note, however, that the theory of the dynamics of the solar system has considerable practical value because it allows man to manipulate his own behavior in the
light of predictions concerning the behavior of the solar system.

[19] Not only is the intellectual tradition in this field heavily nontheoretical, but also
those who have provided financial support for research on international questions
have seldom displayed a serious interest in the development of viable theories.

relevant efforts are so few in number that they can be easily identified
in the context of this discussion.

1. A number of scholars have worked on the problem of constructing
formal models of arms races. Most of these efforts stem from the pio-
neering work of Lewis F. Richardson, who attempted to model arms
races in terms of pairs of differential equations based on a small number of parameters characterizing the actors involved in such races.[20]
Richardson's analyses were based entirely on simple stimulus-response
(or "reaction-process") models that paid no attention to the internal
decision-making processes or to numerous internal characteristics of the
actors involved. It is no doubt for this reason that the Richardson-
process models of arms races have not produced highly accurate predictions of real-world events in those few cases where they have been
cast into empirically falsifiable form. Richardson's work has been carefully explicated by Anatol Rapoport,[21] and the various efforts to build
on the suggestive foundation constructed by Richardson are summarized in a recent essay by Peter Busch.[22]

Some years ago Martin McGuire made an effort to construct formal
models of arms races which go considerably beyond the Richardson-
process models in dealing with the internal characteristics of the actors
involved.[23] McGuire's work is based on the explicit assumption (among
others) that the behavior of the actors will conform to the formal
postulates of rationality, as that concept is generally employed in economic models.[24] Although this work represents a distinct advance over
the original Richardson models, it is based on a set of assumptions
that make its formal conclusions applicable only to special cases which
are difficult to match in terms of real-world events, and the model
requires further development if it is to yield falsifiable predictive statements.

2. The other major stream of formal analysis relevant to the field of
international relations is the theory of games. Game theory is a general

[20] Lewis F. Richardson, *Arms and Insecurity* (Pittsburgh and Chicago 1960).
[21] Anatol Rapoport, "Lewis F. Richardson's Mathematical Theory of War," *Journal of Conflict Resolution*, 1 (September 1957), 249-99, and Anatol Rapoport, *Fights, Games, and Debates* (Ann Arbor 1960), Part I.
[22] Peter Busch, "Mathematical Models of Arms Races," pp. 193-233 in Bruce M. Russett, *What Price Vigilance?* (New Haven 1970).
[23] Martin McGuire, *Secrecy and the Arms Race* (Cambridge, Mass. 1966).
[24] Briefly, rationality can be defined in terms of the following conditions: 1) the actor evaluates alternatives in his environment on the basis of his preferences among them, 2) his preference ordering is consistent and transitive, and 3) he always chooses the preferred alternative.

rubric that subsumes a number of formal models, many of which are carefully formulated and sophisticated in mathematical terms.[25] In essence, however, all of the models of game theory deal with the problem of rational choice in situations involving interdependent decision-making, or strategic interaction between or among purposive actors.[26] The usefulness of game theory for the analysis of international phenomena, nevertheless, is severely restricted. Game-theoretic models fail to produce predictions that correspond at all well to outcomes in the world of international relations.[27] This means that the theory has no descriptive value in this field even though it may be regarded as normatively or heuristically significant. Next, many important international phenomena cannot be adequately represented in terms of the models of game theory. For example, the impact of imperfect information, role conflicts, and indeterminate numbers of strategies, all of which are characteristic of many international interactions are difficult to represent in game-theoretic models. This does not mean that the models of game theory cannot have heuristic value in the field of international relations, but it does limit their practical applicability severely. Game theory also abstracts away many important substantive problems in the field of international relations by assumption. To take a single clearcut illustration: all of the manipulative aspects of international bargaining are left out of game-theoretic models.[28] Finally, as Anatol Rapoport has effectively shown, efforts to analyze international problems in terms of the models of game theory frequently lead to serious distortions of reality rather than to useful insights.[29]

[25] There is now a large literature on the theory of games. A lucid review that is still highly relevant is R. Duncan Luce and Howard Raiffa, *Games and Decisions* (New York 1957). For a more recent overview that is quite sensitive to the difficulties of applying game theoretic models to problems in the field of international relations see Rapoport (fn. 12), together with his *N-Person Game Theory* (Ann Arbor 1970).

[26] Strategic behavior is the behavior of an individual member of a group which involves a choice of action contingent upon that individual's estimates of the actions (or choices) of others in the group, where the actions of each of the relevant others are based upon a similar estimate of the behavior of group members other than himself. Strategic interaction is the set of behavior patterns manifested by individuals whose choices are interdependent in this fashion.

[27] In fact, game theoretic solutions do not even correspond well to empirical outcomes in highly restricted experimental situations. For a helpful discussion of this subject see Anatol Rapoport and Carol Orwant, "Experimental Games: A Review," *Behavioral Science*, VII (January 1962), 1-37.

[28] For discussions of manipulative bargaining see Thomas C. Schelling, *The Strategy of Conflict* (Cambridge, Mass. 1960), and Oran R. Young, *Bargaining* (Princeton Center of International Studies 1970), mimeo, Part IV.

[29] See especially Anatol Rapoport, *Strategy and Conscience* (New York 1964), Parts I and II.

3. Several analysts have attempted to adapt or extend Richardson-process models or game-theoretic models to deal with various substantive problems that manifest themselves within the sphere of international relations. Kenneth Boulding has worked on a general theory of conflict that is based on a set of Richardson-process models and employs some of the conceptual structure of game theory.[30] Similarly, William Riker has formulated a theory of political coalitions by introducing additional assumptions to fill a number of gaps in the analysis of N-person interactions left by the theory of games.[31] Both Boulding and Riker have displayed some interest in applying their theories to the analysis of specific substantive problems within the field of international relations. And both theories have produced perspectives on international phenomena which seem heuristically interesting. These efforts are subject to most of the general criticisms set forth in the preceding paragraphs on arms-race models and game theoretic models, however. And presently they are highly underdeveloped for application to specific problems in the field of international relations. Consequently, while these theories deal with important issues and come off relatively well in terms of the canons of modern logic, in the sphere of international relations they have yet to produce much in the way of falsifiable predictions that correspond well with real-world outcomes.

Beyond these efforts, there is little else that deserves to be placed under the heading of formal theories about international phenomena. There are, however, several theoretical leads, developed largely in other fields, which might be brought to bear on topics within the realm of international relations. A number of aspects of international relations can be conceptualized in terms of problems associated with the supply of collective goods.[32] There are some models of bargaining (other than those stemming from game theory) which could be applied to international relations, though little systematic work has in fact been done

[30] Kenneth Boulding, *Conflict and Defense* (New York 1962).

[31] William Riker, *The Theory of Political Coalitions* (New Haven 1962).

[32] A collective good is any good that cannot be withheld from any member of a specified group once it is supplied to some member of the group. For an interesting, if somewhat preliminary, attempt to construct a theory of alliances based on the concept of collective goods see Mancur Olson, Jr. and Richard Zeckhauser, "An Economic Theory of Alliances," *Review of Economics and Statistics*, XLVIII (August 1966), 266-79, and Olson and Zeckhauser, "Collective Goods, Comparative Advantage, and Alliance Efficiency," in Roland N. McKean, ed., *Issues in Defense Economics* (New York 1967), 25-63. For another analysis of collective goods that could be applied to issues in the field of international relations see Norman Frohlich, Joe A. Oppenheimer, and Oran R. Young, *Political Leadership and Collective Goods* (Princeton 1971).

along these lines.[33] Various scholars have referred to the possibilities of adapting some of the existing stochastic-process models and learning models for the analysis of international phenomena. But it is difficult to point to systematic examples of such adaptations.[34] Some recently developed concepts associated with the analysis of complex organizations and bureaucracies might be profitably utilized in coming to grips with the interactions among collective actors which are a central feature of international relations.[35] But, here again, no formal efforts along these lines have been undertaken so far. Finally, it is worth emphasizing that it is difficult to find any indications that entirely new models are being constructed explicitly for the analysis of international phenomena. This need not, of course, be a bad thing.[36] Nonetheless, it is an interesting reflection of the heavily non-theoretical tradition in the field of international relations.

There is a common tendency in many fields to talk about the development of viable theories as though this were the only objective worth pursuing. This view is clearly false, unless the term "theory" is defined so indiscriminately that it encompasses all worthwhile intellectual operations. Starting with the definition of theory employed in this essay, for example, it is possible to distinguish a variety of useful activities that can be pursued without developing viable theories. Consider the following cases by way of illustration.

Sensitization. It is often of great importance to emphasize concepts, questions, facts, points of view, or diplomatic alternatives that have previously been ignored or de-emphasized, even if this does not lead to important developments in the realm of theory. After all, these are the factors that determine what people think about and which issues they regard as significant. In the field of international relations, this is

[33] For a discussion of these models consult Young (fn. 28), esp. Part II.

[34] For some interesting efforts to construct models of this kind within the general conceptual framework of game theory see Anatol Rapoport and Albert Chammah, *Prisoner's Dilemma* (Ann Arbor 1965). Hayward Alker, Jr. is also interested in the development of models of this kind. See, for example, Hayward R. Alker, Jr. and Cheryl Christensen, "From Causal Modelling to Artificial Intelligence: The Evolution of a U.N. Peace-Making Simulation," to be published in Jean LaPorce, ed., *Experimentation and Simulation in Political Science* (forthcoming).

[35] For a survey of relevant material on complex organizations see James G. March and Herbert A. Simon, *Organizations* (New York 1958). For preliminary efforts to move toward logical models of bureaucratic behavior consult Gordon Tullock, *The Politics of Bureaucracy* (Washington 1965) and Anthony Downs, *Inside Bureaucracy* (Boston 1967).

[36] That is, there may be excellent reasons to treat the problems of international relations as special cases of more general theoretical constructs, rather than develop entirely new theories of international relations.

an important justification for the current growth of interest in studies of "transnationalism" and "bureaucratic politics."[37] Neither transnational activities nor bureaucratic politics are actually new phenomena in the realm of international relations. Nevertheless, there is good reason to believe that both areas deserve greater attention than they have received in recent years.

Conceptualization. Everyone views the real world in terms of some conceptual framework or approach to analysis, even if such a framework is disjointed or never made explicit.[38] Fundamentally, a conceptual framework determines what a person regards as worth explaining and what factors he will look to in the search for explanations. Such frameworks may have a variety of additional consequences especially insofar as they are based upon analytic and substantive presuppositions, incorporate normative orientations, and are affected by cultural biases. In international relations, for example, it makes a real difference whether an individual conceptualizes the world in terms of the tenets of idealism or the tenets of realism.[39] And the formulation of a new conceptual framework is a major event in the sense that it may exercise a formative impact on people's thinking for years to come. It is probably true that the basic conceptual frameworks of high level policymakers are relatively impervious to pressures for change. But every policymaker must acquire his conceptual frameworks at some earlier stage. And it is well known that students are frequently highly suggestible with respect to these conceptual issues. Consequently, teachers of international relations regularly exercise a substantial (if delayed) influence on policymaking by controlling the first word rather than the last word on the subject.

Factual assessment. In a great many cases, policymaking is heavily dependent upon answers to purely factual questions that have little if any bearing on the development of viable theories. Consider the following examples: Was the insurgency in South Vietnam in the late

[37] On transnationalism see Robert O. Keohane and Joseph S. Nye, Jr., eds., *Transnational Processes and International Organization*, a special issue of *International Organization*, xxv (No. 3, Summer 1971). On bureaucratic politics see Graham T. Allison, "Conceptual Models and the Cuban Missile Crisis," *American Political Science Review*, LXIII (September 1969), pp. 689-718, and Richard Neustadt, *Alliance Politics* (New York 1970).

[38] At a minimum, a conceptual framework, or an approach to analysis, is an interrelated set of concepts (with their definitions), variables, and assumptions or premises. For an elaboration of this concept with reference to the field of political science see Oran R. Young, *Systems of Political Science* (Englewood Cliffs 1968).

[39] For a good introductory discussion of these approaches consult John H. Herz, *Political Realism and Political Idealism* (Chicago 1951).

1950's substantially engineered from Hanoi?, Is the Soviet Union presently deploying or developing any new weapons systems that might threaten the second-strike capability of American strategic forces? These examples illustrate the complexity, as well as the importance, of simple factual questions in the policymaking process. In the realm of international relations, apparently simple questions of this kind are notoriously difficult to answer, especially when they ask for facts about motivations as well as information about physical capabilities.

Simple generalizations. There are many situations in which simple generalizations are helpful even if they have no explanatory value. If one knew, for example, that the Russians could always be counted on to adhere to formal treaty commitments, this would be a highly useful piece of information for dealing with policy questions even if one could not explain their behavior. A special form of the simple generalization is the constant conjunction which sometimes emerges from statistical analyses. This knowledge may permit reasonable projections (in contrast to formal predictions). Thus, it may be quite helpful in dealing with certain policy questions to know that there is a high correlation between economic underdevelopment and authoritarian government. Note, however, that the danger of spurious correlation associated with all such constant conjunctions makes it hazardous to rely on them for predictive purposes, let alone for manipulative guidelines.[40]

Correction. Non-theoretical analyses are sometimes helpful in identifying simple generalizations which are erroneous, even though they actually serve as informal guidelines for policymaking. Suppose, for example, that policymakers operate on the premise that there is a strong positive connection in the countries of the third world between the probability of large-scale civil strife and the strength of indigenous Communist movements. If this simple generalization is incorrect (as it almost certainly is), it may well be possible to establish its shortcomings on the basis of empirical analysis without developing a theory of insurgency or civil strife.

Extrapolation. There are situations in which it is possible to extrapolate future trends purely by examining past behavior and assuming the future will be like the past. Extrapolative techniques have recently become quite fashionable in a number of fields, though they cannot be regarded as yielding theory except in the context of simpleminded models whose central assumption is that the future will be a straight-

[40] The practical value of projections derived from constant conjunctions will generally increase as a direct function of the lack of predictions based on viable theories.

forward (e.g., linear) continuation of the past.[41] Population projections, for example, are often made on this basis, and it has recently become popular to project the economic future of countries like Japan on the basis of extrapolations from growth rates over the last ten or fifteen years.[42] It is clear that projections of this kind are sometimes helpful as guidelines for policymaking, especially in areas where there is no viable theory. Nevertheless, the shortcomings of these techniques of projection and forecasting are notorious. This is particularly the case with respect to a variety of subjects that are of interest to the field of international relations and do not appear to operate in terms of simple linear or exponential dynamics. Even with respect to the specific examples referred to above, there are numerous factors that may prevent populations or economies from continuing to grow in the future at the same rate, or on the basis of the same pattern, they have exhibited during the recent past.

Each of these activities represents a significant alternative (or supplement) to the construction of viable theories. Various mechanisms of snobbism have prevented these other activities from acquiring the prestige often associated with theory. They do not offer the predictive and (sometimes) manipulative power of viable theories. And nothing anyone can do, especially in the realm of verbal status seeking, will turn any of these activities into serious theoretical endeavors. Let me repeat, however, that these activities are important and worthwhile. They offer the most useful results that policymakers dealing with international problems are likely to get from outsiders in the immediate future. Their status should be increased. And these activities should no doubt be separated from the pursuit of theory in order to avoid perpetuating the hopeless confusion concerning the nature and state of theory in the field of international relations.

Tormentors of Odysseus

Although I have argued strongly that the field of international relations is strikingly underdeveloped from the point of view of constructing viable theories, this should not be taken as a general indictment of

[41] That is, some may wish to regard these techniques as being based on theories since it is possible to achieve logical closure through the simple procedure of assuming that the future will be like the past and that intervening factors are irrelevant. Even if this argument (which is not very persuasive) is granted, however, there is still the problem that predictions derived from such models do not fare very well in most areas within the social sciences.

[42] For a variety of examples along these lines consult Herman Kahn and Anthony J. Wiener, *The Year 2000* (New York 1967).

those who have labored in the field. Not only is it true that many students of international relations have not been particularly interested in the development of theory, there is also good reason to conclude that the subject matter exhibits some characteristics that inevitably generate severe challenges for theoreticians. A discussion of international relations in terms of several important conceptual distinctions originating in the field of economics will serve to clarify this latter point.

The international system exhibits several of the generic characteristics of an oligopoly, as that term has been employed in the field of economics.[43] Thus, it involves competitive-cooperative interactions among a limited number of purposive actors who have some capacity to communicate with each other. Each of the actors is a relatively complex collective entity whose external behavior is often hard to capture in simple models. The number of the actors in the system is virtually always greater than one. But the number of actors is small enough so that every actor can interact with the others as differentiated entities, rather than having to interact with all of the others together as an aggregated and undifferentiated environment.[44]

The fact that the international system displays these generic characteristics of an oligopoly generates both advantages and problems for the analyst. On the positive side, it means that a fair amount of the conceptual apparatus, and some of the ideas for analytic models, associated with the study of oligopolistic markets can be profitably brought to bear on the analysis of international interactions.[45] At the same time, however, it is important to recognize that oligopoly problems and the study of imperfectly competitive markets in general constitute a notorious weak spot in the development of economic theory. It is widely agreed that the crucial sources of this weakness in economic theories of oligopoly derive from those features of oligopoly which are also displayed by the international system. Accordingly, the fact that the international system exhibits a number of the generic characteristics of oligopoly can be expected to pose serious challenges for anyone interested in constructing viable theories about international relations.

Let me be a little more precise concerning the major analytic problems shared by students of oligopolistic markets and international in-

[43] For clear definitions of the key concepts associated with oligopoly and imperfect competition in general in the field of economics see Paul A. Samuelson, *Economics* (5th ed., New York 1961), chap. 25.

[44] Thus, in economic relationships, oligopoly covers the ground between monopoly on the one hand and perfect competition on the other.

[45] For a good introduction to the study of oligopolistic markets see William J. Fellner, *Competition Among the Few* (New York 1949).

teractions. To begin with, the phenomenon of strategic interaction, or interdependent decision-making, is a major feature of the interactions among the actors in both arenas.[46] Also, a variety of problems connected with imperfect information, and the necessity of making choices under conditions of uncertainty, affect the external behavior of actors in international politics in much the same way that they affect the behavior of firms in oligopolistic markets.[47] There are of course numerous analytic techniques that make it possible to cope with the problems of strategic interaction and imperfect information in a logically satisfactory fashion. And it is certainly true that actors in various arenas continue to make decisions even when they are confronted with problems of strategic interaction and imperfect information. Nevertheless, we have yet to construct logical models capable of dealing in analytic terms with the problems of strategic interaction and imperfect information and capable of producing reasonably accurate predictions concerning real-world occurrences. This is a severe problem in the context of oligopolistic markets. And we have hardly begun to address it seriously in the context of international interactions.

Beyond this, all of microeconomics is based on the assumptions: 1) that individual members of the collective entities called firms will behave in a rational fashion and 2) that the behavior of the members of any given firm can be aggregated in such a way as to form a unified utility function for the firm as a whole which is both consistent and transitive. In practical terms, these conditions have been translated into the assumption that individual firms behave rationally (as integrated entities) in such a way as to maximize their profit.[48] In the field of economics, this set of assumptions has increasingly in recent years come under attack from analysts who point out that many firms are not, in fact, integrated entities and that their behavior in the market is often a function of complex internal interactions.[49] And nowhere is this problem more prominent than in oligopolistic markets which are characteristically dominated by a small number of large firms whose behavior is exceedingly difficult to interpret in terms of the postulates of rational utility maximizing. The resultant difficulties are of great im-

[46] For an extended discussion of strategic interaction and the analytic problems it raises see Young (fn. 28), General Introduction.

[47] For a study of international relations by an economist who emphasizes this link see Schelling (fn. 28).

[48] For an introductory discussion of the application of this assumption to the decision-making problems faced by typical firms see Samuelson (fn. 43), chap. 24.

[49] For a discussion of many of the issues raised by this perspective on the behavior of the firm see Richard M. Cyert and James G. March, *A Behavioral Theory of the Firm* (Englewood Cliffs 1963).

portance for theorists since a workable model of the behavior of the individual actor (i.e. the firm) is a necessary condition for the construction of viable theories of markets. Accordingly, it is hardly surprising that a lively debate has sprung up concerning the existing theory of the firm and alterations which might make the theory of the firm more realistic without sacrificing logical closure.

The same basic problem arises in efforts to develop theories about international interactions, except that a usable theory of the behavior of individual actors has never been developed and that the idea of treating the actors in world politics as integrated and rational utility maximizers seems even less plausible as a fruitful simplification in this area than in microeconomics. This is undoubtedly one of the major reasons why viable theories have never been forthcoming in the field of international relations. Interestingly, recently there has developed a debate about the internal processes of the collective actors who interact in the international system which roughly parallels the current debate on the theory of the firm.[50] Nevertheless, the resultant arguments, which are often set forth under the rubric of "bureaucratic politics," are far more loosely structured and oriented toward description than the analogous arguments in microeconomics which are concerned with such things as rational-choice models of bureaucracy and behavioral "theories" of the firm.[51]

In addition to these fundamental difficulties, there are numerous problems of a more specific nature which frequently arise in analyses of international interactions in much the same way that they come up in studies of oligopolistic markets. Here are some examples.[52] First, the alternative strategies available to a given actor may change in the course of an interaction with the result that the actor's utility function may become inconsistent. Similar problems with utility functions can occur as a consequence of changing information conditions. Second, there is often considerable scope for the actors to manipulate each other's information conditions in the effort to gain advantages for themselves. This prospect opens up a wide range of potential bargaining activities. Third, frequently interactions among a given set of actors simultaneously involve several distinct issues which cannot be inte-

[50] See, *inter alia*, Allison, (fn. 37).

[51] To see this compare such works as Cyert and March (fn. 49), Gordon Tullock (fn. 35), and Anthony Downs (fn. 35), with recent discussions of "bureaucratic politics" such as Allison (fn. 37) and Neustadt (fn. 37).

[52] All of the problems referred to in this paragraph are discussed at greater length in Young (fn. 28), General Conclusion. Accordingly, I have deliberately restricted the present discussion to a rudimentary statement of the issues.

grated into a single set of differentiated alternatives. This makes it possible for different interactions to intersect and influence each other in complex ways. Fourth, interactions sometimes focus on "lumpy" goods (such as who is to control a given segment of the market or a given piece of territory) which cannot be conceptualized in terms of units of some continuously divisible numeraire resource, such as money. In such cases, it often becomes necessary to deal with complex issues involving the possibility of compensation through such devices as side payments. Fifth, there are almost always significant asymmetries between or among the relevant actors. To take a simple example, just as an oligopolist with superior resources may consider initiating a price war, an international actor with a superior monetary reserve position may threaten to take steps to undermine the stability of another actor's currency. Sixth, both oligopolistic markets and international interactions generally produce relationships that are iterative, or at least semi-iterative. Consequently, choices of strategies on the part of the actors are usually affected by the expected future consequences, with respect to factors such as reputation and precedent. Seventh, interactions in both oligopolistic markets and the international system are affected by a variety of contextual factors. Oligopolistic markets are influenced by the extent to which a buyer's or a seller's market prevails, for example. Similarly, international interactions respond to the "competitive position" of the actors in political terms as well as in economic terms. And international interactions ordinarily are significantly affected by a framework of mutually accepted "rules of the game," though these rules are often somewhat weaker and less systematically policed than in oligopolistic markets.

Efforts to construct logical models to deal with oligopolistic markets tend to proceed by abstracting away many of these problems through the introduction of restrictive assumptions. This is satisfying in the sense that it permits the achievement of logical closure. And it may be necessary as a means of initiating the search for viable theories. But it often generates severe problems by sharply reducing the empirical applicability of the predictive statements derived from the resultant models. This difficulty is unquestionably a crucial source of the notorious weakness of economic theories of oligopolistic markets. With respect to international interactions, the difficulty has not yet taken the same form because there have been so few efforts to construct serious logical models. Nevertheless, to the extent that students of international relations wish to work on the development of viable theories, there is no doubt that they will have to tackle the kinds of problems outlined in the preceding paragraph.

This discussion of the analytic similarities between international interactions and oligopolistic markets suggests an additional point that should be emphasized in the present discussion. There is no reason to suppose that the study of international relations will ultimately require the development of theories that are entirely new, in the sense that they bear no relationship to theories in other fields. On the contrary, it seems likely that viable theories of international relations (if they are developed) will often be special cases of more general theories for situations involving strategic interactions among collective entities. That is, even though the specific techniques for handling strategic interaction, the behavior of the individual actors, and so forth may vary to some extent, there is good reason to believe that the basic form and structure of the resultant theories will be quite similar across a number of substantive fields. This is a particularly interesting conclusion since it means that any significant theoretical advances in the analysis of oligopolistic markets, party systems, and even intra-family interactions should have distinct relevance for students of international relations. And any important theoretical advances in the analysis of international relations should prove interesting to students in a number of other fields.

The Current Dilemma

The discussion of the preceding section points to a central dilemma for those who are interested in developing viable theories of international relations in the foreseeable future.[53] It is not difficult to construct logically workable models that have some bearing on international phenomena, but no one has yet constructed models of this type that yield predictive results which are at all impressive. On the other hand, one can begin by working out richer descriptive frameworks or by searching for empirical regularities about international phenomena on an inductive basis. However, so far efforts along these lines have failed entirely to lead toward the predictive and (sometimes) manipulative capabilities associated with the development of viable theories. Consequently, anyone with an interest in constructing theories of international relations immediately faces a difficult choice.

There are three distinguishable responses to this dilemma, and each

[53] Note that this analysis deals only with the development of viable theories and not with other intellectual activities in the field of international relations.

generates its own distinctive pitfalls. First, one can choose to emphasize highly simplified logical models on the grounds that logical closure will always be a necessary condition for the development of theory and that starting with simplistic models may be heuristically fruitful in the sense that it initiates a creative process that may ultimately lead to the formulation of viable theoretical models. This is the position adopted, for example, by those interested in applying game-theoretic models to international relations.[54] The inherent hazard of this procedure is that its products may display little relevance to the real world of international relations for the indefinite future. Second, one can emphasize the development of richer and more "realistic" descriptive categories on the grounds that it is important to attain a high degree of descriptive accuracy before moving on to the problems of constructing workable logical models. This is evidently the position of those who have recently been emphasizing the "bureaucratic-politics" approach to the study of international relations.[55] The built-in danger in this case is that a penchant for descriptive richness is a great enemy of the development of viable theory. It is exceedingly difficult to construct models that exhibit logical closure unless one strips away a great many conceivably relevant factors through the introduction of restrictive assumptions. Third, one can turn to a search for empirical regularities within international phenomena through the application of heavily inductive procedures. The justification here would be that empirical regularities can serve as premises[56] in the development of logically workable models and that the resultant generalizations are of some value in their own right even if they do not contribute to the development of logical models and viable theories (see above, pp. 189-90 on this last point). This general position is exemplified in much of the recent work of a number of well-known scholars in the field of international relations, such as North, Singer, Russett, and Tanter.[57] The inherent pitfall of this orientation is that those who become caught up in the intricacies of inductive procedures (at least in the field of international relations) seldom find it possible to transform their generalizations into the premises of workable logical models. And the generalizations as

[54] For an excellent statement of this view see Rapoport (fn. 12), 186-214.

[55] For a discussion that suggests this conclusion see Graham T. Allison and Morton Halperin, "Bureaucratic Politics: A Paradigm and some Policy Implications," in this issue.

[56] Premises are empirical generalizations, but they play the same analytic role that assumptions play in logical models.

[57] For a convenient collection that illustrates a wide variety of efforts along this line consult J. David Singer, ed., *Quantitative International Politics* (New York 1968).

ends in themselves fail to support very useful projections due to the ever-present hazards of problems such as spurious correlation.

These three responses to the dilemma of the theorist in the field of international relations are not mutually exclusive in any logical sense. Nevertheless, there are several factors that regularly lead individual scholars to emphasize one or another of them. Temperament, for example, is an important determinant of choice in this area. Some individuals find it intellectually stimulating to play with logical models even when they do not yield good predictive results.[58] Others feel uncomfortable about abstracting away any of the descriptive richness of specific empirical situations. And still others find the utilization of various inductive procedures, such as statistical techniques, particularly congenial. Similarly, positions on these issues are sometimes affected by the specific objectives at hand in a given project. Thus, if one's primary objective is to explain or predict outcomes resulting from interactions among the actors in the international system, the pressures will be great to employ a highly simplified model of the behavior of the individual actors.[59] A study whose major purpose is to explain or predict the external behavior of individual actors, on the other hand, can employ a somewhat more complex model of the individual actor without becoming logically unmanageable.

In this section, however, I want to argue that there is a powerful case for emphasizing the construction of simplified logical models *if* one's principal objective is the search for viable theories of international relations.[60] There are several reasons why this is so. First, the ultimate achievement of logical closure is always a necessary condition for the development of viable theories, no matter how subjective or unstructured the initial process of creation may be. Second, simplified logical models sometimes play an important role in revealing the fundamental structure of a set of complex relationships even when the models are not sufficiently realistic to yield good predictions.[61] Third,

[58] In fact, there is good reason to believe that those who do not derive pleasure from playing with logical models will rarely become important theorists (as that concept is employed in this essay) in any discipline.

[59] Note, however, that a viable theory of the behavior of individual actors developed by others might be plugged into the models of those concerned with interactions among actors with excellent results. In economics, for example, this has been the role of the traditional simple theory of the firm for students of market interactions.

[60] This argument need not hold of course if one's primary objective is not the development of viable theories.

[61] For arguments to this effect with specific reference to international relations see Busch (fn. 22), and Martin Shubik, "On the Study of Disarmament and Escalation," *Journal of Conflict Resolution*, XII (March 1968), 83-101.

once you achieve a workable logical model there is always the possibility that its correspondence with the real world can be improved by a disciplined process of relaxing certain assumptions, introducing supplementary assumptions, and so forth.[62] Fourth, though initial models are seldom successful in any scientific endeavor, there is a great deal of evidence to support the view that the very process of creating and manipulating simple logical models generates a creative dynamic that gradually leads to the development of more sophisticated and realistic models.[63] It is this role of simple models in the creative process which has led some scholars to describe simple models as "heuristically fruitful" even when they fail to produce useful predictions. Fifth, there is always an argument for starting with simple models on the grounds that the explanation of some empirical regularities may involve only a small number of factors and that simple models are more powerful than complex ones because they are more parsimonious. It would be an unusual theorist indeed who would deliberately *begin* with a complex model where a simple one might do.[64] Sixth, as I indicated earlier, a heavy emphasis on descriptive richness is a leading enemy of theory. It is of course true that a theory which abstracts away key factors connected with the subject at hand is unlikely to yield good predictions, no matter how satisfying it may be in logical terms. But projects that start out to maximize descriptive accuracy will seldom lead to the development of viable theory. They will ordinarily produce lists of potentially relevant factors which are logically unmanageable. This is the taxonomic fallacy, and it is alarmingly common among those who regard themselves as theorists of international relations.[65] Seventh, though heavily inductive work certainly need not be incompatible with efforts to develop viable theories, in the field of international relations this type of work has all too often become an enemy of theory.[66] This occurs

[62] For some illustrations of these possibilities see, *inter alia*, Frohlich, Oppenheimer, and Young (fn. 32), and John G. Cross, *The Economics of Bargaining* (New York 1969).

[63] There is widespread confusion among social scientists concerning these issues. Whereas physical scientists regard the failure of their initial model as perfectly normal, many social scientists (other than economists) tend quite erroneously to interpret initial failures as evidence that viable theories cannot be constructed about the substantive issues at hand.

[64] On the contrary, as I indicated earlier in this essay, some theorists regard simplicity as so important that they are willing to hang onto a simple and elegant model for a time even in the face of initially negative empirical evidence.

[65] One striking example among many in the field of international relations is Richard C. Snyder and others, eds., *Foreign Policy Decision Making* (New York 1962).

[66] For a more detailed statement of my views on this subject see Oran R. Young, "Professor Russett: Industrious Tailor to a Naked Emperor," *World Politics*, xxi (April 1969), 486-511.

when practitioners become too wrapped up in the search for empirical regularities through the utilization of inductive procedures. They then forget that these activities can only serve the cause of developing theories when they are carefully related to the processes of creating logical models and examining the accuracy of the predictions derived from such models.[67] In summary, none of this demonstrates that an emphasis on simple logical models will in fact lead to the development of viable theories of international relations. But it does suggest quite clearly that such an orientation represents the best research strategy for those who are genuinely committed to the objectives of constructing viable theories in this field.

THE THEORIST AND THE POLICYMAKER

A perennial issue among students of international relations concerns the alleged gap between the academic and intellectual communities in this field on the one hand and governmental policymakers dealing with international issues on the other. Thus, we are constantly told that interactions between the two groups should be more extensive and mutually beneficial, and the academics and intellectuals frequently suggest that the policymakers do not treat their work with sufficient deference and respect.[68] It is not clear to me, however, that these views can be seriously justified, at least with respect to the work of those concerned with the construction of theories of international relations. In fact, I am inclined to believe that the problem of "bridging the gap" is a false issue in this area. The real difficulties stem from the confusions about the state and nature of theory discussed in the preceding sections of this essay.

Viable theory is not a difficult commodity to market. If theorists of international relations could produce even one striking success, it is hard to imagine that policymakers would refuse to pay attention to them. That is, if the theorists could produce consistently accurate pre-

[67] Though heavily inductive work is not logically at odds with efforts to develop viable theories, some of the inductive projects focusing on international relations have probably served to set back the cause of theory in the field. This happens when people unwittingly mistake the inductive studies for the sum total of the theoretical enterprise. Under these circumstances, when the highly limited results of the inductivists breed disillusionment (as is now occurring in the field of political science in general), the whole idea of developing viable theories tends to suffer from its mistaken identification with the heavily inductive work.

[68] This conclusion is relevant primarily to those academics and intellectuals who regard themselves as theorists. A moment's reflection is sufficient to affirm that numerous academics and intellectuals working on essentially nontheoretical projects have exercised substantial influence on policymaking in the international field in recent years.

dictions about any major phenomenon in the realm of international relations (such as power relationships, wars, crises, interventions, or alliances), there is every reason to suppose that policymakers would take their results seriously. Indeed, policymakers might well display a tendency to over-generalize the authority of the theorists' pronouncements in the wake of striking predictive success with respect to any one substantive question.[69] The real problem that many self-proclaimed theorists face at the present time, however, is how to sell the policymaker non-viable theories or, how to market theories that they do not really possess. This is inherently a much more difficult task, and, unfortunately, one whose ardent pursuit can be severely debilitating with respect to the continuation of efforts to construct viable theories.

Perhaps it is also worthwhile making a few comments at this point on the ways in which policymakers ordinarily make use of theory in those areas where viable theories do exist. In general, policymakers utilize the end products of theories without acquiring a thorough working knowledge of the logical structure of the theories themselves. The theorists who can apply and manipulate the theories ordinarily gain authority through the accuracy of their predictions rather than through any elaborate program of instructing policymakers in the intricacies of their theoretical models.[70] Thus, relatively few policymakers dealing with issues involving nuclear energy possess more than a rudimentary knowledge of nuclear physics. And a great many policymakers dealing with economic problems have no more than a general sense of the theoretical bases of modern economics. The nature of this relationship between the theorist and the policymaker produces several important consequences. Theorists and their facilities are often simply brought into governmental agencies lock, stock and barrel or grouped into distinct governmentally supported research centers to which policymakers can turn for advice. This creates certain dangers from the point of view of the policymaker who sometimes feels compelled to accept the conclusions of the theorist more or less on faith and who occasionally exhibits a tendency to respect the views of the theorist on questions that fall outside his range of expertise, due to a kind of halo effect which the theorist acquires as a result of stature in his own field.

[69] Note, in this connection, the deference often accorded to the views of well-known nuclear physicists on numerous issues in the field of national security which are largely political in nature.
[70] Among other things, this suggests that those who wish to obtain influence as theorists of international relations should pay more attention to emphasizing the accuracy and utility of their predictions than to instructing unreceptive policymakers in the intricacies of their theoretical models.

This relationship also generates a distinct and important role for individuals who can act as effective go-betweens because they are sufficiently well trained to understand the work of the theorists and familiar enough with the problems of the policymaker to understand his concerns.[71]

These problems have not arisen in any serious way in the field of international relations due to the absence of viable theories. Periodic efforts by scholars in the field to sell their work to policymakers as though it were theory, however, raise, in my view, some important ethical and moral problems. In brief, an important "sin" committed by some academics and intellectuals in this field is that they go to considerable lengths to try and market their products under false pretenses. It is of course entirely legitimate for such individuals to attempt to influence policymakers as citizens of the state. Perhaps it is even legitimate for them to claim that their judgments are more "informed" than those of most other citizens. But to seek influence for one's nontheoretical conclusions by pretending that they do constitute a theory, and should be accorded the status or prestige of theory, seems distinctly unethical. It is not difficult to understand the psychology of those who commit this "sin" since the identity of an intellectual is often closely associated with the quality or impact of his "expert opinions." And an intellectual who cannot justify his work in these terms may experience a sense of identity crisis.[72] Thus, inflating the importance of one's own work is no doubt a standard form of "hubris" among all intellectuals. Moreover, I suspect it is also true that relatively few academics and intellectuals consciously or deliberately present their work under false colors in order to maximize their influence. The process of falling into this trap is undoubtedly a subtle one that takes place gradually over long periods of time. Depending upon one's sense of justice and charity, therefore, it is possible to argue that the "sins" of various academics and intellectuals in these areas are excusable. This view, however, affords only cold comfort to the policymaker who must ultimately take the responsibility for the consequences of his decisions, even if they are based on the advice of a host of "experts." From this perspective, one

[71] With respect to the field of physics, such well-known figures as Vannevar Bush, Arthur Compton, and James Conant are cases in point.

[72] I recognize that this argument raises questions about the definition of the term "intellectual." One interesting definition of an intellectual, for example, is that he is an individual who regards the exploration and manipulation of ideas as highly valued ends in their own right. Such an individual would not commit the "sin" I am discussing here since he would not, for the most part, be interested in the practical impact of his work. In the text, I employ the term "intellectual" in its more mundane sense to refer to the class of academics, writers, and so forth.

can easily understand (and perhaps even applaud) the apparent hesitancy of many policymakers to place much weight on the advice of those who purport to offer theories of international relations.[73]

It remains only for me to crystalize my prescriptions concerning future relationships between theorists and policymakers in the field of international relations. This can be done directly in a number of brief statements. First, though international policymaking obviously must go on, no one should allow himself to be led into the view that it is or could be based on viable theories at the present time. It does no one any good in the long run to maintain this pretense. And if such a pretense should become very widespread or influential, it could wreak havoc with the quality of policymaking on specific issues. Second, it is entirely legitimate for every citizen (including the academic and the intellectual) to try and influence international policy, but it is not presently acceptable to claim that one's views are superior because they are based on viable theories. It may well be useful to draw a distinction between informed opinion and uninformed opinion on specific issues, although the basis of this distinction is notoriously unclear and imprecise. Efforts to gain influence for one's views by pretending that they are derived from a viable theory, however, seem to me to come perilously close to unethical behavior. Third, those who genuinely wish to work on the construction of theories of international relations, despite all the pitfalls and hazards of this enterprise, should focus primarily on their theoretical interests without concerning themselves to any significant degree about short-term "relevance." It is undoubtedly true that an interest in practical problems has been an important (some would argue the most important) spur to theoretical creativity in most disciplines which have experienced striking theoretical advances.[74] And there is every reason for theorists of international relations to frame their research problems with reference to practical concerns arising from international interactions in the contemporary world. But this in no way alters the facts that an excessive concern with short-term relevance is one of the greatest enemies facing the development of theory in all fields and that relevance ordinarily follows quickly enough after

[73] In fact, it is probably possible to construct an argument to the effect that policymakers have recently displayed too much sensitivity to the advice of those who purport to offer theories of international relations.

[74] This is a well-known proposition concerning the bases of scientific creativity. But the stimulus of practical problems must be clearly distinguished from an excessive impatience to achieve results or find answers directly applicable to real-world problems. The resultant tension constitutes yet another reason why the processes of scientific creativity rest on a set of delicate balances.

striking theoretical success. Beyond this, there is no doubt that the number of individuals who are genuinely interested in devoting themselves to constructing viable theories of international relations on a long-term basis will remain small throughout the foreseeable future. Consequently, as a practical matter it is safe to assume that most students of international relations will devote the bulk of their efforts to various non-theoretical activities, such as those identified in an earlier section of this essay. Fourth, there is a substantial argument in favor of making public funds available to support the work of those relatively few individuals who wish to devote their efforts to the construction of theories of international relations on a long-term basis. The argument is essentially the same as the argument for basic research in all fields and need not be restated here. Note, however, that the kind of theoretical work on international phenomena emphasized in this essay could be adequately supported on the basis of relatively small sums of money, at least for the foreseeable future.[75]

[75] Contrast this with the enormous sums of money that are currently required to support advanced theoretical work in fields such as high energy particle physics.

Unfortunately, the current policy of the National Science Foundation and the major private foundations with respect to research in the field of international relations does not appear to be conducive to basic theoretical work. In short, the present guidelines of the NSF and the large private foundations place a great deal of weight on *short-term* relevance to current issues of national concern as a criterion in the selection of projects to support despite the fact that these organizations have, at least nominally, a greater commitment to basic research about international phenomena than any other major funding agencies within the United States government and American society in general.

THE RELEVANCE POTENTIAL OF DIFFERENT PRODUCTS

By DAVIS B. BOBROW

INTERNATIONAL relations analysts now use a wide range of ideas and techniques. Concepts and styles of reasoning clearly reflect work in economics, organizational behavior, social psychology, operations research and many other fields. Facts thought relevant are the facts customarily used in these other fields. Methods for relating facts to each other and to ideas are increasingly those of logic, statistics and mathematics. What are the implications of this diversity for foreign and defense policy? The only necessary implication is for the length and variety of the menu international relations analysts can offer the policy person. There is no necessary implication for how important or satisfying he will find the offerings.

If we are to arrive at other implications, we need to establish criteria which can be applied to analyses which differ in concepts and methods. These criteria cannot be primarily those of acceptance by the policy community, i.e., of sales in that market. Acceptance is not always a reliable sign of relevance. Transfer to operating users is appropriate at the end, and not at the beginning of a research and development sequence. Acceptance as a requirement to continue work before it moves through development may well abort promising efforts. Acceptance or sales, as we know from consumer life, has only a tenuous relationship to the quality of the product. Explicit quality control standards are necessary for analysts to monitor themselves and their colleagues, and for policy users to make responsible selections. High technical quality does not insure high relevance, but it does help make policy recommendations warranted. Of course, technical quality does not necessarily mean fancy. It does mean rigorous attention to matters of evidence and inference, and a public statement of uncertainties and limitations.

To arrive at a more appropriate set of criteria than acceptance alone, I find it useful to set aside the general category of international relations analysis in favor of parts of it which have very different products. The product categories used in this essay are: metatheory, theory, history, and engineering. Whether or not these labels are acceptable, there are very different types of results involved. And we need to keep them distinct. None is better or worse than another; they are different and a good job on one is very different from a good job on another. Different criteria are appropriate to each. Each differs from the others in the nature of the relevance a good job can have to policy. This essay suggests the criteria and differing relevance potentials of each of the four types of products. Earlier chapters in this volume provide illustrations.

Before we begin, several qualifications may be helpful. First, all of the products to be discussed are empirical as distinct from normative. That is, the results of each are intended to provide information about what is, has been, or will be, and not about what in a moral sense ought to be or ought to have been. Results of an empirical kind may be relevant to one normative purpose and not another. Authors may be motivated by one purpose and not another. Secondly, my purpose is not to provide critiques of the work reported in the preceding articles. The authors' claims are almost uniformly modest. Much of the work reported apparently is drawn from forthcoming publications which buttress the summaries in this volume. The questions of general interest are less about what the authors have done than they are about what we do next and implications of that for policy.

Third, I am concerned that we conceive of policy relevance in ways which do not limit relevance to members of national executive branches. Nor should we assume that all persons in the national policy machinery are an appropriate audience for international relations analysis. Many persons and groups who can or do affect foreign and defense policy are not part of an executive branch. Many persons and groups who affect international matters do so as participants in an international or regional institution, and not from a national base. Many persons and groups who are formally part of executive branch organizations charged with international matters really are not engaged in international affairs. Instead they are involved with a variety of activities found in large organizations, e.g., personnel assignment, contract writing, equipment maintenance, data processing. Social science analysis may be relevant to their activities, but not international relations analysis as we customarily think of it.

Accordingly, I find it helpful to think of the set of policy consumers of international relations analysis as persons and groups who act intentionally to estimate and affect states of affairs involving more than one nation. The relevance potential of the products of international relations analysis is a function of the extent to which they help to: 1) estimate the occurrence and consequences of alternative states of affairs; and 2) design and evaluate means to achieve preferred states (or avoid unwanted ones). Relevance potential varies with the extent to which the analytic product can aid the range of activity of policy persons and groups suggested above. Products may well have a higher relevance potential when they are pertinent to legislators, as well as to members of the executive branch, to the private sector as well as the public sector, to foreigners as well as Americans, to international as well as national actors.

I. Metatheory

By a metatheoretical statement, we refer to a statement which says in effect, "think about X as if it were Y." For example, think about youth as if it were a minority group, or think about international bargaining as if it were interpersonal interaction, or think about the relationship between wealthy and poor countries as if it were class conflict. Statements of this sort are quite different from statements of fact, e.g., "the Chinese leadership fears Japan," or of logical implication, e.g., "great powers tend to exploit small countries; the U.S. and the U.S.S.R. are great powers; the U.S. and the U.S.S.R. tend to exploit small countries." A metatheoretical approach begins with the suggestion of a perspective often in the form of an analogy. For example, Allison and Halperin have been exploring three perspectives. They in effect are saying to us, "think about the behavior of nations as if it were that of (a) rational unitary actors; or (b) large, inertial organizations; or (c) bureaucratic politicians." Because we begin only with a perspective, we start with no advance expectation (prediction) of what we will find, except that we expect the perspective to be helpful to our understanding. Because there is no restriction imposed on political outcomes by the perspective, metatheoretical statements and results are not falsifiable. They are enlightening or unenlightening.

Accordingly, it is not surprising that, for the most part, proponents of a metatheoretical approach attempt to show its value through plausible reconstructions of why what happened did happen. They begin with known outcomes, e.g., the U.S. blockade of Cuba in 1962, the initial Congressionally approved ABM deployment, the Soviet invasion of Czechoslovakia, and then discuss the events leading up to them in the terms of the framework of their metatheory. No matter how skilled such efforts may be, they in no way exclude taking the same outcomes and coming up with numerous other plausible reconstructions from other perspectives. One cannot test the power of one metatheory to explain observations as compared to that of another. Most metatheories can be used to reconstruct any outcome which may be of interest. Relevance comes in the form of metaphor rather than prediction. Evidence cannot be brought to bear to choose between competing metatheories whether they be the three dealt with by Allison and Halperin or those such as role, organism, or machine, used elsewhere in the social sciences. We are left to choose between metatheories on the basis of the extent to which we or persons whose judgment we respect, find them intuitively compelling.

What then are metatheoretical products good for? They can give us a new perspective which leads us to notice facts and conceive of causes and effects which otherwise would have been ignored. For example, the bureaucratic politics perspective leads us to ask a number of questions about the stakes of players in national regimes. It makes us reflect on the need to provide different incentives to particular players if we wish them to behave in different ways with different consequences. It orients us to reconstruct the evaluation of a policy outcome, e.g., a missile deployment, by emphasizing the play within and between complex organizations rather than strategic calculation. It may be useful to note explicitly one subset of metatheoretical products. I have in mind instances where a full-fledged theory from some other domain of science is used as an analogy for the understanding of foreign policy but the formal deductive apparatus and the constraints built into the original theory are left behind. When we engage in partial borrowing of a perspective but not its formal infrastructure, we are in essence limiting ourselves to the payoffs of metatheoretical products. One example is the use of game theory in the analysis of international bargaining. Others involve the use of economic metaphors without the preference structures required for the theory to have predictive power. Analogies imported from other areas of knowledge often seem to provide a rapidly enriched perspective. They may in fact do so but they may also on closer inspection turn out to move us in a misleading direction or simply to provide new labels for old bottles.

One problem which both the research and the policy users of metatheories face is that the metatheory itself is not susceptible to rigorous analysis to determine its value. Firm answers can be arrived at only after people stimulated by the new perspectives have gone beyond the analogy to produce one or another of the types of products we discuss subsequently. In the interim we can arrive at a tentative judgment by asking:

— Does the new perspective suggest novel and potentially useful implications?
— Does the new perspective take into account considerations which seem important but which existing notions and methods tend to ignore?

— Does the new perspective imply that we should ignore considerations we have reason to think matter?

If the answers to the first two questions are positive and the answer to the third negative, the metatheory probably merits work to build its focus of attention into theories, historical hypotheses and data collections, and engineering models.

Metatheoretical products are certainly commonplace in international relations and in the social sciences generally. And it is not difficult to formulate ones which seem to speak to the concerns of operators and citizens. Accordingly, it is particularly important to be clear about the limits of the contributions metatheoretical products can make to foreign policy. A metatheory suggests that policy persons entertain certain considerations in arriving at estimates and choices. It speaks to their information search and processing. That sort of advice has a long and honorable tradition among students of politics.[1] Unfortunately, the metatheory *per se* does not imply that some particular estimate or choice is more likely to produce a desired goal than another. It simply contends that estimates and choices which have not taken certain considerations into account may well be disappointing. It does not state, or logically entail, or provide a vehicle to test for the necessary and sufficient conditions to achieve a particular real world state of affairs. This severe limitation operates whether the metatheory is one of bureaucratic politics, of the importance of cultural tradition (e.g., more Chinese than Communist), or of personality determinants of elite behavior. Because products based on such metatheories do not tell us what the right answer to an action problem is, e.g., how to get the Russian missiles out of Cuba, how to establish positive relations with China, they at best serve as heuristics and not algorithms. That is a contribution, but less than what we all need. To argue otherwise would be to agree with Tom Lehrer's comment on the new math, "the important thing is to understand what you're doing rather than to get the right answer."[2]

Innovative metatheoretical products suggest that the policy community do some work—in particular that it obtain and evaluate information in addition to that already processed. Under what conditions are operators likely to assume or assign that additional work load? Dissatisfaction with estimates and choices not informed by the metatheory

[1] For example, Niccolò Machiavelli, *The Prince* and *The Discourses*; Henry Taylor, *The Statesman*.
[2] Tom Lehrer, "New Math," ASCAP 1965.

clearly is one condition. For example, if users are dissatisfied with estimates of future Soviet strategic weapons inventories based on a rational actor perspective, they are more inclined to implement an organizational behavior perspective.

Another is that some element of the policy community expects payoffs from allocating resources to the information which the fresh perspective emphasizes. These payoffs may have nothing in particular to do with the content of foreign policy but may themselves be a function of bureaucratic competition and organizational processes. A third and perhaps the most common facilitating condition is that the metatheory fits with the personal or group orientation of some part of the policy community. That sort of congenial situation has no necessary implication about the extent to which a metatheory provides enlightenment rather than illusion. Familiarity alone should lead us to expect, for example, that social psychologists will be attracted to social psychological metatheories of international relations, and that political leaders who see themselves as involved in a constant manipulative struggle with their subordinates and bureaucratic competitors will be attracted to a metatheory which takes that perspective on the foreign policy process. This line of reasoning suggests that those metatheories are accepted which have a fundamentally conservative relationship to the current perspectives of those who accept them. If that is the case, we should expect acceptance of new metatheories to produce at best changes in the efficiency with which policy operators pursue goals but not changes in ends themselves or gross resource allocations. Such fundamental changes in the substance of foreign policy will not take place unless the diffusion of the metatheory is accompanied by changes in the distribution of power to sets of policy actors with different orientations.

II. THEORY

Theory, as Oran Young points out in his essay, has a tradition of diverse meanings in international relations analysis. A catholic stance may be warranted if we regard theory construction as of a higher status than work directed to other sorts of products. I do not so regard it and accordingly suggest a narrow and demanding formulation. Having stated the formulation in a skeletal fashion, we can then examine the preceding papers for fit with the requirements of theory construction. The requirements which follow are not incompatible with the perspective in the Young essay but may serve more readily as an evaluative check list.

By theory, we refer to a system of internally consistent statements which allow us to explain or predict deductively.[3] The core elements in a theory consist of three kinds of statements: definitions, assumptions, and scope conditions. Definitions assign meaning to our key terms (concepts). Appropriate definitions for a theory differ from those for other purposes in that they try to avoid being applicable in only some part of the space and time of human experience. Our definitions should be context free, i.e., ahistorical. For example, let us suppose we are defining power. If we define it as nuclear weapons superiority, we limit our concept to the nuclear age. If we define it as the ability to make others do what they would rather not do, our concept can be used in all historical periods. Assumptions state "if . . . then" relationships between concepts, e.g., if some members of a group are relatively under-rewarded, they try to achieve the same rewards as other members of a group. Scope conditions state the necessary characteristics of situations or actors for the assumptions to hold. For example, with reference to the illustrative assumption about equity given above, a list of scope conditions might well include that the under-rewarded members are aware of the inequity. Assumptions are not then limited to "always true" statements, e.g., about all members of all groups at all times. We need explicit scope conditions which identify that subset of situations to which the assumptions and thus the theory are held to apply.

A theory then is a system of statements which include concepts and relationships. In contrast to a metatheory, it enables deductive reasoning and allows for some behaviors and not others. In contrast to a model for applied problem-solving, a theory tends to be simple rather than complex, and context-free. Since a theory is a system of statements, we do not test it by testing any one statement in that system. A meaningful test involves checking some statement which is the joint product of at least two elements (assumptions and/or scope conditions) of that system. Parenthetically, if we do not have a system of statements, as I suggest we do not in the event-interaction formulation used by Tanter, we are not dealing with a theory.

When we do have a system of statements, as we do in the public goods formulation of Frohlich and Oppenheimer, we can proceed with theory construction. In order to get from our core set of definitions,

---

[3] Explanation and prediction have the same structure but different starting points. When we explain something we start from an observed outcome and work backwards to explain it. (X has occurred; it occurred because of Y.) When we predict something, we start with a set of principles and work out the consequences they imply. (Because of X, Y will occur.) We are working inductively when we start with some observed facts and construct a generalization(s) compatible with them. We are working deductively when we logically derive consequences from some system of generalizations.

assumptions, and scope conditions to testable statements and valid tests a number of steps are necessary. The first is to arrive logically at derivations, that is, general ahistorical statements, which are implied by the theory. A number of the freeloader statements of Frohlich and Oppenheimer are examples of logical derivations. The second is to locate a specific situation, which can be an artificial laboratory situation, where the scope conditions are met. For example, a number of theories pertinent to international relations have been tested in simulations and laboratory experiments where scope conditions of restricted strategic choice and particular information and uncertainty mixes can be assured. Familiar examples include work on Prisoner's Dilemma and pacifist bargaining strategies.[4]

A third necessary step is to state the derivation in a specific form applicable to that historical situation, that is in terms of actors and relationships present and possible in the situation. We have to make that derivation operational in the form of a prediction or observation which can be checked out in the specific instance at hand. This clearly is a long and arduous process. Accordingly, we act efficiently when we check each step as much as we can before we proceed to the next step. We can inspect our assumptions to see if they are consistent with or contradictory to each other. They need to be consistent. We can inspect our derivations to see if they follow strictly from our assumptions and scope conditions. They should do so. We can inspect our selected historical situation to make sure that the scope conditions are all present. If they are not, we are not testing the theory under examination. Finally, we can reflect on our operational statement to make sure that it corresponds to the relevant derivation. The last two checks are not hard and fast, but judgmental. Nevertheless, the burden rests on he who tests theory to convince us that scope conditions and rules of correspondence are met.

The authors whose chapters provide illustrations all state explicitly that they have not conformed fully to the sequence and criteria just presented.[5] It still seems useful to note here some of the gaps between what they have reported and my view of theory construction. The illustrations may give us a clearer idea of what steps remain to achieve theory as I have described it.

[4] For example, see: Anatol Rapoport and A. M. Chammah, *Prisoner's Dilemma* (Ann Arbor 1965), and Gerald H. Shure and others, "The Effectiveness of Pacifist Strategies in Bargaining Games," *Journal of Conflict Resolution*, ix (March 1965), 106-17.

[5] The relevant chapters are those by Frohlich and Oppenheimer, Morse, Choucri and North, Tanter, Allison and Halperin.

The theory requirement met most generally in the preceding chapters is that of ahistorical definition of terms. Accordingly, we are given some general language for description. The extent to which the other core elements of any theory are made explicit varies markedly. Only Frohlich and Oppenheimer are explicit and formal enough for us to be clear about 1) the identity of the assumptions; 2) their logical compatibility; and 3) the nature of the scope conditions. The lack of comparable specification in the other essays means that we cannot ascertain with reasonable clarity to what situations the formulations apply, what derivations from the theory are offered as indications of its fruitfulness, or what are reasonable operational hypotheses for testing the theory.

When the line between assumptions and derivations is blurred, we cannot make a reasonable judgment about the extent to which the theory under construction has or will have rich implications. In the Choucri-North and Allison-Halperin papers, have they given us their assumptions or rather the set of derivations which their theory can generate? The statements may be intrinsically interesting and deal with important phenomena. For example, from Choucri-North, "Competitions and conflicts between two or more high lateral pressure countries frequently lead (directly or through colonial or client wars, or through some combination of local and more diffused conflicts) into arms races and crises."[6] The lack of clarity about the assumption—derivation status of statements may also be illustrated by two items in the Allison-Halperin presentation of "suggestive propositions": a) "Decisions of a government seldom reflect a single coherent, consistent set of calculations about national security interests," and b) "Ambassadors and field commanders feel less obliged to faithfully implement decisions because they typically have not been involved in the decision game. They feel they know better what actions one should want from another government and how to get those actions."[7] Other authors, especially Tanter and Morse, leave us uncertain about what statements have the status of assumptions, derivations, or operational hypotheses. Accordingly we cannot clearly evaluate the implications of examples and data they present for the confirmation of a theory. Because only Frohlich and Oppenheimer give a central place to general propositions which clearly derive from explicit assumptions, only their formulation is at the point where one can turn appropriately to the task of selecting a test situation and operationalizing hypotheses.

Accordingly, it is not surprising that most of the authors explicitly

[6] See above, p. 95.   [7] See above, pp. 53-54.

disavow having performed a test.[8] Allison-Halperin and especially Choucri-North go a long way toward operationalizing their conceptual framework in an explicit way which indicates progress toward testing. However, in the Allison-Halperin case it is not always clear what general proposition is being operationalized in testable form rather than only being illustrated. For example, they indicate that patterns of information availability are an important constraint within which their propositions operate. However, rather than a set of measures for determining information availability they provide a situational illustration, "how did the U.S. government become aware of the Soviet construction of missiles in Cuba in 1962?"[9] As Choucri-North point out, in their summary Table 1, they have yet to fully operationalize, i.e., provide a structural equation for, the core element of "demands" which drives their theoretical structure.[10] As the reader will recall, they formulate demands as resource requests produced by an interaction of population and technology. Increases in demands lead to lateral pressure and through second-order effects to military competition and external violence. Until they can operationalize demands, they cannot test propositions which contain this fundamental element of their theoretical structure.

The Tanter essay comes closest to reporting a test.[11] We can use his contribution to illustrate difficulties with rules of correspondence and also the implications of test results for theory construction. The difficulties involve operationalizing terms and relationships in ways consonant with the theory under examination. More specifically, they involve the choice of units of analysis, statistical relationships and data. For discussion purposes, let us assume that theories do exist from which one can derive the propositions Tanter associates with the organizational process, event interaction, and organization/interaction formulations.[12] Let us also assume that the scope conditions of these theories are met by the 1961 Berlin crisis. In Tanter's paper, the organizational process approach is held to suggest that foreign policy behaviors of

---

[8] The formulation which provides a source from much of the thinking in the Frohlich-Oppenheimer essay, Mancur Olson's *The Logic of Collective Action* (New York 1968), has been subjected to at least one carefully designed test. The findings support Olson's theory. See Philip M. Burgess and James A. Robinson, "Alliances and the Theory of Collective Action," in James N. Rosenau, ed., *International Politics and Foreign Policy* (rev. edn., New York 1969), 642-53.

[9] See above, p. 55.   [10] See above, p. 103.   [11] See above, p. 21.

[12] It is not clear if Tanter views these alternative formulations as theories or even as more historically limited closed logical structures. If they are neither, they are not open to test. If they are one or the other, the comments which follow apply.

nation-states are: a function of their internal processes (the organizational process approach); that they are a function of the behavior of
the states (the event interaction approach); and that they are a function of both, i.e., one controls or modifies the effects of the other (organ-
ization/interaction). His operationalization consists of testing for the
extent to which the behavior of each of the two alliances (NATO and
Warsaw Pact) is a function of the previous behavior of the other alliance, of its own previous behavior, or, he states, of both. His technique
is to calculate path coefficients for time lag relations between the behavior of each of the alliances at time one and time two and between
the behavior of a single alliance at time one and time two.

The fit between the treatment of the Berlin crisis and the theories
which are to be illuminated is open to question on at least three counts.
First, the use of alliances rather than nations as units does not seem to
correspond with at least one of the theories being tested. The organizational process formulation emphasizes processes within nations, as
distinct from processes within alliances.[13] Accordingly, it is not obvious
that it is being tested with the 1961 Berlin data. Second, the combined
alternative (organization/interaction) is apparently not tested as a distinct alternative. Coefficients are not reported when one possible determinant (x_2) is used to modify the effect of the other (x_1) on the
dependent variable (y) of subsequent NATO or Warsaw Pact behavior.
This point may be clearer if one compares the diagram of an interaction effect test given below with those presented in the Tanter essay.[14]
Third, neither the event interaction or the organizational process
frameworks stipulate that an actor's behavior is determined by other

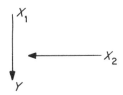

[13] The most accessible formulation is that by Graham T. Allison, "Conceptual Models
and the Cuban Missile Crisis," *American Political Science Review*, LXII (September
1969), 689-718. One can of course try to extend the organizational process formulation
to handle organizational processes within alliances. That seems inappropriate in this
case for two reasons. First, the formulation remains to be tested in the initial area
of concern, i.e., within a nation. Second, the extension would require modifying the
event interaction formulation to exclude interactions between allies.
[14] On this and other problems and possibilities see Raymond Boudon, "A New Look
at Correlation Analysis," in Hubert M. Blalock, Jr. and Ann B. Blalock, eds., *Methodology in Social Research* (New York 1968), 199-235.

actions about the particular action arena which is treated as the dependent variable. That is, neither specifies that behavior vis-à-vis Berlin is determined by behavior of self or other about *Berlin only.* An event interaction framework would include the set of actions relevant to NATO-Warsaw relations during the time period; an organizational process framework, the set of events within actors relevant to their actions during the period. The data used for the analysis consist solely of "events for the Berlin Crisis."[15] In sum, the argument that the rules of correspondence are met seems sufficiently shaky to make dubious any strong claims that the findings of such analyses might have clear implications for the confirmation status of the theories under examination.

For discussion purposes, let us waive these problems and use the Berlin crisis analysis to suggest how one might draw the results of a test into an ongoing process of theory construction. Most generally, the results reported in Figure 3 of the Tanter essay suggest that none of the "theories" is as broadly applicable as its proponents might claim.[16] The power of each seems to vary according to crisis stage and whether one is trying to predict NATO or Warsaw Pact behavior. These findings suggest that the different theories stand in need of substantial work to specify the scope conditions within which they apply.

The previous discussion was intended not to imply that the authors are unaware of work still to be done, but to communicate what remains to be done. While we must withhold judgments about the extent to which fruitful theory will result from their efforts, we do not need to be content with equal uncertainty about the relevance potential of these or any other theories once they have been confirmed. What policy relevance do established theories have? First, none for cases which do not fall within their scope conditions.[17] That is the core of Young's remarks on the limited applicability of arms control models, game theory, and much of microeconomics. When theories are built on the presence of certain decision-maker attributes, e.g., transitive preferences stipulated by Frohlich and Oppenheimer, we forego relevance to policy situations where those attributes aren't there. Second, theory is not con-

[15] See above, pp. 22-24.

[16] See above, p. 28.

[17] When we apply a theory to situations outside of its scope conditions we are engaged in one of two enterprises. We may be trying to establish that the scope conditions are unnecessarily restrictive. In that case we can make no claims for the applicability of the theory until after our attempt to relax the scope conditions has proven successful. Alternatively, we may wish to analogize between situations to which the theory applies and those which it does not. That is, we choose to use the theory as a metatheory. Accordingly, it should be judged as such.

structed to provide optimal detail and determinacy for any particular situation or case. When we build theory we seek to construct and confirm a system of statements applicable across time and space. We want to use case detail only instrumentally. When we have a theory, we can explain and predict behaviors which are members of general classes and not situationally unique. Third, most theories are constructed and confirmed in ways which severely limit their applicability to most practical situations. Most theories contain only a small number of independent and mediating variables. Most theories are confirmed through procedures which ignore many characteristics of a situation, insure that these less relevant characteristics have no biased distribution, or hold them constant. The problem, of course, is that in any particular real world situation one may wish to predict or explain for policy purposes those less relevant characteristics may be very difficult to ignore. They may be distributed in a highly biased fashion. They cannot be held constant at the convenience of the analyst. If these other characteristics do not interact in important ways with those included in the theory, predictive and explanatory power do not suffer. If they do, it is a different matter. Unfortunately, the process of theory construction usually will not have determined whether or not some "hidden interactions" are present for many of the situations in which practical problems arise.[18] All other things may well not be equal and the theory does not tell us what to expect when particular "inequalities" are present. Theory construction and foreign policy management are both highly demanding enterprises. The difficulty arises in the almost non-overlapping sets of constraints and options available to the practitioners of each craft.

We have argued up to this point for the substantial lack of direct relevance of theory to foreign or any other sector of policy. We do not mean to suggest that consumers of international relations analysis have no stake in the state of theory. It remains the case that if we are ignorant of the specifics of a situation, if we know only that it meets the scope conditions of a well-tested theory, we have a better basis for judgment than if we do not have such a theory. More importantly, the quality and delivery time of products with greater direct relevance potential are very dependent on theory. A strong body of theory gets historical and engineering efforts, as discussed subsequently, off to a fast

---

[18] The problems posed by confirmation based on highly controlled tests, which are the only ones likely to meet rules of correspondence, are presented with unusual clarity and insight by A. Chapanis, "The Relevance of Laboratory Studies to Practical Situations," *Ergonomics*, x, No. 5 (September 1967), 557-77.

and helpful start. A deductive theory provides initial focus on what are the important considerations and on what are the consequences of their relationships. What then remains is, first, to operationalize the derivations of the theory for the situation of interest and, second, to take additional considerations into account. We are led to focus on the additional considerations which have significant interaction effects with the elements built into the theory. We can pay slight attention to others. The facts of the matter, as the previous essays demonstrate, are that international relations has little in the way of deductive theory and what there is has not been confirmed to a significant extent. This does not say the task is impossible. It does suggest that the task needs to be pursued in its own right while eschewing unwarranted claims of relevance.

III. History

By historical products, we refer to efforts to describe, foresee, or explain events in a particular time or space, e.g., the 19th Century, the Cuban missile crisis, the world of the 1980's. We include in this category all international relations analysis: 1) whose concepts limit it to a particular time and place; and 2) which does not begin with the purpose of building a model to design policies or to design information systems to monitor the state of the world for policy implications. Accordingly, the analyses we classify as historical may deal with the future as well as the past. Parenthetically, many analyses which use information about the past are not historical. They may instead use information about the past to illustrate a metatheory or test a theory. The key is how information is being used and for what purposes. For history as we use the term, a description or explanation of a particular situation is the central point; for theory it is but a convenient test case; for metatheory, a particular situation is merely a convenient illustration. The major burden of explanation in historical work rests on specifics of the situations under study. In historical work, these specifics tend to be extremely numerous and do not follow generalized scope conditions. The dependence on situational specifics which are not placed in a class of ahistorical properties limits the explanations to the situations being analyzed. As we know, the use of numbers, quantification, does not distinguish theoretical explanation from historical explanation. Words or numbers may be used for history as they can be used for theory.

Historical products differ in scope and method. That is they differ, first in the number and time span of cases included and, second, along a continuum which runs from a synthesizing essay illustrated by supporting examples to a statistical analysis of data on a number of measures, where the data are chosen in explicit ways designed to insure objectivity. Whatever the scope and method of a particular historical product, it has no necessary policy implications and allows for no deductions. Historical products have relevance when and only when policy users already entertain issues and use frameworks which intersect with the facts and explanations of the analysis. For example, a historical study of international law about the oceans becomes relevant when policy persons are interested in the oceans and choose to view international law as a possible important consideration. A demographic forecast of the Chinese population becomes relevant when issues are on the agenda involving China and frameworks in use relate population to goals and means germane to those issues. The dependence on prior information demands by members of the policy community makes readily understandable the familiar observation that historical products which stress variables not thought to be important, e.g., cultural differences in time horizon to policy goals, or situations not already singled out for attention, receive little play in the policy community. The constraint also suggests that additional unconventional historical products are unlikely to gain relevance without the support of salient events at home and abroad which create new fads and fashions in the policy community.

Scope and method differences matter within the boundaries discussed above. The treatment of a single case may increase our understanding of it, e.g., political development in Indonesia, economic cooperation in the Common Market, nuclear proliferation in the Middle East. However we do not get from that product explicit criteria for determining which, if any, other cases are similar. Except for analogies drawn from the case, we must begin from the ground up when confronted with a different case. And to analogize from a single case (e.g., Vietnam is like Malaya or like Munich) is essentially to use the historical product as a metatheory. It has the same problems and potential benefits. The use of numerous cases, e.g., all independent nation-states, broadens the coverage of the product, but it does not necessarily increase its relevance. One reason is that the cost of broader coverage often is loss of detail about, and the uniqueness of, particular cases. The product may consist of results which are in a loose sense only average properties of the set of instances examined. It may be difficult or downright misleading to infer that properties of the set are properties of any specific member of the set. Relevance is lost under the preceding conditions when users are interested in one or another subset of cases included and not in the whole.[19] Historical products also differ as they treat one or a number of points in time. Obviously, the latter provide information about change and stability which the former cannot.

Methods introduce additional differences in potential relevance. As one extreme let us consider the synthesizing essay which uses illustrative supporting examples. First, we do not know whether the examples given are representative and what portion of the pertinent behavior has negative rather than supporting implications. Second, we are not helped to approach other cases more efficiently because the analyst does not communicate to us his explicit procedures which might narrow our information search and processing. Third, while a number of points in time may be treated, we are not given precise portraits of the amount and rate of change in key considerations. Accordingly, we have only very limited ability to project the results ahead, or to describe and explain the dynamics of the situations analyzed. Finally, we are left with only a vague basis for policy implications. We are not shown, although we may be told, precisely how important each key consideration is. We are not shown what the probable consequences of change of X amount in one will be for the others, and when those consequences will occur. Accordingly, we have no firm basis for suggesting that a particular policy action or program will, or would have, produced a result different from that reported in the analysis.

A more statistical approach promises greater benefits if done well, i.e., if the measurements are reasonably valid and reliable and if the statistical treatment reasonably appropriate. Such work can provide explicit procedures which enable us to proceed more efficiently with other cases using similar measures. If the measurements are made for a number of points in time, we will have a factual grasp of the nature of trends and be in a position to project these trends ahead for the set of cases under analysis.[20] If there is conventional wisdom about the phenomenon under analysis (e.g., domestic violence and international war) we will have a clearer idea of how well that wisdom conforms to the array of pertinent facts. We can gain relatively precise information on 1) how much change in one or several key characteristics ac-

[19] The subsets of interest to policy users are frequently isomorphic with their role in the bureaucratic division of labor. If the bureaucracy is organized along geographical lines, interest and relevance go to a geographically bounded part of the set analyzed. If the organization is along functional lines (as used by the State Department), the part of the analysis pertinent to the function receives attention.

[20] Projections rest of course on a variety of continuity, in a sense stability, assumptions. If we have no basis for accepting or rejecting such assumptions, projections, as Hume pointed out some time ago, are useful if worrying.

counts for change in others and 2) how that ability to account for variance involves time lags. Knowledge of the last kind can have important evaluative implications for policy already in force or under consideration, and for estimating future situations.

If one wishes to use history to generate policy suggestions, their plausibility gains strength if certain forms of evidence are provided. As an example, let us use Morse's suggestion that the United States establish a central foreign economic policy mechanism. In using this example, I do not mean to suggest that his intent or presentation are exclusively historical as we use that term. Two sorts of historical approaches would seem to provide substantial support for such a suggestion. The first would involve the analysis of the comparative foreign economic performance of a substantial number of nations which had and a substantial number which did not have such a central mechanism. If the class of nations with the mechanism tended to perform substantially better than those without, and their international economic interdependence was approximately equivalent, one might conclude that the mechanism was valuable regardless of societal differences. As an alternative one might focus on a single example of success characterized by such a mechanism, e.g., France. The problem of historical explanation would then be to establish through some sort of model of the French system that its performance was more sensitive to the central mechanism than to other features Morse mentions which are unlikely to be present in the U.S. case, e.g., relative insulation of foreign policy from domestic pressures, support from the E.E.C. Commission. Since neither sort of historical demonstration is reported, we have no basis for assigning priority to the creation of a central mechanism relative to other coping measures and few substantial reasons to assign any particular level of benefits to its establishment. We may still accept the suggestion; the above argument is not sufficient reason to reject it. However, if we find the suggestion persuasive it is more because we are habituated to centralization as a reflex when control seems inadequate than because of evidentially based reasoning for the effectiveness of a command center.

To conclude our discussion of historical products, it seems useful to note a particular class of relevant byproducts that quantitative history can in principle provide. These involve improving the information processing capability and reducing the information cost of policy actors. The conduct of quantitative historical research often involves the development and demonstration of computer based methods for organizing, accessing, and using international relations information.

Indeed, I would suggest that in terms of relevance to the policy community the major payoff from the data analysis and archival activities recently salient in international relations has been the methods developed for information handling.[21] These methods may well have a relevance which is not nullified by fluctuating policy preferences and issue-agendas among policy actors. They can assist with problems of organizational memory and short decision deadlines without waiting for international relations scholars to significantly advance their theoretical and engineering capabilities.[22] The methods allow policy actors to use whatever verbal and numerical records they believe of value to explore those historical patterns and policy options which the operators think have relevance. Indeed recent developments including the emphasis on coherent country and regional planning of U.S. foreign policy, the increased numbers of foreign policy officials with some training in modern economic and management science analysis, the cuts in foreign affairs personnel, and increasingly tough budget reviews, all create incentives to use information handling methods developed in contemporary international relations analysis.

IV. Engineering

In his 1968 Compton lectures, Herbert Simon addressed the possibility and content of what he called the "sciences of the artificial."[23] He pointed out the existence of a body of professions whose fundamental task resembles that of policy relevant international relations. "Engineering, medicine, business, architecture, and painting are concerned not with the necessary but with the contingent—not with how things are but how they might be—in short with design."[24] The point of these

---

[21] I have deliberately stressed information-handling methods as distinct from data and findings. For helpful examples of such methods and their applications, see: John V. Gillespie and Betty A. Nesvold, eds., *Macro-Quantitative Analysis* (Beverly Hills 1971); John E. Mueller, ed., *Approaches to Measurement in International Relations* (New York 1969); and J. David Singer, ed., *Quantitative International Politics* (New York 1968). I do not mean to imply that all the articles in these references are instances of quantitative history or indeed that any are pure cases.

[22] For example, one can see potential policy value in the CASCON and CACIS systems discussed by Tanter without sharing any of his theoretical views. For discussion of the considerations involved in academic and official development and use of computer based information systems, see: Davis B. Bobrow, "Data Banks, Foreign Affairs, and Feasible Change," prepared for delivery at the Conference on Data Banks for International Studies sponsored by the U.S. Department of State and the International Studies Association, Washington, May 14-16, 1971; Raymond Tanter, "The Policy Relevance of Model Building in World Politics," prepared for delivery at the American Political Science Association Annual Meetings, Chicago, September 7-11, 1971.

[23] Herbert A. Simon, *The Sciences of the Artificial* (Cambridge, Mass. 1969).

[24] *Ibid.*, xi.

professions is to design instrumentalities for outcomes based on human purposes and goals.

The perspective of professional work to produce designs conducive to the achievement of human purposes underlies the fourth class of products I wish to discuss.[25] From the standpoint of international relations, "engineering" products are designed capabilities for two sorts of performances. The first is that of monitoring and anticipating the external environment. The general design problem is to provide an information system which provides signals about when some intervention or change is needed in terms of a given goal, e.g., U.S. balance of payments surplus, international peace, free access to Berlin, economic growth in excess of population growth. Perhaps the most familiar example of such a system is the set of economic indicators used to signal when some change in U.S. economic policy is needed given particular employment and inflation goals. The second purpose is that of achieving or avoiding some particular real-world state of affairs. The goals involved may be the same as those which motivate the design of a monitoring system, but the task is to achieve them rather than only to know how one is doing with reference to them. The goals may differ greatly in subject and scope, e.g., arrange a Presidential visit to Peking, produce self-sufficiency in food-grains in a developing country, avoid nuclear war. Products for achieving substantive international policy goals are prescriptive in nature. They are constructed for specific problems and situations within which the prescription is intended to work. They set forth what set of actions will accomplish a goal and the procedures to carry out those actions at a particular time and place. For example, if the goal is agricultural development, the engineering design will address itself to the set of strategies (biological, financial, and institutional) needed to produce development for a particular country with particular soil and climate, disposable income and taxation, and landholding and labor force organization characteristics.

Before we discuss the properties which "engineering" products must have to serve as designs for policy, it may be helpful to note explicitly how our fourth class of products differs from history and theory. Engineering models resemble history in their emphasis on the characteristics of a particular time and space. Engineering models differ from history in that they flow from an explicit, advance plan and provide a detailed prescription for a socially useful capability. This prescriptive commitment to a design that will achieve a preset performance goal,

[25] I am indebted for many fruitful ideas to Minnesota colleagues Frederick Bailey, Robert Holt, and James Lyday.

as illustrated above, is not present when we point out implications of historical analyses. In those cases we are only using the historical framework to provide analogies to contemporary policy problems, or, in the case of quantitative history, to provide information about states of some part of the real world, e.g., international trade, public opinion, which constrains foreign policy.

Engineering models resemble theory in that both require understanding of why particular outcomes occur. One must understand the necessary and sufficient conditions for the occurrence of X or Y, e.g., an arms freeze as contrasted with arms reduction, to design programs and policies to achieve X or Y. However, engineering does not require that understanding in advance. That is, engineering does not require an ahistorical understanding of cause and effect. Engineers can build models which work in the absence of a formal deductive system by relying on experience, intuition, trial and error, and a long series of adjustments ("tuning"). That is in fact what has been done in complex programmatic sectors of foreign policy, e.g., general war forces, development assistance. Sometimes such an approach works. Unfortunately, we have sufficient experience to know that, first, the *ad hoc*, pragmatic approach does not work much of the time in either the military or civil sectors of foreign policy and, second, that the costs incurred in a long and fruitless adjustment process of a basically inappropriate policy design can be prohibitive. "Engineering" in international relations resembles that for other complex systems. It requires the ahistorical deductive structure of theory if it is to be successful time after time and if it is to be efficient. Trial and error implies wasted resources on dead ends and unreliable performance. And the waste multiplies due to the growth of organizational and personal commitments by foreign policy actors. Even if that inertial force can be held down, the problems posed by a complex system such as international relations are simply too numerous and too interconnected for us to try out all the possibilities we can argue persuasively for.

If engineering products are to provide relevant prescriptions and designs, they must have certain attributes. It seems useful to note these and then turn to the chapters by Choucri-North and Allison-Halperin to illustrate their implications. First, the engineering model must specify a real-world goal in terms of some set of performance requirements. For example one set of requirements might be to increase the standard of living of the masses in a developing country by a particular percentage while holding the power of a pro-American elite at its current level. If we alter any requirement, e.g., abandon the elite, we change the design problem also. While our language in talking about the requirements attribute may be unfamiliar, substantive equivalents are familiar in the policy community, e.g., instructions to representatives in international negotiations, accuracy and weight standards for missiles.

Second, the engineering product needs to provide the necessary and sufficient conditions, if there are such, for achieving the goal in the historical situation of interest. Standard statistical relationships which well surpass tests of significance are inadequate in the absence of process models.[26] The analyst requires process models in order to determine what happens to interventions and what interventions, in the sense of purposeful actions, will result in the pre-selected goal. It is inadequate to know, for example, simply that alliance membership is positively associated with war involvement. The links must be understood to prescribe a design for reducing war involvement or for monitoring its probability. In addition, the understanding of process must be sufficiently precise to illuminate, for example, whether changes in alliance policy will in and of themselves reduce the chances of getting into war as much as desired and, if not, what other policies are required. We must be able to perform sensitivity analysis to evaluate strategies and that is best done when we have process models.

Third, engineering products must consciously take time into account. A relevant prescription calls for actions to be taken at some point in time in order to achieve a goal at some other specified point in time. The time frame should itself be part of the performance requirements. If time is not treated explicitly, the product does not clarify when one intervenes to achieve a particular future, e.g., arms control before a decision must be made on a new generation of delivery vehicles, a trade agreement before a scheduled change of government in our own or another nation. In order to meet the need for time-dependent prescriptions, the process model must specify how long it takes for change in one element to affect another. For example, if our interest is in food self-sufficiency for a poor nation, we need to understand the possibly differential rates of change in food grain availability and seed production. Failure to be informed about rates of change can lead to actions taken too late to be effective or to premature resource commitments which close options and reduce resource stocks. If we are

---

[26] On the need for process models, see: Ronald D. Brunner and Klaus Liepelt, "Data Analysis, Process Analysis, and System Change," Institute of Public Policy Studies, University of Michigan, Discussion Paper #20 (1970); and Davis B. Bobrow, "International Indicators," prepared for delivery at the American Political Science Association Annual Meetings, New York, September 2-6, 1969.

to determine what time-relationships should be built into our process models, we need to have acquired time-series information about the elements of the model. With it we can determine important leads and lags (e.g., what happens how long before trade imbalances develop; what happens how long after a revolutionary party gains power). One final point about time merits our attention. It is the need for some fit between the time-frame of the engineering model and the time-frame of the policy actors for whom the model prescribes action. Action implications should fall within the timespan actors treat as relevant to what they do. Obviously, the length of that span varies across cultures, organizations, persons, and issues, but whatever its value the engineer must take it into account. In doing so, he may prescribe that the time-span of policy actors must be changed for them to achieve their goal. Such suggestions are not a new idea although they receive relatively little attention in international relations analysis. Perhaps the most familiar examples are extending the tour of duty of military and foreign service personnel in particular assignments, and moving from a single year to a multi-year budget authorization for development assistance.

Fourth, since the purpose of the engineering activity is to prescribe policy or action, the elements and relationships in the model must be sufficiently manipulable to be subject to change through deliberate interventions. The exact degree and type of manipulability required depends on the actors who are supposed to follow through and implement the design. It does little good to prescribe a course of action which an accessible audience cannot implement even if it would like to do so. The implications of this condition are severe for international relations where a national actor seldom fully controls the behavior of any others. It may often mean that the goals of the design and thus of a policy must be modified substantially. However, failure to come to grips with manipulability constraints can often produce policy designs which are at best irrelevant and at worst generate false expectations of efficacy.

Finally, engineering models are most helpful when they contain some updating and adjustment mechanism. As the reader will recall, engineering products depend on numerous specific historical conditions. They may well change in less time than it takes to design and implement a policy intervention. Indeed this sort of instability has often been cited as a major barrier to the conduct of engineering in social as distinct from technological areas. Because the conditions can change quickly relative to the pipeline of delivery from a policy, engineering products need a monitoring capability to free them from unwarranted stability assumptions. Familiar long delivery time items in foreign policy include weapons systems and massive development projects. Familiar important determinants of their value which may change before the weapons are deployed or the development projects are productive include an opponent's military capabilities and intentions and the political orientation of a host country regime.

The prospect of engineering products for international relations analysis is attractive. If we are successful in such efforts our relevance would clearly be much greater than is now the case. It would be a different form of relevance from that of analysts who use more customary intellectual approaches. The chapters by Allison-Halperin and Choucri-North indicate both substantial progress toward and shortfalls from engineering products.[27] On the encouraging side, both papers suggest central elements in processes of foreign policy and move toward specifying their relationships. Both deal with behaviors through a set of time periods. Both stress the extent to which variables are and are not manipulable. Both differentiate between variables according to that criterion. Both include variables which change relatively quickly. Both generate prescriptions for policy actors. However, because they differ in substance and research strategy, the two contributions appear ultimately to have different purposes and, for engineering relevance, different development needs.

Choucri and North are engaged in designing a long-range monitoring system to provide information about the probabilities of international conflict. The paper can be seen as an effort to design an international relations monitoring capability. They present a general formulation of the processes which result in conflict between nations. They report their effort to develop a model embodying these processes for major international actors for the 1890-1914 period. Their formulation implies, but the data analysis reported does not show it, that long-term relatively non-manipulable processes overwhelmingly constrain the leeway of national decision-makers to avoid conflict. The data do show a varying ability for the equations stated to account for four rates of change.[28] If we are to have a long-range conflict warning system, we look forward to the extension of the reported work in at least the following ways. First, equations which provide a good fit are needed to link a structural equation of demands to lateral pressure, intersections,

[27] The authors stress the need for further development. I do not mean to imply that they are unaware of the limitations I suggest.
[28] See above, pp. 103, 121.

and military competition, and the ultimate concern of external violence. Second, the time relationships between changes in one and another component need to be worked out to relate warning to the leadtimes which policy coping programs require. Third, there is a need for sensitivity analysis to determine the impact of unit changes through public policy, e.g., in military budgets, on the components of the structural equations. In particular, we need to know the impact of changes on the terms which link one structural equation to another, and we need to allow for additional possible non-linear relationships. Fourth, judging solely from the coefficients reported in Table 2 of their paper,[29] the equations need to be modified, and possibly specified on a national basis, to explain the rates of change of particular actors more fully.

Even at the stage reported, we can see that Choucri-North have established two important points. First, specific variables with long and short time constants seem to have important relationships to major aspects of international affairs. Accordingly, time-series for these variables are a warranted investment. Second, modeling approaches from economics can be usefully applied to international relations analysis. These suggest estimating procedures which clearly show the limits (uncertainty) of their findings. Their effort also illustrates engineering with a high relevance potential to legislators and citizens, not only to executive branch officials. If successful, the product clearly will have relevance to an international as well as to an American community.

What are the necessary and sufficient conditions for the information a finished version of the Choucri-North system provides to be heeded? How would the actions it suggests be chosen and implemented? Allison-Halperin are working toward the process knowledge to answer that sort of question. In contrast to Choucri-North they are not designing with reference to an explicitly desired state of international affairs. Instead, judging from the Planning Guide appended to their paper, their concern is to provide process knowledge necessary for an executive to be effective (achieve goals).[30] Clearly it is much farther from a model which can be tested and tuned in a technical sense. What they have done in a compelling manner is to suggest elements and relationships to be included when one sets out to design a course of action to produce a particular foreign policy. In principle one could use their outline to evaluate the feasibility of particular goals and means. One can specify at least one set of conditions necessary for goals to be achieved. One can specify the conditions under which one strategy is more effective than another. We have here a partial design guide, but not the design of a

[29] See above, p. 121.   [30] See above, pp. 77-79.

strategy which a particular actor can use in a particular situation to accomplish a specified goal.

Systems engineering of international relations requires that we construct models which put together the concerns of the two papers we have been discussing. We need the information monitors to know the state of the world and how it changes as a consequence of national policy outputs. If we are to design capabilities to produce more effective outputs and to modify those resulting from established policy, we also need to deal with the intervening bureaucratic and political processes. Engineering products are designed to be used. Use requires that their designer include as parts of his problem the hurdles to adopting and implementing his suggestions. If he designs for the real world rather than a utopian or a simulate world, his artifices must take into account the persons and groups whose behavior shapes foreign policy performance. The desirability of combining constraining macro-state variables, such as Choucri-North emphasize, with micro-state variables, such as Allison-Halperin treat, is not unique to international relations. It is common in the physical sciences and the ability to affect such a synthesis is the mark of a very advanced science indeed. It is also the case that useful models can be produced prior to the ability to combine the two streams.

The remarks on engineering, and indeed on the other forms of products as well, have been more concerned with questions of technical criteria than with those of persuasive communication to foreign policy officials. Relevance involves both sets of questions but the strategies and tactics involved differ very substantially.[31] They overlap principally in terms of some of the inherent relevance potential properties we have discussed.

I do not know if international relations analysis is yet up to systems engineering as described above. I am sure that it will never be unless we try a few times. Without attempts, we cannot know what are priority efforts to increase our relevance potential. Odysseus was mentioned in an earlier chapter. It seems to me that the depressing aspect of his perils was that he and his companions went through so much and really did not do much for anybody. I suggest we attempt international systems engineering in the hope that the same will not be said of us.

---

[31] Problems of and strategies for influence are discussed in two recent papers: Charles F. Hermann, "The Knowledge Gap: the Exchange of Information Between the Academic and the Foreign Policy Communities," and Davis B. Bobrow, "Analysis and Foreign Policy Choice: Some Lessons and Initiatives." Both were prepared for delivery at the American Political Science Association Annual Meetings, Chicago, September 7-11, 1971.

THE SCHOLAR AND THE
POLICY-MAKER

By ALLEN S. WHITING

INTRODUCTION

EVER since Plato advocated his ideal of a philosopher-king, the intellectual has sought to guide the destinies of state. Sometimes he has been openly explicit in articulating advice, as with Machiavelli. More often, however, the intellectual has abjured so crass a role. Instead, he has sought to influence through private persuasion or has rendered counsel indirectly through scholarly essays. Only in China did the dichotomy between scholar and statesman disappear some two thousand years ago with emergence of a political system that monopolized bureaucratic control in the hands of the literati, that infinitesimally small proportion of the population that could master the classical adages which comprised the examinations for entrance into government. Elsewhere the sword proved to be mightier than the pen, at least in determining affairs of state.

In the United States, hostility toward and suspicion of intellectuals remained relatively steadfast through almost two hundred years of the republic, Professor Woodrow Wilson's election to the White House notwithstanding. President Franklin D. Roosevelt's academic advisers or "brain trust," pejoratively so called, were customarily caricatured in cartoons of the day as cross-eyed crackpots with professor's robes askew. Then, in 1961, President John F. Kennedy's inauguration opened up a "New Frontier" in government for a flow of distinguished scholars recruited from campuses and research centers across the country. Intellectuals proliferated throughout the Department of Defense, the Department of State, the National Security Council staff in the White House, and embassies abroad. Others played an inside role from the outside as private consultants or in close association with the Rand Corporation and similar institutions in the Washington and Boston area. Contracts for conferences and special studies burgeoned, spawning a new generation of advisers fresh from graduate school to counsel such luminaries as Secretary of Defense Robert McNamara and Ambassador Maxwell Taylor.

This phenomenon reached its apex in the American political system with the appointment of an esteemed Harvard scholar, McGeorge

Bundy, as "special assistant" to President Kennedy. Over the next ten years this critical position was consistently occupied by noted social scientists with Walt W. Rostow following Bundy, to be succeeded in turn by Henry Kissinger. Indeed, so far had the intellectual risen in the policy process by 1971 as to evoke concern from Senator J. William Fulbright, himself a former professor, over alleged lack of accountability and responsibility whereby men of reputedly high intellect produced bad policy yet remained beyond the control of Congress.[1] To be sure, differing assessments of this symbiotic relationship between men of research and men of politics are inevitable, given the varying perspectives of individual participants, publicists, and historians. But regardless of how the ultimate consensus may eventually apportion credit or blame for U.S. policy in the nineteen-sixties, Senator Fulbright is not alone in his disappointment over the intensive interaction between academic and bureaucrat.

This context adds particular interest to a supplementary issue of *World Politics* which examines anew the potentiality for theory in world politics to facilitate foreign policy making. Fortunately the context does not define the contributions of the volume. Raymond Tanter and Richard Ullman wisely did not seek retrospective assessment of how social science impacted on past policy. Insofar as such judgment can be made at all so soon after the event, it is amply available elsewhere. Instead, they solicited a series of thoughtful essays which offer a sober but constructive contribution to understanding the limitations as well as the advantages which theory might offer practitioners of world politics. Yet whatever their conscious design, the memory of accusations and recriminations exchanged amongst critics and defenders of the Vietnam War may have tempered the mood of the authors and made them even more tentative than scholarly modesty and intellectual prudence might otherwise dictate. As a result, the promise of scholarly solutions to international problems is nowhere evident. If the "sixties" were criticized as exemplifying the arrogance of professors as well as of politicians in America, the "seventies" have begun with a humble search for self-confidence and direction, verging on self-criticism as exemplified by the authors.

This renders difficult my task of highlighting those aspects of the papers most relevant to policy-makers in the Department of State and its counterpart, the National Security Council. However, perhaps part

---

[1] *United States Relations With the People's Republic of China*, Hearings Before the Committee on Foreign Relations, United States Senate, 92nd Congress, June 28, 1971, p. 235.

of the problem may be seen in different perspective and to that extent be susceptible to more positive an approach. C. P. Snow has lamented the existence of two cultures which separate men of letters from men of science.[2] Anyone who moves across the boundary line between "insiders" and "outsiders" soon learns, however, that there is still a third culture which separates the bureaucrat from the other two realms of intellectual endeavor. As one who has shared this nomadic wandering, I would like to focus on specific characteristics of this third culture which theory must confront if it is to serve policy. Because my area of responsibility embraced Asia, illustrations tend of necessity to be oriented toward China and Vietnam policy. This focus is not, however, for the purpose of reraking past errors. My aim is to provide positive as well as negative observations which may guide research and theory in international affairs as practiced by the United States.

GENERAL THEORY VERSUS SPECIFIC EXPERTISE

Oran Young's cogent critique of the academic marketplace bluntly cautions the policy-maker against what passes for theory in his exchange with professors. So strong is Young's statement, that it might be subtitled *caveat emptor*, let the buyer beware. Pointing out that what appears to be a tested hypothesis is often little more than shrewd hunch, he notes, "The policymaker sometimes feels compelled to accept the conclusions of the theorist more or less on faith." Moreover, he "occasionally exhibits a tendency to respect the views of the theorist on questions that fall outside his range of expertise due to a kind of halo effect."

Having said this, Young stops short of indicting intellectuals for past policy errors, claiming "These problems have not arisen in any serious way in the field of international relations due to the absence of viable theories." This invites a double rejoinder. The absence of viable theories did not inhibit successive presidents from escalation in Vietnam nor from the felt need to dress escalatory policies in theoretical garb. Both scholars and their product were recruited for the rationalization of policy. Whether at the more abstract level of game theory or in the concrete realm of counter-insurgency, theories and models (or what passed for such) became the warp and woof of memoranda that implemented policy in Washington and manuals which defined practice overseas.[3] Occasionally this amounted to little more than emulating models ad-

[2] C. P. Snow, *The Two Cultures and the Scientific Revolution* (Cambridge 1959); also *The Two Cultures: A Second Look* (Cambridge 1964).

[3] An extremely useful survey of the literature, completed in September 1962, may be found in *A Counterinsurgency Bibliography*, compiled by D. M. Condit and others, Special Operations Research Office, The American University (Washington 1963).

vanced by Mao, Che, and Giap. Often, however, it invoked theories of nation-building and political development.[4] While the scholar's language misleadingly implied a capability in human engineering derived from analysis of transitional societies in the modernization process, Young's warning also obtained, namely that "policymakers utilize the end products of theories without ever acquiring a thorough working knowledge of the logical structure of the theories themselves."

In this regard, Young's critique of game theory as a basis for prediction in world politics is particularly well taken. Had the policy-makers probed into the logic behind war games played in the Pentagon, they might have been less willing to project the future by this method or, alternatively, they might have demanded more of the academic contribution. During the mid-1960's the Joint War Games Agency regularly recruited civilian and military specialists to pursue alternative scenarios of conflict in Southeast Asia.[5] Rarely did the umpires or evaluators of these games include specialists in either Vietnamese culture or communist politics. On one exceptional occasion, the "Red" team included a predominance of both types, but more generally the specialists were consigned to the so-called working level while the superiors consisted primarily of senior bureaucrats and academicians. Interestingly enough, on the single occasion when "Red" was heavily weighted with Asian and communist experts, the war ended in a stalemate. This outcome proved very disturbing to the Chairman of the Joint Chiefs of Staff who evaluated the game for top ranking individuals from the White House, State and Defense Departments. He explicitly chided "Red" for not taking the game seriously while commending "Blue" for its contribution. It was virtually inconceivable to these graduates from America's most distinguished military and civilian academies that the persistence with which Hanoi's simulated representatives countered U.S. strategies could correspond with the real course of events. In fact it took two years of U.S. military effort in Vietnam before the game became accepted as grim reality.

To be sure, the scholarly gamesman would be the first to object that he is not depicting reality. Moreover, refiners of the method have added the need for multiple runs to achieve an N-factor sufficient to provide

---

[4] See, for instance, Walt Whitman Rostow, *Stages of Economic Growth* (Cambridge 1960). In his calculus of the North Vietnamese willingness to comply with U.S. policy when accompanied by the threat of U.S. air strikes, Professor Rostow cited Hanoi's industrial investment for modernization as the most promising target for leverage on North Vietnamese decision-making. See *The Pentagon Papers*, Bantam Books (New York 1971), p. 241, as one instance of this position argued at greater length in other memoranda and in oral discussions.

[5] The author was a participant in these games.

some credible basis of analysis. In addition, area specialists plead against ethnocentric biases while others caution against ideological blinders, both excellent criticisms for American policy-makers attempting to anticipate Asian Communist behavior on the basis of game theory and systems analysis.

Another approach, however, is suggested by the success of intelligence specialists in the Central Intelligence Agency and the Department of State in forecasting developments in the Indochina War. As noted at various points in the so-called "Pentagon Papers," intelligence estimates proved quite prescient in predicting the failure of various U.S. escalatory policies to achieve their desired ends in either South or North Vietnam.[6] Contrary to conventional impressions conveyed by the word "intelligence" however, these estimates were not based on "hard" evidence clandestinely acquired. Instead, they emerged from many years of close association with evidence of Asian communist motivation as manifested in behavior and public pronouncements. This evidence was further refined by a mixture of insight and intuition which, whatever else machines may do better, is still the unique property of man.

This consensus between two different agencies within the government existed from the very earliest estimates in 1964 through the close of the McNamara history in 1968. This suggests a more systematic approach at work than the subjective impressionism implied by such pejorative terms as Kremlinology and China-watching. Unfortunately, neither by inclination nor opportunity did analysts in the Department of State and CIA explicate their methodological assumptions and techniques. Conceivably they were consistently right for consistently wrong reasons. More likely they worked with partial theory and learning, generating what Young calls "informed opinion."

To profit from their experience, scholars could systematically interrogate government analysts, requiring the latter to articulate the assumptions which underlay predictions and then, if security considerations permitted, compare predictions with actual behavior so as to better evaluate success versus failure. Provided that individuals were assured sufficient safeguards to preserve their professional anonymity, considerable gain might emerge from carefully collected interview data. In return, scholars could offer to test new research techniques, refine theories, and train ongoing analysts in their use. Computer methods of content analysis, for instance, hold promise of major breakthroughs for

[6] *The Pentagon Papers* (fn. 4). The author took part in all of the estimates down to mid-1966 as Director, Office of Research and Analysis for Far East, Bureau of Intelligence and Research, Department of State.

overworked and understaffed officers responsible for interpreting foreign media. Data banks and information retrieval systems have yet to realize their full potential primarily because of inadequate funding. Retrospective coding and the almost inevitable subjectivity thereby entailed, is another obstacle to be overcome if any near-future gains are to be realized from more extensive computer analysis for trend prediction and contingency event forecasts.

Raymond Tanter's paper is instructive in this regard. Tanter tests implications of alternative models and argues for synthesis between a system interaction approach and a foreign policy decision-making focus. Integration of academic game theorists, man-machine simulators, and governmental area specialists provides a useful analogue to his approach. Admittedly, the governmental expert is less structured in his analysis of decision-making in country X than are his academic counterparts who provide the models for Tanter and others. Prolonged probing, however, is likely to reveal a fairly cohesive model in the mind of the analyst who sifts the daily intake of data for clues to the political dynamic of his particular country, from which he predicts actions and reactions in alternative future contexts.

This fusion of the academic theoretician in world politics and the government area specialist offers more promise than past efforts at purely academic interdisciplinary inquiry. Area specialists on most campuses are heavily oriented toward the humanities and history, with relatively less emphasis on contemporary political inquiry. Government analysts, for obvious reasons, are more compatible with international relations scholars in their time and problem focus, if not in their methodological framework. Even in this latter instance, however, their resources can significantly augment those of the outside scholar whose language and source limitations often confine him to a relatively inadequate data source such as the *New York Times* for event coding.[7] Every newspaper is a product of pressurized output involving a long chain of inputs determined by varying criteria along the way, from reporter through copy editor to final compositor and typesetter, resulting in cumulative selection, distortion, and error. It is also a culturally and politically biased medium. Subjective reporting of what is considered "news" reflects what can be learned from open sources or sources which will not be foreclosed by publication. In short, the newspaper can pro-

---

[7] From 1949 to 1970, the *New York Times* had no correspondent in the People's Republic of China and only an occasional correspondent stationed in the Republic of China. Reporting from Hong Kong relied on a two-man bureau, supplemented by dispatches from Tokyo. This provided a limited basis for covering the interaction between the Communists and Nationalists, plus covert involvement by the C.I.A.

vide only partial coverage of events that are perceived by persons in other governments. Admittedly, "I saw it in the *New York Times*" may, as in the irate rejoinder of the Soviet ambassador in *Dr. Strangelove*, become a fact of international life itself, contrary to the actuality.[8] Nevertheless, moving from newspapers to the incorporation of data derived from government monitoring and reporting into banks and retrieval systems oriented toward theory-building would constitute a quantum leap in the resources of scholars. In turn their refinement of methods and development of theories could enrich government analysis.

It would be specious to suggest this joint effort would result in symmetrical payoffs. Oran Young's persuasive disclaimers against undue expectations in theory-building suggest that for some time to come the academic would be the greater beneficiary. This argues for the initiative and the funding to come from outside the government, especially in a tight budget situation. The high cost of computers and the time-consuming nature of interviews and interaction between government and academic specialists requires a major commitment by private institutions over a period of at least five, and perhaps ten years. This may not be a wholly unfeasible proposal. For instance, one organization expressly oriented toward world politics and currently in transition under the new leadership of a former government official responsible for intelligence forecasts, the Carnegie Endowment for International Peace, might be a prime candidate for such an undertaking. Only after sufficient time and testing for the results to be beneficial for policy-making should the government be expected to take over ongoing research and development costs, preferably through a wholly non-policy oriented agency such as the National Science Foundation.

ADDRESSING THE POLICY-MAKER

Graham Allison and Morton Halperin provide an insightful and illuminating analysis of the policy process, as practiced in the United States, with suggestive application to large bureaucracies whose internal values may be similar, as in Soviet Russia. Their article is a useful counter to an exclusive preoccupation with the objective validity of theory and methods since quite often the policy game is not truth but consequences. Thus, according to Allison and Halperin, it is the politics of policy rather than its logic which determines the outcome. While this oversimplifies their argument, it nonetheless helps to adjust our focus to

---

[8] The exchange occurred between the Soviet ambassador and the American President, the latter denying he had ever authorized development of a "doomsday machine." See *Dr. Strangelove or How I Came To Love The Bomb*, screenplay by Terry Southern.

the problem of the policy-maker which may be different from that initially addressed by the scholar in at least three respects. First, he is not addressing a problem *de novo* but finds himself thrust into an on-going situation freighted with precedent and established views, and sub-ject to multidimensional tugs both within the government and from the outside.[9] Second, his authority is usually limited to a specific country, region, or problem, the specific details of which dictate his sense of choice and his policy needs. Third, he has a personal time-span of in-dividual responsibility which rarely exceeds four years and more likely one or two, in terms of his current assignment. He may have a lifetime association with an area but he often leaves a particular office or desk in the near future.

These problems deserve examination at greater length if the scholar is to design theory and make its application to policy consonant with constraints relevant to the bureaucrat's needs. This first problem, that of arriving in the midst of a policy struggle instead of prior to its inception, leaves little that can be done. Theoretically, of course, the scholar could try to alert the policy-maker to future issues to be addressed well in advance of their becoming critical. Robert North and Nazli Choucri exemplify the classic case of those who see trouble ahead and attempt to forestall disaster by raising the perspectives of political men from their preoccupation with selfish and short-term goals to the long-term con-sequences of action or inaction. Specifically, they stress the interaction of technological development and population growth on resource require-ments, resulting in lateral or expansionist pressures which in turn lead to conflict. Objectively, their case has much merit and should command the attention of policy-makers throughout the world. Subjectively, how-ever, it runs afoul of the bureaucratic fact of life, so provocatively de-picted by Allison and Halperin, that tomorrow's problem can be taken up next week but today must still be devoted to yesterday's agenda. Unfortunately today is always with us; next week never seems to come.

Intervening on yesterday's agenda today, however, renders the scholar liable, willfully or not, to becoming party to one side in an ongoing policy dispute. The common complaint, "They didn't really understand what I had to say, so naturally my ideas were misused," often masks a more complex situation. To be sure, understanding may be partial, re-sulting from limitations both in the communicator and his audience.

---

[9] The continuity of policy problems into which officials find themselves thrust is amply illustrated by Harry S. Truman, *Memoirs* (Garden City 1956), Volume I; Ar-thur Schlesinger, Jr., *A Thousand Days* (Boston 1965); and Dean Acheson, *Present At The Creation* (New York 1969).

More likely, however, the policy audience has heard only that portion which is useful to its side in the dispute already under way. New evidence or a new approach, particularly if it bears the prestigious stamp of a professor or an institution in high repute, can be useful in advancing one's cause against an adversary.[10] If this requires citing theories and addressing models in order to benefit from their political implications, so be it.

The structure of decision-making presents a more fundamental problem which is both political and functional. Regardless of where one draws the line for determining the "policy-makers," in the government as a whole or in specific agencies, the perceptual and behavioral constraints posed by information inputs and operational outputs are primarily country-oriented, secondarily region-focused, and only rarely global or functionally determined. It is true that trade and tariff policies, assistance programs, narcotics controls, and a host of activities are ostensibly global in scope and should bear a reasonable degree of conformity across geographic lines. In addition, to the extent one superpower policy confronts another, extending its adversary role even further through global ideological divisions, the policy framework can transcend country or regional limitations. However, neither of these situations eliminates the constraints altogether. Moreover, as U.S. policy has given rise over time to a greater sophistication concerning communism and the Soviet alliance systems, so too has it become more particularized as compared with its global range at its inception in the years immediately following World War II.

In sum, a principal consumer of the scholar's product in the policy realm is a country or region specific desk officer. Yet a main thrust of academic inquiry in world politics over the past two decades has been systems specific.[11] Whether the system under examination is global or partial, the generalizations offered for and deriving from behavior seldom aim at particular relationships. On the one hand, area studies are abjured as unscientific or incapable of generating sufficient predictive capability to advance general knowledge in world politics. On the other hand, prudent theoreticians admonish their audiences that we still know too little to venture specific estimates of single country actions or reactions and must rest content with larger, looser conglomerates in tendency or trend probability forecasts.

[10] Colin S. Gray, "What RAND Hath Wrought," *Foreign Policy*, No. 4 (Fall 1971), traces the interaction between "outside" strategic analysis and "inside" decisions.
[11] Among the foremost contributors to systemic analysis in international relations are Bruce Russett, Karl Deutsch, Hayward R. Alker, Richard A. Brody, Rudolph J. Rummel, and J. David Singer.

Finally, trend forecasts and futurist projections usually address events at least five years distant, and insofar as the projection is made over longer time it is within five or even ten year increments. The policy-maker, however, is preoccupied with the immediate or the near-future, the latter defined as six months to a year or two at most. As a minimal objective, he seeks to leave problems no worse than when he inherited them; at most, he looks for visible success within his tenure of respon-sibility. For the President this maximum tenure is eight years, with only four or less certain; the same holds for the Secretary of State. An assistant secretary, however, is likely to have only two years in the job, while desk officers can rotate even more frequently according to the vicissitudes of personnel assignments throughout the Foreign Service.

These problems are not uniquely those of the professor. They apply in equal measure to officials in the Policy Planning Council and its suc-cessor at State when they prescribe general long-range policy guidelines for a Department which is country and problem specific in its daily orientation.[12] It is no coincidence that policy planning has enjoyed far more prestige among professors than policy-makers, even allowing for the inevitable friction of competition that the Council's presence arouses amongst the regional bureaus. Unlike the full-time official, however, who can promote his theories and pursue their (mis)application on the spot, the social scientist carries a far greater burden of anticipation and communication through his written product which must float on the ocean of paper that rolls over every policy-maker without surcease.

Thus, applicability to perceived policy needs is half the battle. Feasi-bility constitutes the other half. Washington is far more insular in its perceptions and conservative in its estimates of the possible than most academicians appreciate. If professors are criticized for living in an ivory tower, the Washingtonian inhabits a labyrinthine honeycomb with the queen bee directing her court as they, in turn, direct the hive.

Ethnocentricity versus Universality

It is appropriate for American social scientists to focus on U.S. deci-sion-making if they aim to improve policy, since their influence is infinitely greater here than elsewhere. It is also tempting to generalize from behavior in Washington since data is so much more accessible there than in most other capitals. But the question of ethnocentricity remains for the student of world politics who must make his observa-

---

[12] Insightful reflections on problems of the Policy Planning Council are offered in George Kennan, *Memoirs, 1925–1950* (Boston 1967); also Charles Burton Marshall, *The Limits of Foreign Policy* (New York 1954).

tions pertinent to at least several dozen governments capable of affecting the international system by actions short of war, as well as the more obvious five nuclear powers whose military capabilities place them in a separate category. More than 120 nations can officially claim status as nominally equal members of the international system through participation in the United Nations. How relevant for understanding, much less predicting, their individual and collective behavior is data overwhelmingly derived from a European state system, through scholarly perspectives which both reflect membership in and focus primarily upon the so-called "great power" relationships?

Happily, the authors in this volume fare better in this regard than might appear at first glance. Edward L. Morse, for instance, specifically notes that his essay deals with "crisis diplomacy in international economic relationships among the Western industrialized states." Despite this disclaimer, however, he offers a prescription which has far wider applicability, to wit, "A new prudential statecraft is called for which establishes priorities among existing objectives and depreciates a few so that governmental control at the national level can be reasserted." Morse arrives at this conclusion through a comprehensive model of interdependence and transnational activity which breaks with the traditional paradigm of nation-state relations as essentially government to government. He argues that the definition of new priorities should "involve the reimposition of barriers to international interchange" lest greater influence drives out lesser, resulting in eventual superpower domination of all weaker national and cultural entities.

Morse's analysis touches on one of the major issues of the "Great Proletarian Cultural Revolution" wherein Mao Tse-tung wrested control of China from Liu Shao-ch'i, *inter alia* destroying the power of the Chinese Communist Party. The policy struggle involved, among other things, political priorities of social revolution versus economic priorities of development.[13] The argument included international and transnational relations with the Soviet Union at two levels. First, was China to remain dependent upon and subservient to Russian politico-military policy and power, accepting a junior partnership in return for the

---

[13] Two writers who experienced events in China first-hand offer differing assessments: Stephen Fitzgerald, "China Visited: A View of the Cultural Revolution," and Ray Wylie, "The Meaning of the Cultural Revolution," in *China and Ourselves: Explorations and Revisions by a New Generation*, edited by Bruce Douglass and Ross Terrill (Boston 1969). A wide set of interpretations may be found in *China After the Cultural Revolution* (New York 1969). Monographic research on selected aspects appears regularly in the *China Quarterly*. The mass of documentation and the problem of probing the murky politics underlying the struggle have thus far precluded an overall authoritative study.

strategic benefits of an alliance? Second, was socialism in China to accept the Russian model, passively or actively emulating the socio-economic value system which had evolved through twenty-five years of Stalinist policy?[14] Mao acted in full accord with Morse's analysis as well as his prescription, arguing that the Soviet relationship had to be wholly broken and rebuilt anew on drastically limited terms if the communists were to succeed in their avowed revolutionary objective of restructuring Chinese society from a hierarchical to an egalitarian culture.[15] Outside observers saw only that part of Mao's struggle with "socialist revisionism" which involved control over the international communist movement.[16] Far more basic, however, was his concern over the transnational penetration of Chinese society by Russian models antithetical to his revolutionary goals.

Curiously enough, Allison and Halperin's bureaucratic model also appears relevant to the political upheaval which wracked China from 1966 to 1968 since many of the Maoists' allegations ascribe to their opponents behavior parallel to that detailed by Allison and Halperin.[17] The Washington scene may indeed have had its counterpart in Peking with consensus emerging as the residue of interaction largely predetermined by bureaucratic politics and organization constraints. The vested interests of each individual and unit in the decision-making process, and more particularly in China the decision-implementing process, culminated in the priority which top political figures gave to personal status, power, and authority. Admittedly the Maoist indictment is political and self-serving; no hearing can be given to the opposition's case since it has simply disappeared from the scene. However, the charges gain credibility by the model advanced by Allison and Halperin —and surprisingly so in view of the degree to which their observations are limited to wholly different political and cultural systems.

In one sense, this brings the wheel full circle. Max Weber and Karl August Wittfogel long ago sensitized Western social scientists to the centuries of traditional Chinese bureaucracy and its influence on behavior

[14] A brilliant probing of this problem is presented in Franz Schurmann, *Ideology and Organization in Communist China* (2nd edn., Berkeley 1969).

[15] The fullest statement of Mao's position is "On Khrushchev's Phoney Communism," joint editorial by *Jen Min Jih Pao* [People's Daily] and *Hung Ch'i* [Red Flag], July 14, 1964, reprinted in A. Doak Barnett, *China After Mao* (Princeton 1967).

[16] The classic study is Donald S. Zagoria, *The Sino-Soviet Conflict, 1956–1961* (Princeton 1962). See also William E. Griffith, *The Sino-Soviet Rift* (Cambridge, Mass. 1964).

[17] Selected aspects of this confrontation are examined in *China: Management of a Revolutionary Society*, edited by John M. H. Lindbeck (Seattle 1971); and *Party Leadership and Revolutionary Power in China*, edited by John Wilson Lewis (Cambridge 1970).

in the world's oldest continuous political system.[18] If we juxtapose their retrospective analysis against the contemporary Allison-Halperin model, we can better appreciate the difficulty of Mao's struggle to break up bureaucratic politics with its incrementalist fixation on short-term goals that are parochial rather than national. Morse's analysis, in turn, adds the necessary dimension of foreign policy to make the Chinese case relevant for students of world politics. The interlock between foreign policy and domestic politics involving transnational influences which permeate bureaucratic behavior is exemplified by Mao's initial struggle with Kao Kang who, from 1949 to 1953, ran Northeast China as the model for subsequently "liberated" areas. Kao's heavy dependence on Soviet assistance aroused suspicion among observers both in China and abroad that Stalin was building a satellite political rival to Mao Tse-tung's much vaunted independent leadership of the Chinese Communist Party.[19] After Stalin died, Mao purged Kao for allegedly establishing an "independent kingdom."

Just as vested economic interests fused internal and foreign policy in Northeast China, so did the military bureaucracy come to arouse Mao's suspicions because of its emulation of the Soviet model as well as its dependence on access to Russian supplies of modern weapons and nuclear technology. In 1959 his suspicions erupted in confrontation with Marshal P'eng Teh-huai, ostensibly in argument over the "Great Leap Forward" but also involving the threat this economic experiment posed to the modernizing, elitist military interests.[20] Those interests were in turn linked to Moscow which looked askance at Mao's domestic policies. While the Stalin-Kao Kang relationship remains exceedingly obscure, Khrushchev's interaction with Chinese policy arguments in 1958–59 was overtly reflected in his contemptuous comments on Peking's highly touted communes and backyard furnaces.[21] Whether P'eng, as Minister of Defense, actually colluded with Soviet opposition as alleged or merely paralleled Moscow's criticisms, Mao's accusations are consonant with the hypotheses inherent in the Allison-Halperin and Morse models.[22]

[18] Max Weber, *The Theory of Social and Economic Organization* (Oxford 1947); Karl August Wittfogel, *Oriental Despotism* (New Haven 1957).

[19] Schurmann (fn. 14); Professor Roy Grow, Brandeis University, is completing a doctoral dissertation examining this problem in detail.

[20] David A. Charles, "The Dismissal of P'eng Teh-huai," *China Quarterly*, No. 8 (October-December 1961); Alice Langley Hsieh, *Communist China's Strategy in the Nuclear Era* (Englewood Cliffs, N.J. 1962).

[21] Zagoria (fn. 16).

[22] Charles (fn. 20), seems partly supported by later Cultural Revolution accusations, although these are polemical and undocumented. See *Peking Review*, Vol. 10, No. 36, p. 14.

This turns our attention anew to the linkage between domestic politics and foreign policy, a problem central to Tanter's analysis. One major obstacle to past application of the Allison-Halperin model to communist policy-making has been the absence of reliable data. Tanter suggests that imaginative but rigorous use of computer methods can provide an oblique approach to the role of internal as opposed to external inputs in the foreign policy process. Refining this still further through quantitative content analysis holds promise of probing bureaucratic models in communist and other systems whose inner workings are heavily screened from outside observation, to the extent that different media reflect different interests either in their point of origin or in the audiences to which they are addressed.[23] Traditional studies in this area have relied heavily on subjective methods for inferring conflict from essentially qualitative textual indicators.[24] The General Inquirer raised new possibilities for content analysis, however, with important implications so far as the various problems of training research personnel and of reliable data acquisition are concerned.

To continue with our Sino-Soviet illustration, the entrepreneurial model with its emphasis on cost calculation and collective goods offered by Norman Frohlich and Joseph Oppenheimer is also relevant, at least heuristically. They concede that their purpose "is not to formally derive hypotheses which will be of immediate application to the policy-maker, but rather to indicate how this theory might be applied to situations of interest . . . how the theory draws attention to a number of variables and interactions which may prove important in specific applications." This modest set of objectives is justified by the very early stages of development in their model so far as its explicit relevance to world politics is concerned. Nevertheless, their exposition of its potential utility for analysis of alliance relationships illuminates one disruptive dynamic which eroded the Sino-Soviet alliance. Mao Tse-tung expressly perceives most contemporary socialist states as vulnerable to socio-economic tendencies similar to those prevailing in capitalist systems.[25] For him, the entrepreneurial model fits Soviet, albeit of course not Chinese, behavior. His view apart, however, the model may avoid some of the problems which more ideologically oriented interpretations encountered when

---

[23] Suggestive evidence along these lines emerged in the author's research for *China Crosses The Yalu* (Stanford 1968); further probing of the hypothesis is under way by graduate students at the University of Michigan, Stanford, and the University of California, Los Angeles. While these are separate efforts, they occur within a common framework and should prove comparable for assessment.

[24] Hsieh (fn. 20), is a brilliant example of this approach.

[25] "On Khrushchev's Phoney Communism" (fn. 15).

faced with open conflict between the two communist partners. One Frohlich-Oppenheimer calculus, for instance, seems particularly relevant: "States in which there is potential for political competition at relatively low cost would make the best allies." As Khrushchev learned, political competition with Mao came at relatively high economic, political, and even military risk-taking costs.[26] From a Russian calculus, the alliance's disutilities came to outweigh its utilities.

To be sure, some of the authors' admonitions on intervention policy seem less applicable to Soviet behavior as practiced in East Europe since World War II. Frohlich and Oppenheimer assert that "with increasing communication and decreasing costs of transportation throughout the world, it is hard to imagine a country which could not form an alliance with a second outside state to prevent subsequent interventions." Certainly Soviet behavior in Czechoslovakia in 1948 and 1968 showed no such consideration to constrain Moscow as is true for other Russian interventionist decisions in East Germany and Hungary.

THEORETICAL VERSUS PRACTICAL FEASIBILITY

These illustrations suggest the greater dimension of breadth and depth with which the policy-maker might have perceived the Sino-Soviet dispute had he been able to synthesize the models offered by Morse, Allison-Halperin, and Frohlich-Oppenheimer. Instead of crudely dichotomizing alternative single-factor explanations, he would have obtained a sense of the multi-dimensional sources of strain which underlay the alliance and which ones drove Mao Tse-tung to initiate the break. Such advice is premature, however, in view of the very primitive and rudimentary state of these and other models in world politics analysis. Once designed, they must be tested and cross-correlated if, as Tanter shows, the policy-maker is to have enough confidence in assigning weights to the independent variables so as to design his behavior optimally for eliciting a desired reaction. Khrushchev, for instance, may have assigned an unduly high priority to the bureaucratic interest coalition model in his attempt to pressure Mao by manipulating Soviet nuclear and technical assistance in 1959–60. If so, he miscalculated Mao's ability to mobilize support, essentially following the Morse model of transnational threats to independent sovereignty.

Even should an ideal, multi-dimensional model be realized in theory, however, its practical adoption in the Department of State and its

[26] John Gittings, *Survey of the Sino-Soviet Dispute* (Oxford 1968), conveniently groups exchanges between Moscow and Peking according to issue areas which highlight the policy differences.

foreign ministry counterparts is unlikely so long as policy-makers exclude analysis of their own behavior and decision-making process. If a nation's foreign policy derives from more than interaction with other states, as is cogently argued in various forms by all of the essays in this volume, then total comprehension of prospective policy developments must include analysis of one's own behavior as well as that of one's opponents. Traditionally, however, such analysis is taboo in foreign ministries. Ironically, this taboo persists in the Department of State despite the fact that the politics of Washington often preoccupy higher level officers as much or more than foreign affairs. Time and energy are drained away in interagency battles fought at conference tables, on the Hill, and through the press. One consequence of this taboo is that Foreign Service officers are often more expert on policy-making in other countries than in the United States, explaining in part their failure to compete successfully in the bureaucratic battle.

This taboo justifies further the fusion between academic and government specialists discussed earlier. Interesting experiments in this regard have been carried out through the work of Andrew Marshall at Rand, Graham Allison, and various officials, primarily in the Department of Defense. Alexander George's studies in crisis decision-making similarly turn the official's gaze inward for a conscious examination of how structure, function, and personality condition policy wholly apart from the behavior of other states.[27] The Tanter emphasis on computer data desensitizes the problem of individual policy-makers who traditionally avoid outside observation lest professional or personal embarrassment result, permitting coded inputs that mask the players from subsequent identification with specific recommendations and decisions. Thus the perils of the "Pentagon Papers" need not be relived by officials who work with scholars. However, these papers merit attention in the way they reveal the bureaucratic phenomena which cumulatively define "national interests" and then proceed to implement these interests according to particularistic and parochial interpretations. The published documents illustrate the importance of such inputs to policy, independent of external stimuli. Indeed, interaction analysis which focuses exclusively on nation-states as actors seems woefully weak in explanatory power when placed against this account of U.S. thinking and planning for the Vietnam War.

---

[27] For the fullest examination of theoretical and evidential literature in his continuing development of this field, see Alexander L. George, "The Case For Multiple Advocacy In Making Foreign Policy," prepared for delivery at the 1971 Annual Meeting of the American Political Science Association.

Whether one aspires to a general model which encompasses all of the studies in this volume or one focuses more particularly on the Tanter synthesis, greater co-ordination of academic and government research seems mandatory. The pitfalls of such an alliance are both objectively verifiable and subjectively perceived by hostile critics. Nonetheless the need justifies the hazards. No academic center can hope to match the foreign policy decision-making insights possessed by a government with respect to most other countries in the world. Reciprocally, it is unlikely that systems-oriented analysis will take widespread root in a bureaucracy so entrenched in country and geographic orientation. The piecemeal approaches through individuals crossing the academic-governmental barrier, through contractual and consultative arrangements, and through so-called "think tanks," has failed to achieve any significant theoretical breakthroughs. However, the linking of systems-oriented analysis and decision-making models through research conducted by an avowedly governmental academic institution for foreign affairs has genuine promise. If, for instance, the Foreign Service Institute could gain the intellectual stature and the financial resources long advocated by proponents of a civilian counterpart to the national service academies, one of its major contributions could lie in the fusion of academic and governmental research strengths, perspectives, and needs.

In the absence of this larger effort, better use could be made of former government specialists now in academia or retirement. As the ranks of past "participant-observers" of the policy process grow and as Presidential libraries proliferate, so too does the potential payoff of systematic integration of academic theory-building with direct evidence of systemic interaction and domestic decision-making. To be sure, the effort demands a group approach. Individual research can scarcely hope to go much beyond single case studies or the synthesis of existing diplomatic histories and political memoirs. A group effort goes against the scholarly tradition, but the growth of co-authoring reflected in this volume may be a harbinger of greater collective venture in social science, as is already the case in the physical sciences.

Whether one is optimistic or pessimistic concerning the future contribution of theory to policy depends on one's expectations for each side of the relationship. In this regard, an interesting contrast exists between the assumptions of the Allison-Halperin model and those underlying the analysis of Nazli Choucri and Robert North. Choucri and North demonstrate that parochial concern for short-range security can prejudice long-run security interests because of the interrelationship between the technology of arms races, their demands on resources, and the resultant lateral pressures or expansionist tendencies which in turn raise the risk of conflict with competing countries. In effect, they call for coalition politics whereby those responsible for resource conservation join with those concerned with economic development to address problems normally reserved for groups immediately concerned with arms control and defense. This does not necessitate bureaucratic confrontation since their theoretical framework relates long-term security to short-run measures prejudicial to interstate relations, thereby producing consensual interests between defense and development specialists.

However, the Choucri-North consensus model contrasts with the Allison-Halperin emphasis on bureaucratic interests as determining interaction within governments, with consensus emerging essentially as compromise in power struggles rather than from integrating logical convergences of view. Once again our Chinese example is relevant. In 1958 and again in 1966, Mao Tse-tung appeared quite willing to sacrifice short-term economic growth and even middle-range national security capabilities for pursuit of change in domestic and foreign political relationships. His opponents, however, felt Mao's goals were not only utopian but dangerous, not least of all to their vested interests. Mao's prescriptions on population control, together with his emphasis on self-reliance and production with minimum capital and technological investment, combine to meet the challenge posed by the Choucri-North analysis. Despite the logic of his position, however, he collided head-on with a bureaucracy motivated by the vested interest factors as delineated by Allison and Halperin. Whether or not Mao succeeded cannot be finally determined until he leaves the scene and we can analyze the durability of the patterns he moulded. However, the magnitude of the turmoil unleashed by his Cultural Revolution suggests the degree to which the subjective logic of organizations may prevail over the objective logic of environmental factors.

Thus, the best theory may encounter the worst response so far as policy is concerned. Nonetheless, the scholar's first responsibility is to theory, not policy, and the fact remains that theory is more likely to be outside than inside the government. The bureaucrat is much less well placed to challenge the premises of policy or even to re-examine its basic assumptions. Moreover, daily involvement in incremental developments denies the perspective necessary to explicate analytic models or to develop sound hypotheses. Those who do rise above these obstacles to present a "fresh look" rarely can test their models and hypotheses systematically because of ongoing demands of the job. Even the stimulus of professional journals and scholarly studies is stultified by the constant flow of bureaucratic paper which requires scanning, if not careful reading. Finally, those bureaucrats who are assigned expressly to undertake policy-oriented research almost invariably succumb to the temptation of pursuing policy while leaving research behind.

Perhaps we are self-centered and anachronistic in thinking that twentieth-century governments, functioning in the era of thermonuclear weapons and instant global exposure through satellite television, can be guided in their course like Plato's philosopher-king or Machiavelli's prince. It is increasingly difficult to hope that intellectual output can determine the foreign policy of contemporary chiefs of state, pulled and pushed as are many regimes by ever increasingly intensive and extensive a range of interests which impact daily on their individual and collective perceptions. If, however, we can reduce at all the hazards of statecraft under these conditions and thereby assist in lessening the likelihood of thermonuclear war, we shall have justified our effort. It is in this spirit that the papers solicited by Tanter and Ullman may provide a modest, self-critical contribution to the future role of world politics theory in foreign policy.

CONCEPTUAL INDEX

By STEPHEN M. SHAFFER

INTRODUCTORY NOTE

Approaches to the study of international relations employ a wide variety of concepts and indicators. The interrelationships among these concepts often are specified in conceptual schemes, models, or theories. This supplementary issue of *World Politics* presents several approaches to international relations theory which utilize familiar concepts, such as decision-making, crisis, and interdependence, and also concepts (frequently borrowed from other disciplines) that are less familiar, e.g., entrepreneurial and consumer roles, free riders, and externalities. The diversity of approaches and the variety of models specified by the contributors led the co-editors to commission an index focusing on concepts and the variables used to tap the concepts (indicators) rather than a more traditional listing of names, places, and events.

A conceptual index provides an opportunity to do more than merely list various concepts and indicators; the index can serve as a vehicle for illustrating a general scheme assumed by the authors. Although such a scheme may be useful as a tool for summarizing each contribution and for comparing across articles, its use does not assume that each contribution fits the same theoretical or policy orientation. Nevertheless, there seem to be more similarities than there are differences.

All of the contributors to this issue explore the relationship between theories or models of international relations and the needs of the policy-making community. Moreover, each author focuses on the policy-making process either directly, by explicating concepts and variables which influence a nation's foreign policy behavior, or indirectly, by pointing out the stumbling blocks in efforts to build policy-relevant theory and models in the discipline.

Despite the variety of the specific models employed by the authors, a common theme is discernible which resembles one voiced in much of the international relations literature, viz., *interaction* among actors in which the behavior of one actor is considered to be the result of prior behavior of another actor and of the effects of intervening variables. Thus, the outcome is some consequence of both a set of inputs and a set of intervening variables. Two examples illustrate this point. Graham Allison and Morton Halperin suggest that the input—a deadline or an event (external or domestic)—triggers intervening conditions—bureaucratic politics and organizational processes—which then determine the outcome.[1] Edward Morse constructs a model which says that the effect of incompatible goals or objectives (input) on the use of economic diplomacy to achieve political goals (outcome) will depend upon the *amount* of interdependence existing between two nations.

---

[1] A functional relationship of this sort is a developmental sequence in which there is no direct effect of input on outcome. Rather, the input causes the intervening variables which in turn cause the outcome. See Herbert Hyman, *Survey Design and Analysis: Principles, Cases, and Procedures* (Glencoe, Ill. 1955), 254-63.

Hence, the input will have a very different effect when no interdependence exists than when the actors are highly interdependent.[2]

While this general organizing framework may appear quite familiar to some readers, a brief exposition might prove useful. A complete interaction sequence consists of inputs, intervening variables, and outcomes for *each* actor; we look, then, at only one-half of the total interaction. We do not mean to suggest that the specific input factors and intervening conditions will differ across actors; in *most* cases, they will be the same.

Each index entry consists of a concept central to a given article and indicators or definitions used to operationalize the concepts. These entries are located in a cell formed by the intersection of the entity or unit of analysis to which the concepts refer, and the role as input, intervening variable, or outcome that the concepts play in each author's model.

Input refers to the conditions which may prompt the foreign policy-making or theory-building process, and also to attributes or characteristics of the actors which may be salient explanatory factors. For example, in the paper by Morse, crisis is seen as "driving" the system. The conflictive behavior of another alliance is a major input in Raymond Tanter's paper, and Allison and Halperin seem to regard strategic policy, such as deterrence or coercive diplomacy, as an input. Oran Young suggests that theory-building begins with simplified logical models and focuses on behavioral characteristics of actors in international politics such as arms races or bargaining and negotiation.

Intervening variables include those conditions which suggest *why* one particular outcome as opposed to some other plausible result occurs, given certain inputs. Characteristics of the interaction process itself also are treated as intervening variables. For example, Norman Frohlich and Joe Oppenheimer point out that the structure of the exchange relationship is an important intervening condition between rational intentions and exchange behavior. Nazli Choucri and Robert North note that the relationship between the growth of national capabilities and international conflict is dependent upon the perceived domestic and foreign costs of an expansionist foreign policy. According to Tanter, the amount of interdependence among alliance members intervenes in the explanation of inter-alliance conflict using the prior interactions of the adversary alliance as a predictor or input variable.

Finally, outcome is the dependent variable(s) the author wishes to explain. While most of the contributions are concerned with conflictive and cooperative national behaviors, outcomes of concern to three of the authors (Bobrow, Whiting, and Young) are viable international relations theory or policy-relevant models.

In evaluating the utility of this index, an important criterion that might be kept in mind is the amount of useful information the index supplies. The

[2] This is what is often termed a nonadditive relationship which states that the effect of the input varies as a function of the level of the intervening variables. The input thus can affect the outcome directly or influence the outcome via the mediation of the intervening factors. For a discussion of nonadditivity, see Hubert Blalock, "Theory Building and the Statistical Concept of Interaction," *American Sociological Review*, xxx (June 1965), 374-80.

generality of the organizing framework permits the index to summarize the articles, and the communality of the framework for *all* articles facilitates comparison across authors. For example, the papers by Frohlich and Oppenheimer and Tanter both seek to explain foreign policy behavior. But, while Tanter focuses on explaining conflictive interaction between alliances using organizational and system properties, Frohlich and Oppenheimer deal with attributes of individuals and groups to explain foreign policy (conceptualized as choice and exchange behavior). To this extent, the index might be helpful in pointing out similarities and differences across related studies as well as "holes" where the authors have failed to take into account potential explanatory or confounding variables.

Classifying according to units of analysis is also a convenient means of assessing the respective author's theoretical orientations. One question which could be answered using the index, for example, is the extent to which a particular author is oriented more toward decision-making, national, or international system perspectives.

CONCEPTUAL INDEX

Raymond Tanter, "International System and Foreign Policy Approaches: Implications for Conflict Modelling and Management"

Unit of Analysis	Input	Intervening Variables	Outcome
Individual	Rational intentions, 8-11, 14, 15, 17, 18, 20 Value-maximizing processes Learning behavior, 13, 14-16, 17, 20	Information levels, 10, 37 Perceptions, 9, 16	
Group			
Organization*		Bureaucratic processing, 7, 8, 10, 12, 31 Organizational processes, 7, 8, 10-12, 13, 17-20, 30, 31-32, 34-35, 36, 37, 38 Standard operating procedures Search processes Communication patterns, 10, 36 Stress, 37	
Nation	Prior interactions of adversary, 7, 9, 17 Demands, threats, deeds		
Dyad			
Alliance	Prior interactions of adversary alliance, 10, 11, 12, 16, 17, 20, 21, 23-24, 27 Demands, threats, deeds	Intensity of interaction, 16-18, 20-21, 22-28, 31, 33, 36-38 Action intensity Interdependence, 16-17	Conflict behavior, 12-13, 14, 16-18, 20-39
System†	Structure of international system, 7, 9, 13-14 Internation relationships System processes, 13, 20 Interactions		

* Organization refers to "formal," "complex," or "bureaucratic" organizations. The principal elements of formal organizations include the following: (1) an organization is a group which has clearly defined roles and shares certain basic goals; and (2) an organization is a group which makes decisions with regard to means and ends and the operation of the group on a continuous basis.

† System is defined as the patterns of all *interactions* among the various units studied.

Graham Allison and Morton Halperin, "Bureaucratic Politics: A Paradigm and Some Policy Implications"

Unit of Analysis	Input	Intervening Variables	Outcome
Individual	Rational intentions, 43 Value-maximizing processes	Information, 50, 52, 55, 61, 71, 72, 73-75 Perceptions, 44, 45, 47, 48, 50, 56, 57-58, 60-61, 62, 71, 73 Roles, 44, 47-48, 59, 73 Resources (power), 47, 50, 52, 57, 62, 78 Personal interests, 43, 44, 48-49, 57-59, 62-63, 73, 78 Skills, 50 Degree of involvement in decision, 50, 54	Policy choice/Decision, 43, 45, 46, 50-51, 52
Group			
Organization	Rational intentions, 48-50, 53-54, 58-59, 61, 62-63, 72-73, 75 Maximization of organizational interests	Bargaining, 42-44, 51, 56, 57, 58, 60, 72 Organizational processes, 42, 43, 51-52, 54-56, 59, 61-62, 71, 75, 76, 77 Standard operating procedures Competing goals, interest, priorities, 42, 47, 48, 53, 55, 57, 68-69, 72 Resources, 48, 50, 52 Number of players, 42-43, 47, 54 Variety of inputs, 42, 47, 53 Action channels, 45-47, 50, 52, 77	Policy choice/Decisions, 42-43, 45-47, 50-51, 53-54, 76
Nation	Strategic policy, 41-43, 45, 46, 51, 57-58, 61, 70-72, 75 Strategic objectives or goals, 40, 66-67 Intentions, 41 Interests, 41 Alternatives, 41 Costs and benefits, 41, 42 Behavior of adversary nations, 41, 57-66, 69-72	Resources, 57, 62, 78	Policy outcomes, 42, 44, 45-47, 51, 52, 60, 61 Results of action
Dyad			
Alliance			
System			

Nazli Choucri and Robert C. North, "Dynamics of International Conflict: Some Policy Implications of Population, Resources and Technology"

Unit of Analysis	Input	Intervening Variables	Outcome
Individual	Goals, 84, 85, 113 Preferences, 84, 85, 113 Intentions, 84	Images, 83 Perceptions, 83, 84, 88, 89, 96-97, 99-100 Role, 99 Motivation, 85	
Group			
Organization	Goals, 113	Constraints, 98-99, 113, 120 Bureaucratic politics and organizational processes	
Nation	National attributes, 82-95, 98, 100, 105-112, 114 National capabilities, 82-95, 98, 100, 105-112, 114 Rates of population growth Access to resources Knowledge and skill Rates of growth of technology	Constraints, 85, 89 Efficiency of government—ability to organize and mobilize Internal dynamics, 86-89, 90-92, 93, 97, 101, 103, 104-107, 109-112, 116, 117, 118, 119 Internal demands Lateral pressure Manipulation of policy relevant variables, 81, 82, 83, 84, 86, 87, 88, 89, 92-93, 97-98, 100, 101, 106-107, 108-109, 110-112, 114 Breakpoints, 97, 104-105, 115-122 Shift from internal to external dynamics Costs of lateral pressure, 94-95	

Edward Morse, "Crisis Diplomacy, Interdependence and the Politics of International Economic Relations"

Unit of Analysis	Input	Intervening Variables	Outcome
Individual		Elite socialization, 131	
Group			
Organization		Perceptions, 133, 134	
Nation	Strategic behavior, 134-136 Economic crisis, 123-125, 126-128, 135, 140-142, 143-146, 147 Conflicting goal patterns Incompatible values or objectives	International economic policy, 124-125, 128-132 Domestic welfare policy, 130-131 Full employment economy Policy objectives, 136-138, 144, 148-149 Governmental expenditures Policy instruments, 136-138, 144, 148-149 GATT, Kennedy Round Permeability of national boundaries, 135-136 Interactions/Transactions	Decreased political autonomy, 136-138, 143-144, 147 Control over foreign activities of citizens Relationship between policy objectives and policy instruments, 136-138, 144, 148
Dyad			
Alliance			
System		Interdependence, 124, 127, 132-150 Outcome of actions that are mutually contingent Strategic interdependence, 134, 138-139 Strategic "distance" Psychological interdependence, 139 Communication and transportation technology Transmission of ideas Economic interdependence, 134, 139 Externalities Trade in dollars Imports	Politicization of economic interactions, 123-124, 128, 131-132, 147 Linking political demands to economic threats Politicized economic crisis, 125-126, 128-132, 133, 135, 142-146, 147-150

Norman Frohlich and Joe Oppenheimer, "Entrepreneurial Politics and Foreign Policy"

Unit of Analysis	Input	Intervening Variables	Outcome

Individual	Rational behavior, 154-156, 159
	  Value-maximizing processes
	Entrepreneurial and consumer roles, 151, 153-154, 155-163, 165-173, 175, 177-178
	  Set of costs and benefits
	Consumption units, 155-163, 178
	  Good the consumer received in exchange for good he gives up
	Production unit, 155-163, 178
	  Good held by entrepreneur
	Profits, 159-162, 165-167, 173-175
	  Political gains
	Costs, 159-162, 165-167, 173-175
	  Political losses
		Preference schedules, 166, 170, 171, 175-176, 178
		Expectations of aggregate behavior of others, 161-162, 164-165, 169, 175
		  Free-riders
		Rewards, threats/punishments, 168-175
		Competition, 162, 166-167, 168-176
		Capabilities, 162, 168-170, 175
		Supply of goods controlled
		Cross-cutting memberships, 162-163
		Consumers can receive goods from more than one entrepreneur
			Exchange behavior, 155, 157, 158-159, 168-173, 177

Group	Consumption unit, 155-163, 178 Production unit, 155-163, 178	Structure of exchange relationship, 156-159, 160-163 Number of consumption units a given production unit supports Degree to which consumption units are granted on an individualistic basis	
Organization			
Nation			
Dyad			
Alliance			
System			

Oran Young, "The Perils of Odysseus: On Constructing Theories of International Relations"

Unit of Analysis	Input	Intervening Variables	Outcome
Non-unit specific	Simplified logical models, 194-199	Short-term policy relevance, 202-203 Predictive accuracy, 180, 181-183, 184-186, 190, 192, 197-198, 199-200 Descriptive richness, 185, 196, 198 Taxonomies	Theory, 180-187, 190, 195-203 Set of general statements such that some imply others and implications can be tested Power of theory, 181, 196, 198 Parsimony Sensitization, 187-188 Conceptualization, 188 Factual assessment, 188-189 Simple generalizations, 189 Correction, 189 Extrapolation, 189-190 Heuristic fruitfulness, 181-182, 185, 186, 196, 198 Guides to further theorizing
Individual		Temperament, 197 Research objectives, 197 Relationship between policymakers and theorists, 183, 188, 199-203	
Group			
Organization			
Nation	Arms races, 184, 186	Complexity of behavior of single actor, 184-185, 191, 193-195 Changing utility functions, 192-193 Multiple issues, 193-194	

Davis Bobrow, "The Relevance Potential of Different Products"

Unit of Analysis	Input	Intervening Variables	Outcome

Non-unit specific	Metatheory, 204, 206-209
	  Use of analogous perspectives
	Theory, 204, 209-217
	  System of internally consistent statements which allow deductive explanations or predictions
	History, 204, 216, 217-221
	  Description, explanation, or prediction of events in particular spatial-temporal domain
	Engineering, 204, 216, 221-228
	  Methods of monitoring external environment
	  Methods of designing foreign/defense policies
		Empirical fit, 216
		Predictive accuracy, 206-208
		User's established perspective, 209
		Operationalization of implications, 210-217
		Definitions, 210-217
		  Meaning of concepts
		Assumptions, 210-217
		  If . . . then relationships among concepts
		Scope conditions, 210-217
		  Situation of actor
		  Characteristics necessary for assumptions to hold
		Generality/specificity of theory, 210-211, 215-216
		Information demands of policy consumers, 208, 218-219, 221
		Specificity of model, 217-219
		  Number and type of variables
		Size of spatial-temporal domain, 217-221
		Foreign policy issue areas, 222, 223
		  Military or civil sectors
		Costs of inappropriate policy, 223
		Performance requirements—goals, 222-224, 227
		Process models—necessary and sufficient conditions, 224, 266, 227
		Relevant time span policy consumers focus on, 224-225, 226
		Manipulability of variables, 225, 226
			Policy relevance potential, 205-208, 215-217, 218-221, 226-227
			  Ability to estimate the occurrence and consequences of alternative states of affairs
			  Design and evaluate means to achieve preferred states
			Utility, 206-208
			  Aid to understanding past outcomes
			Implications
			  Explanation and prediction of general behaviors of nations, 215-216
			  Information processing, 208-209, 217, 219, 220-221
			  Control over alternative outcomes, 221-222, 228
			  Awareness of limited control, 225

Allen Whiting, "The Scholar and the Policy Maker"

Unit of Analysis	Input	Intervening Variables	Outcome
Non-unit specific	Scholarly research and models, 231-232, 235-247	Funding, 234, 235 Precedent, 235-236 Structured situations Temporal domain of research, 234, 236, 238 Past vs. future orientation Utility of results for short-range vs. long-range policy, 234, 236, 238, 245-246 Feasibility, 238 Ethnocentric character of U.S. scholarly research, 238-243, 246 Data availability, 234, 239, 241-242 Policymakers' awareness of their own decision processes and procedures, 243-244	Linking of system-oriented research and decisionmaking models, 234, 242-245
Individual		Interests and demands on policymaker, 235-238 Implicit models, biases, and assumptions of policymaker, 234, 236-237 Country-specific or regional focus of policymakers, 234, 236-237 Length of service, 236, 238	
Group			
Organization			
Nation			
Dyad			
Alliance			
System			

Books written under the auspices
of the Center of International Studies
Princeton University

Gabriel A. Almond, *The Appeals of Communism* (Princeton University Press 1954)

William W. Kaufmann, ed., *Military Policy and National Security* (Princeton University Press 1956)

Klaus Knorr, *The War Potential of Nations* (Princeton University Press 1956)

Lucian W. Pye, *Guerrilla Communism in Malaya* (Princeton University Press 1956)

Charles De Visscher, *Theory and Reality in Public International Law*, trans. by P. E. Corbett (Princeton University Press 1957; rev. ed. 1968)

Bernard C. Cohen, *The Political Process and Foreign Policy: The Making of the Japanese Peace Settlement* (Princeton University Press 1957)

Myron Weiner, *Party Politics in India: The Development of a Multi-Party System* (Princeton University Press 1957)

Percy E. Corbett, *Law in Diplomacy* (Princeton University Press 1959)

Rolf Sannwald and Jacques Stohler, *Economic Integration: Theoretical Assumptions and Consequences of European Unification*, trans. by Herman Karreman (Princeton University Press 1959)

Klaus Knorr, ed., *NATO and American Security* (Princeton University Press 1959)

Gabriel A. Almond and James S. Coleman, eds., *The Politics of the Developing Areas* (Princeton University Press 1960)

Herman Kahn, *On Thermonuclear War* (Princeton University Press 1960)

Sidney Verba, *Small Groups and Political Behavior: A Study of Leadership* (Princeton University Press 1961)

Robert J. C. Butow, *Tojo and the Coming of the War* (Princeton University Press 1961)

Glenn H. Snyder, *Deterrence and Defense: Toward a Theory of National Security* (Princeton University Press 1961)

Klaus Knorr and Sidney Verba, eds., *The International System: Theoretical Essays* (Princeton University Press 1961)

Peter Paret and John W. Shy, *Guerrillas in the 1960's* (Praeger 1962)

George Modelski, *A Theory of Foreign Policy* (Praeger 1962)

Klaus Knorr and Thornton Read, eds., *Limited Strategic War* (Praeger 1963)

Frederick S. Dunn, *Peace-Making and the Settlement with Japan* (Princeton University Press 1963)

Arthur L. Burns and Nina Heathcote, *Peace-Keeping by United Nations Forces* (Praeger 1963)

Richard A. Falk, *Law, Morality, and War in the Contemporary World* (Praeger 1963)

James N. Rosenau, *National Leadership and Foreign Policy: A Case Study in the Mobilization of Public Support* (Princeton University Press 1963)

Gabriel A. Almond and Sidney Verba, *The Civic Culture: Political Attitudes and Democracy in Five Nations* (Princeton University Press 1963)

Bernard C. Cohen, *The Press and Foreign Policy* (Princeton University Press 1963)

Richard L. Sklar, *Nigerian Political Parties: Power in an Emergent African Nation* (Princeton University Press 1963)

Peter Paret, *French Revolutionary Warfare from Indochina to Algeria: The Analysis of a Political and Military Doctrine* (Praeger 1964)

Harry Eckstein, ed., *Internal War: Problems and Approaches* (Free Press 1964)

Cyril E. Black and Thomas P. Thornton, eds., *Communism and Revolution: The Strategic Uses of Political Violence* (Princeton University Press 1964)

Miriam Camps, *Britain and the European Community 1955-1963* (Princeton University Press 1964)

Thomas P. Thornton, ed., *The Third World in Soviet Perspective: Studies by Soviet Writers on the Developing Areas* (Princeton University Press 1964)

James N. Rosenau, ed., *International Aspects of Civil Strife* (Princeton University Press 1965)

Sidney I. Ploss, *Conflict and Decision-Making in Soviet Russia: A Case Study of Agricultural Policy, 1953-1963* (Princeton University Press 1965)

Richard A. Falk and Richard J. Barnet, eds., *Security and Disarmament* (Princeton University Press 1965)

Karl von Vorys, *Political Development in Pakistan* (Princeton University Press 1965)

Harold and Margaret Sprout, *The Ecological Perspective on Human Affairs, With Special Reference to International Politics* (Princeton University Press 1965)

Klaus Knorr, *On the Uses of Military Power in the Nuclear Age* (Princeton University Press 1966)

Harry Eckstein, *Division and Cohesion in Democracy: A Study of Norway* (Princeton University Press 1966)

Cyril E. Black, *The Dynamics of Modernization: A Study in Comparative History* (Harper and Row 1966)

Peter Kunstadter, ed., *Southeast Asian Tribes, Minorities, and Nations* (Princeton University Press 1967)

E. Victor Wolfenstein, *The Revolutionary Personality: Lenin, Trotsky, Gandhi* (Princeton University Press 1967)

Leon Gordenker, *The UN Secretary-General and the Maintenance of Peace* (Columbia University Press 1967)

Oran R. Young, *The Intermediaries: Third Parties in International Crises* (Princeton University Press 1967)

James N. Rosenau, ed., *Domestic Sources of Foreign Policy* (Free Press 1967)

Richard F. Hamilton, *Affluence and the French Worker in the Fourth Republic* (Princeton University Press 1967)

Linda B. Miller, *World Order and Local Disorder: The United Nations and Internal Conflicts* (Princeton University Press 1967)

Henry Bienen, *Tanzania: Party Transformation and Economic Development* (Princeton University Press 1967)

Wolfram F. Hanrieder, *West German Foreign Policy, 1949-1963: International Pressures and Domestic Response* (Stanford University Press 1967)

Richard H. Ullman, *Britain and the Russian Civil War: November 1918-February 1920* (Princeton University Press 1968)

Robert Gilpin, *France in the Age of the Scientific State* (Princeton University Press 1968)

William B. Bader, *The United States and the Spread of Nuclear Weapons* (Pegasus 1968)

Richard A. Falk, *Legal Order in a Violent World* (Princeton University Press 1968)

Cyril E. Black, Richard A. Falk, Klaus Knorr and Oran R. Young, *Neutralization and World Politics* (Princeton University Press 1968)

Oran R. Young, *The Politics of Force: Bargaining During International Crises* (Princeton University Press 1969)

Klaus Knorr and James N. Rosenau, eds., *Contending Approaches to International Politics* (Princeton University Press 1969)

James N. Rosenau, ed., *Linkage Politics: Essays on the Convergence of National and International Systems* (Free Press 1969)

John T. McAlister, Jr., *Viet Nam: The Origins of Revolution* (Knopf 1969)

Jean Edward Smith, *Germany Beyond the Wall: People, Politics and Prosperity* (Little, Brown 1969)

James Barros, *Betrayal from Within: Joseph Avenol, Secretary-General of the League of Nations, 1933-1940* (Yale University Press 1969)

Charles Hermann, *Crises in Foreign Policy: A Simulation Analysis* (Bobbs-Merrill 1969)

Robert C. Tucker, *The Marxian Revolutionary Idea: Essays on Marxist Thought and Its Impact on Radical Movements* (W. W. Norton 1969)

Harvey Waterman, *Political Change in Contemporary France: The Politics of an Industrial Democracy* (Charles E. Merrill 1969)

Cyril E. Black and Richard A. Falk, eds., *The Future of the International Legal Order*. Vol. I: *Trends and Patterns* (Princeton University Press 1969)

Ted Robert Gurr, *Why Men Rebel* (Princeton University Press 1969)

C. Sylvester Whitaker, *The Politics of Tradition: Continuity and Change in Northern Nigeria 1946-1966* (Princeton University Press 1970)

Richard A. Falk, *The Status of Law in International Society* (Princeton University Press 1970)

John T. McAlister, Jr. and Paul Mus, *The Vietnamese and the Revolution* (Harper & Row 1970)

Klaus Knorr, *Military Power and Potential* (D. C. Heath 1970)

Cyril E. Black and Richard A. Falk, eds., *The Future of the International Legal Order*. Vol. II: *Wealth and Resources* (Princeton University Press 1970)

Leon Gordenker, ed., *The United Nations in International Politics* (Princeton University Press 1971)

Cyril E. Black and Richard A. Falk, eds., *The Future of the International Legal Order*. Vol. III: *Conflict Management* (Princeton University Press 1971)

Francine R. Frankel, *India's Green Revolution: Economic Gains and Political Costs* (Princeton University Press 1971)

Harold and Margaret Sprout, *Toward a Politics of the Planet Earth* (Van Nostrand Reinhold Co. 1971)

Cyril E. Black and Richard A. Falk, eds., *The Future of the International Legal Order*. Vol. IV: *The Structure of the International Environment* (Princeton University Press 1972)